Lessons from the Field

APPLYING
APPRECIATIVE INQUIRY

CO·EDITORS SUE ANNIS HAMMOND
AND CATHY ROYAL

A Special thanks to all those who participated in the Book Writing Conference in
October, 1996 in Taos, New Mexico
especially Jane Seiling who helped
organize the conference.

This book is dedicated by Sue to the
wonderful creative, imaginative spirit of
Chase M. Hammond and by Cathy with
thanks to my healing circle, your love
nurtures my creative energy and my soul!!
You make my dreams possible.

Co-editors, Sue Annis Hammond
and Cathy Royal
Copy assistance from Dana Joseph
Art Director: Alisann Marshall
Cover Illustrator: Kyle Dreier
Thin Book Publishing Co.

ISBN: 09665373-3-5

Thin Book Publishing Co.
P.O. Box 260608
Plano TX 75026-0608
Toll-Free (888) 316-9544
www.thinbook.com

The marks in this book are from:
Arts and Crafts Ornaments Font
available from P22 Foundry. P.O. Box 770,
Buffalo, NY 14213

THEORY

CASE STUDIES

APPLICATION OF THEORY

COMMUNI

ICATION

THEORY

APPLICATION OF THEORY

APPLICATION

THEORY

ASE STUDIES

APPLICATION OF

COMMUNITY APPLICATION

What is Appreciative Inquiry?

Ap-pre'ci-ate, v., 1. Valuing; the act of recognizing the best in people or the world around us; affirming past and present strengths, successes, and potentials; to perceive those things that give life (health, vitality,excellence) to living systems. 2. To increase in value, e.g. the economy has appreciated in value. Synonyms: VALUING, PRIZING, ESTEEMING, and HONORING.

In-quire' (kwir), v., 1. The act of exploration and discovery. 2. To ask questions; to be open to seeing new potentials and possibilities. Synonyms: DISCOVERY, SEARCH, and SYSTEMATIC EXPLORATION, STUDY.

Appreciative Inquiry (AI) begins an adventure. The urge and call to adventure has been sounded by many people and many organizations, and it will take many more to fully explore the vast vistas that are now appearing on the horizon. But even in the first steps, what is being sensed is decisive new direction in our language and theories of organization and transformation – an invitation, as some have declared, to "a positive revolution in change."

In the ten years since the theory and vision for *Appreciative Inquiry In Organizational Life* was published in *Research in Organization Development and Change* (JAI Press, 1987), there have been literally hundreds of people involved in co-creating new practices for doing AI and for bringing the spirit and methodology of AI into organizations all over the world. The velocity and largely informal spread of the ideas continues to escalate and points clearly to the need for more rapid sharing – new tools, training designs, example interview protocols, case stories, cross-cultural learnings etc. Put simply, new practice is outpacing theory. And that is what this wonderful book is about.

More than just a "fieldbook," this volume is aiming at something higher. Its meta-message is about building learning community, and about the need to dramatically reduce the time lag between innovations in the field (no matter how nascent or fresh) and our free and open sharing with one another as creators, colleagues, co-theorists, and co-conspirators.

It is a time for re-thinking human organization and change. Deficit based modalities are increasingly falling short. And cynicism, about the very idea of planned change, is rampant. But Sue Hammond and Cathy Royal and all the other generous co-authors of this book offer a message of hope. Through each and every one of these compelling stories appreciative inquiry is given strength as a work in progress. Read this book as an invitation to your own experimentation, say the authors and then let's share again!

David L. Cooperrider
1998

What you are about to read

The purpose of this book is to share stories of our applications of Appreciative Inquiry processes and theory. We asked people to write the stories or case studies in their style and words, writing from the heart. We have retained their voices with little editing. For that reason, we believe the book *sings* as contributor Alexsandra Stewart described what she hoped the book would do for the reader.

Our hope for you the reader is to read the contributions one at a time and learn from the authors' experience. Each contribution shares what the author(s) did and learned. Each experience creates an opportunity to inquire into the possible, and in that sense allows us to reflect in the positive on what is perfect. This opens us up to new possibilities at each inquiry. That is the beauty of the poetic underpinning of an/the Appreciative Inquiry experience.

Each chapter stand on its own but the sections are groups that emphasize a distinct flavor and purpose. The graphic models are for the visual learner. The case studies reveal rich detail and examples. The wonderful community applications reveal where most of the new ground has been broken in AI. The application of theory chapters share the creative use of AI by practitioners. Finally the two essays ground you in the roots of AI. The resource section is literally hot off the press, the latest in current publications and forthcoming work.

Many will ask questions about "Pure AI". The applications are the works in progress that give us the learning that continues to create possibilities for the use and implementation of AI in organizations and communities. Each application and example is an opportunity to study the impact of AI in the organization that chose to look at what it was doing well. As the use of AI spreads and more systems realize that working in the realm of the positive is possible, we will have more conversations about the pure application of AI. Each is a welcomed dialogue. The more we inquire and examine the philosophy the better. Just as we emphasize dialogue in our client systems, we encourage a dialogue on the best possible application and theory for AI amongst practitioners and dreamers. We emphasize that Appreciative Inquiry is a large system change philosophy. Most of us apply the philosophy in ways that we think are appropriate to the client's needs and our understanding of the philosophy. Of course, we all wish we could do it "right", as we know it has the most impact when we can engage the entire system. But in each case, we have applied the principles as we saw opportunities and possibilities.

One emotion is clear throughout the book. We all have a passion about our work with Appreciative Inquiry. That passion is dramatically demonstrated in the community application section. As we read the community cases we see all the elements common in organizations; group dynamics, politics, budgets, leadership, and differing visions. The diverse cultures from Chicago, to Dallas to South Carolina to The Bronx and Nepal represent a microcosm of the world of organizations and we are delighted to share their stories in this book. Indeed, when we are at our best, a culture community application and corporate application inform each other and we work to "think beyond the positive" in each arena, discovering a new possibility at each new horizon.

We honor those pioneers who allowed us to practice, dream and imagine. We challenge all those in organizations who want to know "What other Company (preferably Fortune 500) has used this?" before they will try something new. The challenge is simple, leadership for the sustainable organization will and has always required a pioneering spirit. Look to AI and the art of the possible, as a process and intervention that will enhance the climate and productivity of your unique organization.

We look forward to future volumes of this book and other works-in-progress, as we continue to learn. We gratefully acknowledge all the passion of the contributors. Each contributor has retained his or her copyright so please contact the author for reprints or questions. Many thanks to Jackie Kelm and Lia Bosch for the needed assistance from time to time. Dana Williams again proved her mastery as a Copy Editor and we don't know what we would do without her help. Alisann Marshall continues to amaze us with her talented design. She gave major editorial assistance while designing the pages. Finally, we feel privileged in our role as editors and producers to publish these stories. Enjoy your journey and let us know how it goes.

Cathy Royal and Sue Annis Hammond

CASE STUDIES

COMMUNITY APPLICATION

APPLICATION OF THEORY

THEORY

H₂ DO IT

"What is"

"What"

"What will Be"

"What

1 Begin with the **TOPIC**

2 Create **QUESTIONS** To Explore the topic

3 Conduct **INQUIRY** interviews

4 Share information to uncover **THEMES**

5 Create provacative **PROPOSITIONS**

6 Transform into **ACTION**

a philosophy for ▲

A?

ASSUMPTIONS Shared

6 If we ☐ parts of the past forward they should be what is ☆ best

7 It is important to value ☐ ● differences ▲

8 The ☐ we use creates our reality.

COULD BE. **WE STRETCH WHAT WE**

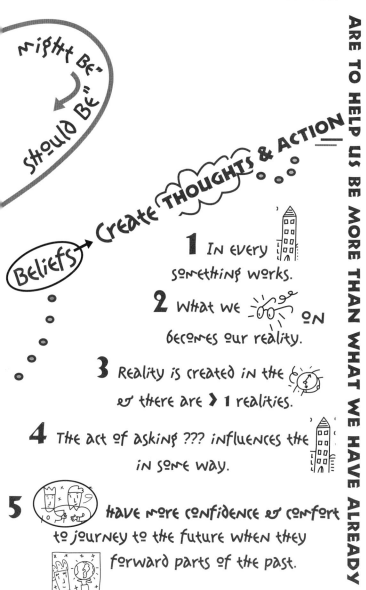

might Be.

should Be.

Beliefs → Create THOUGHTS & ACTION

ARE TO HELP US BE MORE THAN WHAT WE HAVE ALREADY BEEN

1 IN every something works.

2 What we ☀ ON becomes our reality.

3 Reality is created in the 🕐 & there are > 1 realities.

4 The act of asking ??? influences the IN some way.

5 have more confidence & comfort to journey to the future when they forward parts of the past.

SUCCESSFUL AT. WE ENVISION A

ABOUT THE AUTHOR

CHARLOTTE S. POLLARD is founder of PO.LAR Associates, a consulting firm dedicated to providing customized solutions to business problems. She works with management teams who have a need to work together more effectively to resolve both interpersonal and business issues. She also works with subject matter experts to design customized training, develop training materials, and facilitate training programs for organizations in a variety of industries. She and her clients enjoy the engaging activity that results from appreciative inquiry. She enjoys creating mind maps just for fun. And, she learns better that way.

For more information, contact:
Charlotte Pollard
505-474-4228

NOTE: The information in the mind map is from *The Thin Book of Appreciative Inquiry* by Sue Annis Hammond.

Why Appreciative Inquiry?

People have asked me: Why is AI able to build so much positive momentum while other change methods soon find themselves on the shelf? My answer is simple. I think any organizational change or management method will be powerful if it responds to three "facts" about all human beings: exceptionality, essentiality, and equality of voice.

By exceptionality I mean that every human being is an exception to the rule – no one has ever been born quite like you and no one in the future will ever again be quite like you. To the extent to which our management methods understand and value people for the exceptionalities they bring, to that extent people will respond to those methods.

Conversely, those methods that do not see people for the exceptional people they are (or treat people as problems to be solved) will be resisted and ultimately become tired and ineffective over time. The same can be said for essentiality. We all have a basic human want to be recognized as "essential" to any human group (family, work, community) we belong to. We do not need to be central but we need to be appreciated and recognized as essential. That is, we would be missed if we left or perhaps even died.

Finally I think all human beings, in every group they are part of, feel some sense of equality, especially equality of voice. We all have a desire to be able to share, without censorship, our hopes and visions of the true, the good, and the possible. So this is precisely why appreciative inquiry is powerful. It deliberately seeks to discover people's exceptionality — their unique gifts, strengths, and qualities. It actively searches and recognizes people for their specialties—their essential contributions and achievements. And it is based on principles of equality of voice — everyone is asked to speak about their vision of the true, the good, and the possible. Appreciative Inquiry builds momentum and success because it believes in people. It really is an invitation to a positive revolution. Its goal is to discover in all human beings the exceptional and the essential. Its goal is to create organizations that are in full voice!

David L. Cooperrider
2001

THIS MODEL IS THE BEST PLACE TO BEGIN TO SHOW

THE DIFFERENCE BETWEEN THE TWO PARADIGMS.

PROBLEM-SOLVING — APPRECIATIVE INQUIRY

Problem Solving		Appreciative Inquiry
"Felt Need" Identification of Problem	▼	**Appreciating and Valuing The Best of "What Is"**
Analysis of Causes	▼	**"Envisioning "What might Be"**
Analysis of Possible Solutions	▼	**"Dialoguing "What Should Be"**
Action Planning	▼	**"Innovating "What Will Be"**
BASIC ASSUMPTION: **An Organization is a Problem to be Solved**		**BASIC ASSUMPTION:** **An Organization is a Mystery to be Embraced**

Adapted from Cooperrider and Srivastva (1987) Appreciative Inquiry Into Organizational Life In *Research in Organizational Change in Development.* Pasmore and Woodman (EDS) Vol 1, JAI Press

13

CASE STUDIES

Every transformation of the (human species) ...

has rested on a new metaphysical and

ideological base; or rather, upon deeper stirrings

and intuitions whose rationalized expression takes

the form of a new picture of the cosmos and

the nature of (humanity).

— L. MUMFORD

CASE STUDIES

LAGUNA BEACH EDUCATION FOUNDATION,
SCHOOLPOWER™

BY MICHAEL PINTO
AND MARY CURRAN

Introduction

We have probably each spent a life-time in appreciative inquiry but only recently discovered that it has a name and also come across a project in which we could apply more consciously, a point of view that has been so intuitively familiar. I had selected for my dissertation topic an inquiry into what has made Schoolpower so successful. With the positive approach of Appreciative Inquiry, it seemed a perfect lens through which to view this school-oriented philanthropic foundation. Mary Curran, as an academician well versed in the techniques of AI, agreed to chair my dissertation committee.

A graduate of Case Western Reserve in Cleveland, Mary heard of Appreciative Inquiry seven or eight years ago and has been deepening her understanding of it ever since. She is always looking for new applications and eagerly accepted my invitation. This joint description of the process I followed is one more step to increasing our own appreciation for AI as a point of view, a process and a series of relationships.

When I began my graduate work, I understood the dissertation research project to be just another obstacle to overcome in completing a series of tasks leading to conferral of a Ph.D. It was business as usual: define a goal, line up and sequence the tasks, then get to work on them one at a time. I would not expect to be changed by the tasks, but rather they would bend to my will and conform to my wishes and goals.

What happened though, was quite the contrary. I found that throughout the first two years of my core doctoral program, involvement with group processes in a reflective way proved to be quite transformative. Additionally, though I had studied in the fields of sociology of knowledge, philosophy and cultural anthropology, I was not prepared for the live experience of cultural clash and conflicting perspectives in a cohort model of learning that put flesh on the bones of the academic knowledge I had gained during my graduate years in the sixties. I was beginning to feel what differing forms of knowledge construction were like, and my familiar role of separated and immovable observer no longer worked nor felt as comfortable as before.

During my dissertation research this transformation moved to a much higher plane. As with my initial understanding of the core program, I thought that the research study could be cleanly outlined, described, implemented and completed. What I found instead was a tiger whose tail I could barely hold onto. Nothing stayed the same, from definition of the problem statement to research methodology. I began in one direction, then was moved to take another. I struggled to define the appropriate research methodology, finally defined it, then completely changed it when introduced to Appreciative Inquiry.

I found that when engaging in a qualitative study, just as the focus shifts from finding a "truth" to unearthing "meaning," so the capacity to control variables greatly diminishes as they vastly expand with the many people that join the project as co-researchers. Stance changed for me from the controller to the facilitator, from the leader to the cheerleader, from the one to the one amongst many. I could no longer solely focus on my goals, my plans, and my interpretations, but had to recognize that meaning came from a process of social construction provided by the many co-researchers and other Schoolpower members that were part of this study.

Introduction to Schoolpower

Throughout America there are thousands of public school foundations. They developed from the recognition that the political, economic and organizational environments were changing and that the community, especially parents, needed to be more involved in the direct funding of public education.

With two-earner families more dependent on institutional resources for educating their children, their expectations simultaneously increased while at the same time involvement in their child's education frequently decreased. This created a double-edged quandary for both the school systems and parents.

Numerous studies have shown that parental expectations and involvement are key to the success of their child's educational experience (Haller, 1986; Muro, 1995; Newby, 1985). The desire for excellence was there, yet for many years as our culture evolved into the two-earner family, the child was left without the family's energy and involvement necessary to excel in school. As the baby boomer generation began to have children, pay taxes, and settle into their own careers, there was growing recognition that more time was needed for changing or at least improving an educational system they perceived as needing help.

It was during the time of these intersecting forces that the public school foundation movement emerged. Starting fitfully in the seventies and accelerating into the eighties, public school foundations became vehicles for parents to express themselves outside the political arena of elections. By helping to raise money and through parent participation in the schools, public school foundations could take a district-wide perspective of the educational program and then do something about it, as was mentioned by numerous interviewees during our study.

Additionally, when an organization has the capability to fund large projects, the school administration takes notice and works closely with it as they would any large donor. And because this financial capacity is ongoing and not a one time gift, there can develop a symbiotic relationship between the foundation and the administration that leads to a more open, consultative relationship that is empowering to the parents and leads to greater involvement on their part in the schools.

The public schools of Laguna Beach were faced not only with the above factors, but also with a tax shifting law (Proposition 13) which reduced property taxes (the primary source of money for public education in California) by over 50%, as well as a series of court decisions (The Serrano-Priest rulings) that limited the growth in income of wealthy school districts as it shifted funds to poorer areas. All of these factors, in addition to the significant inflation in costs during the middle to late 70's as well as a reduction in school population as couples had fewer children, created a financial crisis for the Laguna Beach School District.

Beginning in 1974 a series of public meetings were held that focused on the problems in the Laguna Beach public schools. These meetings were open to everyone in the community and formed the basis of

a partnership between parents, community, teachers and administration. Throughout the process, the School Board was very supportive and, in fact, several members took a leadership role. Though the meetings were infrequent, they created a consensus in the community around cooperative involvement in solving public school problems.

However, what these meetings could not do was to solve the growing financial crisis in the district. Towards the end of the 70's financial conditions had deteriorated to the point where one school had to be closed due to declining enrollment, teachers were laid off, and finally a teacher strike was threatened because financial needs and district capability were just too far apart. It was around this time that parents and community members, initially led by the Board of Education, resurrected a non-profit corporation (501c3) originally established in 1969 by the Laguna Beach Board of Education to conduct fundraising that in fact never happened. At the time of its resurrection, this foundation was one of the first in the United States and the first of its kind to be established in Orange County, California.

This time, the newly resurrected corporation was to form the legal basis for a community ready and willing to help the schools. Its name was the Laguna Beach Educational Foundation, but soon the nickname *Schoolpower* was adopted. From its inception, the foundation was almost exclusively a volunteer lead and staffed organization, with only

one paid staff member. The mission of the foundation was two fold: to raise money for the public schools of Laguna Beach and to show the community's support and appreciation for the teachers.

Within a very few years, the good work of the foundation helped heal the wounds between the teachers, administration and community and from then on, the key mission of the foundation remained the raising of money for the public schools. Additionally, it was decided that the money would be given directly to the Board of Education with no strings attached, the reasoning for this being that the members of the foundation Board did not want to get involved in any political decisions over how moneys should be spent.

Throughout its fifteen-year history, Schoolpower has been considered a successful public school foundation raising in excess of $100 per student per year. Additionally, it completed a $3 million capital campaign as well as establishing an endowment fund. My case study was created to focus on the question, "What elements have led to the success of Schoolpower?" **Unlike many case studies that look at what is wrong with an organization and attempt to come up with some plausible solutions, this study wanted to unearth what was right and to ask how those elements could be extended.**

Research Design Overview

In this case study of one organization, my intention was originally two-fold: 1) to help the insiders reveal their latent knowledge and wisdom in order to further the cause of the Foundation, and, 2) to make the research findings available to members of other organizations. The results of the study were thus limited to a description of how one organization had proven successful in conducting fundraising and development on behalf of the public school system in Laguna Beach.

The process of organizing and conducting the case study was broken down into several phases:

1 Development of the research proposal and presentation to the Board of Directors of Schoolpower

2 Recruitment of the research teams

3 Conducting the initial interviews

4 Analysis of the individual interview transcripts

5 Development of the interview guide for the focus groups

6 Conducting the focus groups

7 Analysis of the focus group transcripts

8 Team members writing up their impressions and ideas

9 Final analysis of transcripts and research team members writings

10 Final writing

11 Presentation to the foundation and suggestions for continuing involvement in the research findings

As the research was to be conducted as a collaborative enterprise based on the action research methodologies so well propounded by Peter Reason (1994), it was necessary for me not only to recruit members to the team but also to educate them in the methods of collaborative research methodology and Appreciative Inquiry. With that in mind, I produced several papers that described Appreciative Inquiry and contrasted it with standard models of organizational development (see Appendices H&I).

I was fortunate to have as my first volunteer a member of Schoolpower's executive committee who had done her doctoral work in the field of sociology back in the 60's (A). She was familiar with case studies and was excited about collaborative research methodologies as well as AI. She, in turn, recruited a second member (B) a friend from her alma mater who had completed her doctoral work in sociology. Finally, the third member (C) of the team was a friend of mine who had extensive research experience, taught research methodologies at the university level, and was open to the concept of qualitative research and collaborative inquiry.

It was with this team that I started the study. We began with a two-day retreat during which we discussed the basic outline of the research strategy as described in the approved research proposal. As a qualitative study that was to be a collaborative process of organization insider involvement, we recognized that the research protocol was subject to change as the research developed, but we wanted to flesh out issues of leadership, organization, responsibilities, and initial action steps. As the person responsible for completion of the dissertation, I took the role of overall research leader. There was to be no formal organization, but rather each member would contribute based on his or her skills, experience and time available. I was responsible for overall coordination of the research, A would work closely with the Board of Trustees of Schoolpower to help recruit members to the research team, and B&C would make themselves available as necessary.

The initial focus of the research was on the interview process and the stories that people had to share (Fetterman, 1989; Patton, 1990). Using the processes of Appreciative Inquiry, we focused on two interview elements:

1) Open-ended interview techniques in which the interviewer asked questions with minimal leading of the interviewee

2) Questions that were positive in nature such as "Can you relate to us some heart-warming experiences that you had with the organization?"

There were two sets of interviews: for the first group of individual interviews, and to avoid inside-researcher bias, a randomized sampling of past and present Board members was conducted using the standard table of random numbers. Through the course of Schoolpower's history there have been approximately 176 Board members (of which 40 were executive officers) who could be described as informed and effective people in the Schoolpower organization. Of this total, multiple positions in the

organization were held, i.e., one of the executive directors had previously been a Board member and President of the organization. Twenty interviews were conducted by members of the research team.

I developed an interview guide (Appendix B) based on Patton's work (1990) and the process of Appreciative Inquiry (Cooperrider, 1987, 1991).

The Interview Guide highlighted the following: the interviewer would ask the following questions, probing only for clarification, elucidation and depth: *"Can you tell me a story about some experiences you had with Schoolpower that was particularly heartwarming?; Can you please describe what you believe helped make Schoolpower successful? "* The guide ended with the following statement: "The purpose of open-ended and unstructured interviewing is to find out what is in the interviewee's head, not to put something there. The task of the interviewer is to make it possible for the person being interviewed to bring the interviewer into his or her world." From the data developed during these interviews as well as the personal experiences and knowledge of the research team members, the group interview guide was developed.

The second set of interviews was conducted within the context of ten small groups. We used focus groups for several reasons. First, it was a way to include many more people in the study without stretching our resources in time, money and personnel. Second, a group of people with common experiences can many times help one another in reconstructing past events and experiences.

Additionally, as people reflect on a question and hear one another's responses, memories are triggered that may correct prior statements, thus adding an element of crosschecking to the narratives. **Finally, the use of small groups is a very efficient way of using the interviewer's time; during a span of five days, we were able to interview over 60 people within the course of ten hours.**

Each session was scheduled for one hour and all ended within five minutes of the allotted time. Two interviewers conducted each interview session. One would begin as the primary interviewer while the other observed the interviewees and noted important points. Later in the session, the other interviewer often took the lead and the original lead interviewer then became the primary observer. Additionally, each interviewer would back up the other, asking for elucidation of key points and helping to get interviewees to further develop interesting lines of discussion. Strict confidentiality was maintained between the interviewer and interviewee, all respondents being referred to anonymously during the taping as well as on the transcripts. Finally, all interviewees were given the opportunity to review transcripts of their sessions to validate and clarify any points.

An analysis committee was formed that included most of the interviewers plus additional Board members that were now available to be part of the research team. In all, nine people plus myself formed the analysis team. An initial meeting was held in which each team member was given several transcripts to read and to code (see instructions,

Appendices F&G). Of the ten focus group interview transcripts, each was reviewed by at least three people.

Additionally, team members were encouraged to write down their personal thoughts and observations about any area of the research, the data, or the process of the collaborative research experience. Several did so, though a great deal of what was shared took place during informal discussions either after a formal meeting or one-on-one at a later date.

Finally, the actual writing of the findings and conclusions sections were one in which several analysis team members participated. There was a general consensus among the members that I, though the principal investigator, could not write these sections alone but must fully share the process, as I had the interview and analysis stages.

Findings and Conclusions

The findings were developed from three levels of data gathering: the individual interviews, a cross comparison of the two team's analysis of the interviews, and an analysis of the focus group interviews. Finally, members of the research team were invited to submit their personal conclusions on all the data as well as the research process. A summary table of those findings and their data sources is at right.

These twelve elements form the core of Schoolpower's values and are the foundation stones of its culture. However, findings 10, 11 and 12 have been particularly important as energizing elements contributing to the flexibility of the orga-

FINDINGS

THEMES FROM INDIVIDUAL INTERVIEWS

1. The importance of limiting tenure on the Board.

2. Motivating factors that affect parents.

3. The compatibility of the Board members.

4. The importance of giving back to one's community.

5. The organization's reputation.

6. The role of community in the success of Schoolpower .

7. The dynamic relationship between the community, the schools and the various support organizations that are devoted to enhancing the educational system.

REFLECTIVE LEARNINGS OF THE RESEARCH TEA

8. The Board was reflective of the entire community and not one segment.

9. The organization's public relations strengths and how they can be further enhanced.

MAJOR FINDINGS OF THE STUDY AFTER ANALYSIS

10. The dynamic tension between organizational needs and the näive volunteer. This prevents the operational paradigm of the organization from becoming frozen and inflexible.

11. Continuous organizational re-invention as the needs of the community change.

12. The organization's goals are never ending

*1 - Teams A & B independently derived data from individual interviews;

DATA SOURCES

ONE	TWO	THREE
x	x	x
x	x	x
x	x	x
x	x	x
x	x	x
x	x	x
x	x	x

AFTER ANALYSIS OF THE INDIVIDUAL INTERVIEWS

ONE	TWO	THREE
	x	x
	x	x

AND REFLECTION ON THE FOCUS GROUP INTERVIEWS

ONE	TWO	THREE
		x
		x
		x

2 - Additional data developed together by Teams A & B;

3 - Data derived from Focus Group Interviews.

nization and its visionary mission. There is no hierarchy of value between these three, but rather an interrelationship, each moving into, supporting and enhancing the other two.

In addition, themes 10, 11 and 12 that emerged from our reflections on the focus group interviews have been revealing. They speak not only to the success of Schoolpower but to challenges that many organizations face:

1 the importance of balancing an organization's needs for structure and continuity with the dynamic energy and current community concerns that newcomers bring.

2 The numerous elements that contribute to continuous organizational reinvention such as the "näive" volunteer (näive in the sense that they bring new eyes to the organization no matter what outside experience they have), the incomplete event documentation that allows for re-invention by new volunteers, and the lack of what sociologists would call a professional class culture embedded in the organization's past that may prevent it from seeing new possibilities for the future.

3 The importance of goals rooted in a quest for excellence and an eternal vision of hopefulness toward the future that is never ending and always unfolding.

The significance of the three key concepts 10, 11 and 12 is that they are circular in nature, each nourishing and building on one another. None stands alone, but continuously dips into as well as builds on the other as a synergistic dance of self-enhancing parts that constitute the organic whole of an active and evolving organization.

ORGANIZATION GOALS ARE NEVER ENDING - DYNAMIC TENSION BETWEEN ORGANIZATIONAL NEEDS AND THE "NAÏVE" VOLUNTEER - CONTINUOUS ORGANIZATIONAL REINVENTION - ORGANIZATION

Appreciative Inquiry

These interwoven elements of organizational re-invention, never-ending goals and and the tension between organizational needs and the näive volunteer, led to another key finding in this study, the importance of Appreciative Inquiry as a process for organizational development. As the role of Appreciative Inquiry became such a central feature of the methodology, a new goal for this study emerged. That was to help the insiders experience a collaborative and empowering process of organization insider inquiry that was critically reflective in a way that enhanced the egalitarian qualities of Schoolpower and helped them to appreciate the value of their insights and the rich harvest of shared wisdom that was embodied in the experiences of past and current Board members.

The key elements in an egalitarian organization include organizational ethos: the general human spirit serving to characterize the disposition of an organization as a dynamically formulated living social system. Within this organization there is a threefold ideal of inclusion, consent and excellence. Shared governance is central to effective leadership.

As an inclusive process, appreciative action research helped to illuminate several important factors that were validated in my literature review:
• It was able to elicit through the focus groups an unearthing of individual and group memory, cross validation of knowledge, and member support for each other in revealing sensitive information about themselves as well as their culture (Fetterman, 1988 & 1989).
• It had the potential to create synergies from which emerge new knowledge greater than the sum of what individual group members had to offer (Reason, 1994)

• It identified a personal stake in the process and outcomes of the study as well as implementation of the findings. It also helped to develop and therefore employ skills the co-researchers learned and practiced during the study.

• It provided an analysis phase for the benefit of the organization's future (Reason, 1994).

There has been a growing focus in the literature on the role of learning as a fundamental element in the long term viability of an organization (Bolman & Deal, 1991; Janov, 1994; Senge, 1990). Engaging insiders in thoughtful data collection and analysis as part of a formal process of critical self-reflection provided the organization with trained and experienced members that became transformative change agents. One of the key researchers in this project said that participating in this research might be the most important action taken by Schoolpower during the 1995-6 school year. As a full participant in the data gathering and analysis stages, he exemplified for all the co-researchers the possibility of extending into the future the study's findings and collaborative processes that were so exciting to him.

From unearthing those elements that have been positive, heartwarming and life affirming, Appreciative Inquiry took the participants through a process of dialoguing about what might be, what should be, and then what will be. It was a process that affirmed each member's unique experience, gave voice to the specialness of his or her knowledge and feelings, and opened up a process that included them in a vision for the future. As one member of Schoolpower said, "Experiencing this process has been renewing, energizing and exciting for the organization. When I look at all the substantive changes taking place this year, what strikes me most is this research project we are engaged in. It, above all the other things, has brought an excitement and energy to the organization."

Appreciative Inquiry focuses on the role of dialogue, for this is fundamentally an inclusive and consensual process that moves attention from individual to collective appreciation. It also works to create an attainable vision through innovating new ways to move the organization closer to a collectively imagined ideal. **Again and again, Schoolpower members spoke of a vision not only for their children but for all the students of the school district.** In fact, there was a sense that the vision went beyond even that to an idea of community, the schools being a cornerstone of an expanded sense of community life.

Some of the evolving reactions to the study by Schoolpower members included a sense of being filled with new discoveries, a desire to join the process and to be included in what's going on, wanting to be heard with the concomitant willingness to take on more responsibilities in the study, and an excitement about what is happening and the long term effects on the organization. One member, reflecting the feelings of many, was continually bubbling over with ideas she had unearthed through interviews with past Board members.

In a recent interview with another investigator, I was asked what advice I would give to communities considering forming a public school foundation. Instead of pointing to such things as a clear purpose and parental involvement, I realized that each community is unique and to plan one's actions based upon another's cultural and social paradigms may lead to an unsatisfactory outcome. **Why not, I suggested, look at other successful volunteer efforts within the community? What are the common elements they share and why not adopt them, with appropriate adjustments, to the unique needs of the particular organization?** In other words, rather than looking for an outsider's template that may not be applicable to the community, why not develop a process that helps "mine the gold" already present in other local organizations?

Appreciate what is, engage in a process that is inclusive and consensual in unearthing the best of what exists, and fashion an organization that reflects the community's culture and social structure. You then have a fabric, as one Schoolpower member described, "...made up of many patches that, though individual, all weave together to form a quilt that covers us all."

Learnings

While the dynamic collaboration that occurred throughout this process within Schoolpower provided many learnings, the collaboration between Mary Curran and me had its own generative quality. She managed the academic interface and continually encouraged me personally and also provided guidance as to the quality of the research itself. This project has verified for Mary a belief she has held for many years about Appreciative Inquiry. While it requires a basically optimistic mental frame to even understand what Appreciative Inquiry is about, not every organization is appropriate for its application. **When the habit of attention and human energy are devoted primarily to problems, it is too much of a stretch for them to move into an energy field of appreciation.** On the other hand, when the focus of the inquiry, as in the case of Schoolpower, is to discover what has made it successful, Appreciative Inquiry is an entirely congruent process to use.

A final thought, and one that I hope to pursue in future studies, is not so much a personally transformative one as it is an intellectual epiphany. I have been most interested in the perplexing problem in organization theory propounded by Duverger (1915) suggesting that all organizations move toward an oligarchic and rigid structure. Through this research and the appreciative process of inquiry, I believe that Duverger's "iron law"of sociological hierarchical imperatives in organization theory may be subject to modification.

My research appears to indicate that organizations can remain flexible and environmentally adaptable, egalitarian and cooperative, through focus on appreciative developmental processes rather than retrospectively defined goals problematically situated. I am excited to imagine the implications this line of inquiry would take and hope to pursue these studies as part of a lifetime goal of scholarship in service to community.

References

Bolman, G. L., & Deal., Terrence E. (1991). *Reframing Organizations.* San Francisco, CA: Jossey-Bass.

Cooperrider, D. L. (undated). Positive Image, Positive Action: The Affirmative Basis of Organizing, an unpublished draft document for the Fourth International Symposium, *The Functioning of Executive Appreciation.*

Cooperrider, D. L. & Srivastva, S. (1987). Appreciative Inquiry in Organizational Life, *Research in Organizational Change and Development*, Vol. 1, (pp.129-169). JA1 Press Inc.

Cooperrider, D. (1991). *Notes on Appreciative Inquiry.* Paper presented at the 1991 Stanford Program on Managing Change in Health Care Organizations.

Duverger, M. (1915). *A Sociological Study of the Totalitarian Tendencies of Political Parties in a Modern Democracy.* London: Free Press.

Fetterman, D. M. (1989). *Ethnography Step by Step.* Newbury Park, CA: Sage Publications.

Haller, P. A. (1986). Non-traditional Fund Raising for Public Schools. *Dissertation Abstracts International,* 47/09, 3310A. (University Microfilm No. 8629363).

Janov, J. (1994). *The Inventive Organization.* San Francisco, CA: Jossey-Bass.

Muro, J.J. (1995). *Creating and Funding Educational Foundations: A Guide for Local School Districts.* Massachusetts: Allyn & Bacon.

Newby, P.E. (1985). Three Local Educational Foundations: Collaborative Inter-Organizational Relationships that Support Public Education. *Dissertation Abstracts International.* (University Microfilms No. 8614262).

Patton, M.Q. (1990). *Qualitative Evaluation and Research Methods.* Newbury Park, CA: Sage Publications.

Reason, P. (1994). (Ed.) *Participation in Human Inquiry.* London: Sage Publications.

Senge, P.M. (1990). *The Fifth Discipline.* New York: Doubleday/Currency.

ABOUT THE AUTHORS

MICHAEL PINTO PH.D. has extensive experience in both the for-profit and non-profit worlds. He founded a successful chain of music stores as well as a wholesale distribution company, retiring from both in 1983. Investing in a full range of commercial properties, he continues to actively manage his portfolio while spending most of his time in the non-profit world. Over the last twenty five years, he has been president of a number of charitable organizations: The United Jewish Welfare Fund/UJA of Orange County, The Laguna Beach Education Foundation, The Laguna Beach Education Endowment and Capital Fund (founder), and The Laguna Canyon Foundation (founder). He is a board member of the Institute for Deep Ecology and is a member of the advisory board of the Center for the Study of Philanthropy (Graduate Research Center, City University of New York). Michael holds a PH.D. in Integral Studies with a research concentration in learning and change in human systems. His doctoral dissertation focused on public school foundations and organizational transformation processes. He is passionate about discovering new paradigms that lead to a synthesis of seemingly disparate interests.

For more information, contact:
Michael Pinto
PO Box 1809
Laguna Beach, CA. 92652
phone: 949.494.7283
fax: 949.497.7222
e.mail address: Mpinto@aol.com

MARY CURRAN, PH.D. has worked with appreciative inquiry for the past 10 years in her Organization Development consulting practice of 25 years. She has taught organization development courses at the California Institute of Integral Studies, Pepperdine and JFK University. She is now living in Redwood Valley, Ca. between a Buddhist and a Byzantine monastery working as a stained glass artist, a therapist and an organizational consultant and trainer. She considers herself partially retired.

For more information, contact:
Mary Curran
phone: 707.485.5249
fax: 707.485.9390
e.mail: maryc123@sonic.net

Appendices:

Letter to past and current Board members introducing them to the study and initial round of interviews:

Dear John :

I have a vision and passion for what we have done through Schoolpower, and believe that there is much more to be accomplished. As a Ph.D. student of Philanthropy and Organizational Development, I have chosen to study Schoolpower for my dissertation as an example of excellence in the Public School Foundation movement.

Last March the Schoolpower board voted unanimously to support this research. I believe this study can accomplish a number of things that will be beneficial to our organization: 1) we will have the opportunity for many past and present members to voice their opinions as to why the organization has been successful, 2) the process of self-reflection may spark new ideas and energy that will help us to grow in new directions, 3) some of the Schoolpower members will be part of the research team and the skills they learn may prove of value to the organization, 4) we will be engaging in a collaborative process that focuses the study on what organization members want to know about Schoolpower, 5) a history of Schoolpower will be written that documents our success, can help us with our public relations efforts, and forms the basis for introducing new members to the culture of our organization, and 6) our historical records will be assembled and organized.

As part of this study, we will be conducting a series of face-to-face interviews. In order to be truly representative of the organization, a randomly selected group of 20 out of 187 people have been identified from the list of all current and past board members. Your name is among those chosen to be interviewed. For the study to be scientifically valid, it is essential that we be able to interview as many of those randomly selected people as possible.

In order to insure confidentiality, all interviews will be numbered and only Dr. Steiner, an outside researcher, will have the key. The taped interview will be transcribed by an independent secretarial service and there will be no identifying names on the transcript. Additionally, the transcript will be available to you for review, correction and comments. I will never hear the tapes nor see the transcript, but will only be given excerpts out of context and unidentifiable as to author.

A research team made up of Schoolpower volunteers and outside researchers will study the documents for emerging themes. I have some strong beliefs in why our organization is successful, and it is only human that those will form a part of how I interpret the data. Yet, by removing me from the data collection and initial analysis stage, I hope to be able to see better your ideas, observations and recollections.

Help us to do a wonderful job for Schoolpower. Please respond with a YES when you are called for an interview.

Interview Guide for Individual Interviews:

SEPTEMBER - OCTOBER, 1995 • THE LAGUNA BEACH EDUCATION FOUNDATION

Welcome the Interviewee

Welcome the interviewee and tell them how important their responses will be to the study. Chat informally for a moment to relax things and to get both parties comfortable. If they should ask, you can tell them that they are one of only 20 people being interviewed face-to-face.

Informing the Interviewee

Before beginning the interview be sure to do the following:

1. Tell the interviewee that this interview is strictly confidential. Other than you, no one else will know who is being interviewed. They will not be identified on the transcript and no one else other than the transcriber will hear the tape.

2. They will be given a copy of the transcription for review.

3. Review the consent form with them and have them sign it. They keep one copy, you the other.

4. They may stop the interview at any time.

5. They may stop the tape recorder at any time.

6. There will be two rounds of interviews. The first is based on the following questions. Their answers will be analyzed and used as the basis for developing another interview guide. It is that guide which will lead the second round of interviews.

The Interview

The interviewer is to ask only two questions, probing only for clarification, elucidation and depth.

1. Can you please describe for me what you believe helped make Schoolpower successful?

2. Can you give me an idea about what things, if any, you believe impeded the success of Schoolpower?

After asking one of the above questions, just let the respondent answer. You can encourage them to speak by using the following techniques:

Probes and follow-up questions.

To deepen the response to the questions, the interviewer can use the following techniques (Patton, 1990):

a. A conversational probe to get more detail

> When did that happen?
>
> Who else was involved?
>
> Where were you during that time?
>
> How did that come about?
>
> What was your involvement in that situation?

b. An elaboration probe to keep the respondent talking more about a subject.

> Nod your head gently to indicate you are listening and would like to hear more.
>
> The verbal corollary of head nodding is the quiet "uh-huh."
>
> You could say:
>
> > Would you elaborate on that?
> >
> > Could you say more about that?
> >
> > I'm beginning to get the picture. Could you say more?

c. A clarification probe

> If the interviewer has not fully understood what the interviewee said, clarification probes tell the respondent that the interviewer needs more information.
>
> You said the program is a "success." What do you mean by "success"?
>
> I'm not sure I understood what you meant by that. Please let me repeat to you what I think you said, then correct or elaborate as you see fit.
>
> Let me ask you to repeat what you said so that I can get your exact thoughts.

The purpose of open-ended and unstructured interviewing is to find out what is in the interviewee's head, not to put something there. The task of the interviewer is to make it possible for the person being interviewed to bring the interviewer into his or her world.

Letter requesting participation in the focus groups:

I need an hour of your time for a research project on Schoolpower. During the week of November 6-10 we will be conducting focus group interviews at the Schoolpower office. As a current or past member of Schoolpower, we feel you have something important to contribute and would like to ask your help in this project.

I have a vision and passion for what we have done through Schoolpower, and believe that there is much more to be accomplished. As a Ph.D. student of Philanthropy and Organizational Development, I have chosen to study Schoolpower for my dissertation as an example of excellence in the Public School Foundation movement.

Last March the Schoolpower board voted unanimously to support this research. I believe this study can accomplish a number of things that will be beneficial to our organization: 1) we will have the opportunity for many past and present members to voice their opinions as to why the organization has been successful, 2) the process of self-reflection may spark new ideas and energy that will help us to grow in new directions, 3) some of the Schoolpower members will be part of the research team and the skills they learn may prove of value to the organization, 4) we will be engaging in a collaborative process that focuses the study on what organization members want to know about Schoolpower, 5) a history of Schoolpower will be written that documents our success, can help us with our public relations efforts, and forms the basis for introducing new members to the culture of our organization, and 6) our historical records will be assembled and organized.

As part of this study, we will be conducting a series of face-to-face group interviews. Each group will contain up to 8 interviewees. The interviews will be led by one or two interviewers and the session will be taped. The taped interview will be transcribed by an independent secretarial service. The transcript will be available to you for review, correction and comments.

A research team made up of Schoolpower volunteers and outside researchers will study the documents for emerging themes. I have some strong beliefs in why our organization is successful, and it is only human that those will form a part of how I interpret the data. However, as I am only one among several data analysts, and as our preliminary results will be shared with the full board of Schoolpower, I am confident that our the Schoolpower story will emerge in a way that will be truly reflective of all our many diverse perspectives.

Help us to do a wonderful job for Schoolpower. Please respond by volunteering to join at least one of our interview groups.

Sincerely,

Focus Group Interviews

Yes, I would like to participate in a focus group interview. I am marking the three groups I qualify for. Number one represents my first choice, two my second and three my third. I understand that selection to any particular group will be on a first come basis and that the selection will also strive to include as many different people as possible.

NAME ────────────────────── **PHONE NUMBER** ────────────────────

GROUP	MEETING DATE AND TIME	CHOICE
1. 1980 Board members	Mon. Nov. 6, 5-6 PM	_____
2. small gift contributors	Mon. Nov. 6, 6-7 PM	_____
3. 80-83 board members	Tues., Nov. 7, 5-6 PM	_____
4. past presidents	Tues., Nov. 7, 6-7 PM	_____
5. committee chairs	Wed, Nov. 8, 5-6 PM	_____
6. large contributors	Wed, Nov. 8, 6-7 PM	_____
7. 84-90 board members	Thurs., Nov. 9, 5-6 PM	_____
8. past exec. comm. members	Thurs., Nov. 9, 6-7 PM	_____
9.. 91-95 board members	Fri., Nov. 10, 5-6 PM	_____
10. people who left their board position before their term ended	Fri., Nov. 10, 6-7 PM	_____

The interviews will focus on the following two questions:
1. "What do you believe has contributed to the success of Schoolpower?"; and,
2. "What instances have you experienced that have been particularly satisfying during your time with Schoolpower?"

Your experiences and insights are critical to the success of this study. Please participate by filling in this form and mailing back to the Schoolpower office immediately. As you can see by the schedule printed above, we are trying our hardest to complete all interviews before the holiday season begins.

Analysis Team Instructions

The following three papers (appendices E, F and G) were given to the research team:

Laguna Beach Education Foundation
Research Project Analysis Guidelines

1. The purpose of analysis in qualitative methodology is to find meaning in the transcripts. As we are using an Appreciative Inquiry approach, you are focusing on the "life giving forces"of Schoolpower, that is, those unique structures and processes that make the organization's existence possible. What emerges from the interview that touches on the energy and spirit motivating the person's thoughts and actions? What ideas, beliefs and values form the foundation of Schoolpower?

2. Organizations are created and maintained around a set of values and beliefs. When we study organizations, we hope to discover fundamental ideas about them that will help us build greater successes in the future. To do this, we build theories around our research data. Those theories that are well grounded in the lived experience of organization members contain five important elements:

   a. They have a conceptual framework that resonates with organization members.
   This framework is like a lens that focuses our attention on things we consider important and diminishes attention to actions and thoughts considered less important.

   b. Within this framework, there is an implicit

understanding, even agreement, among members that things make sense, that is, they are logical. This logical sense allows people to act with confidence and conviction that they are doing the right thing on behalf of the organization.

   c. Any conceptual framework has incorporated within it a system of values. It is those values that guide our awareness and decide what we deem important.

   d. Through this research we help discover our group's common language. By recognizing that we have a common language within our organization, we come to understand its role in transmitting ideas that shape how we see ourselves vis–a–vis Schoolpower. Within this understanding is an important aspect of human science that distinguishes it from the physical sciences. "...The study of human groups differs from (the study) of objects in an important way: Human beings have the capacity for symbolic interaction and, through language, they have the ability to collaborate in the investigation of their own world — the introduction of new knowledge concerning aspects of our world carries with it the strong likelihood of changing that world itself — it is the 'enlightenment effect' of scientific work, meaning that once the formulations of scientific work are made public, human beings may act autonomously either to dis-confirm or to validate the propositions — it is because of this enlightenment effect that the (building) of theory can and does play an important role in the positive construction of society."(Cooperrider, 1987)

   e. Extending Visions of the possible. We study

things in order to help improve them. An extension of this reasoning is that, ultimately, a generative science is one that thoroughly, intensely and persistently works toward the improvement of human life (Cooperrider). A disciplined study of a group by its own members, can help facilitate a more conscious understanding of three critical elements in

the life of an organization:

1. The vision shared by members which motivates them toward excellence.

2. A passion for their involvement that goes beyond the rational basis of action. This passion taps into sentiments, values and dreams that are at the core of a social group.

3. Integrity of the organization as a unified whole; that is much more than the sum of its parts and that is cohesive; that has a common vision grounded in caring; and

finally, that has an internal consistency and coherence to the validity of its vision.

3. During the research process, a form of "affective (emotional) bonding"takes place that is generative for the organization and that re-energizes a group of insiders with a passion for the organization and its purposes. The goals of this kind of research are therefore, not only the development of better understandings but also the bettering of human life. Goals are no longer centered on solving "problems" but rather on helping to evolve the vision and values of members and to enhance their will toward excellence.

4. The core of this research is to appreciate what

has worked and been successful, rather than to focus on what is wrong or "broken." What elements have given "life" to the organization and activated member's competencies and energy? An organization is an open ended system continuously adapting to internal and external changes. This form of research is focused on helping Schoolpower members to guide its development toward a vision of excellence and to understand the elements that affect its progress. By focusing on what is, what could be, what should be and what will be, the energies of the members and of the organization become provocative (challenging) in an organizationally and socially useful way.

5. Collaboration and empowerment are core values in this type of research. There is an inseparable relationship between the process of this research and its outcome, because we act as a group and find meaning through a shared set of values and understandings. In the same way that we collaborate during fundraising events, the collaborative nature of research helps us to share our understandings and to build a common body of knowledge that will be of help to Schoolpower's future. Another core element in this process is that we, as Schoolpower members, determine the outcome of this research: it reflects our concerns and interests, the questions about which we are most passionate, and gives us a sense of power over its design and outcome. We are not being studied but are studying ourselves in collaboration with others whose experience may facilitate the process.

Inductive Research Analysis

Remember that in this research we are looking for illumination, understanding and appreciation of Schoolpower in a way that will provoke us toward a vision and action for excellence. We are not trying to create categories of causal relationships that lead to prediction and control.

STEPS TO TAKE IN THE ANALYSIS:

Form teams of three people each. Each team member should receive six transcripts. These transcripts should be read and analyzed following the steps below. The team should then meet to share its results. Finally, all the teams will meet for a large scale discussion of their findings.

In reading the transcripts, follow these steps:

1. Look for patterns, themes and categories that will emerge from the data: transcripts, observations and documents from Schoolpower. What do you think are the life giving forces that emerge from the transcript and are fundamental to Schoolpower's existence and its successful fundraising and development?

2. We will begin by reading the transcripts and looking for key ideas and concepts. Whenever you identify an idea or concept, mark it. Additionally, look for particularly meaningful passages in the transcript that comment on feelings, inspiration, and other special instances that go to the spirit of the organization and the reasons why a person would want to support Schoolpower.

3. After the first read-through, go back and re-read the marked sections. Give each of them a one or two word description.

4. Once you have categorized the data, look for similarities and differences between the categories.

5. Now share your findings with your committee. Look for similarities in your categories. Look for differences. Then question both the similarities and the differences. By sharing our findings, we are engaged in what is called inter-rater reliability, that is, seeing how our insights match with another's who is looking independently at the same material. Remember that there are no right or wrong answers but only your personal insights into the meaning that emerges for you from the transcripts.

6. We will then all meet together and share our findings. What similarities and themes emerge from our readings?

7. From this data we will create a story about Schoolpower that will focus on the meaning of the organization and the underlying motivations and spirit that bring people to join and to help Schoolpower. Additionally, in order to involve others in this project, we may create an interview guide that touches on key concepts we would like to pursue in greater depth. This interview guide may be used to either direct additional face-to-face interviews with individuals or groups of individuals (focus groups) or to help us create a written survey instrument that Schoolpower members would be asked to complete.

8. The final step is the creation of provocative propositions. Gathering together all the data we have accumulated, we will meet as a large group and develop a series of propositions that bridge the best of what is (what we have found in the readings) with our intuition of what "might be." These propositions are provocative in that they stretch our imagination while at the same time basing themselves on the best of what has already been accomplished. They are inspiring because they challenge us to create a new vision for the future while at the same time honoring our past. Provocative propositions build on the life giving forces of Schoolpower and heighten our attention, releasing powerful forces that help make visions a reality.

Srivastva and Cooperrider suggest that there are three aspects of organizational life that provocative propositions address: they are novel in that they help elicit an element of surprise, challenge and intrigue; they insure that there is continuity between the past and the future; they insure a smooth transition between the familiar and the unfamiliar, our past and present successes and our future dreams. It is at the intersection of these three elements that provocative propositions are most powerful and energizing.

The Laguna Beach Education Foundation
Action Research Project Appreciative Inquiry

Now that the interviews are behind us, we can begin the analysis of the transcriptions. There are three phases to this process, though you may find that they overlap to some degree. The phases are:

1. Code and summarize data

2. Look for themes, patterns and relationships in the data

3. Attempt to develop explanations for the success of Schoolpower.

The themes identified during the individual interviews were the following:

REP 1. The organization's reputation

MOT 2. What motivates parents

COM 3. The role of community in the success of Schoolpower

TEN 4. The importance of people limiting their tenure on the board

ELITIST 5. Perception of Schoolpower being elitist as compared to the actual experience of board members

COMPAT 6. The compatibility of the board members

PR 7. Our public relations strengths and how we can build on them

RELATION 8. The dynamic relationship between the community, the schools and the various support organizations like PTA and Schoolpower

IDEALS 9. Our ideals: commitment and dedication, direct benefit to the schools, a sincere effort, personal gratification for a job well done, and action for the community rather than personal pride...no glory hounds

We now want to read the transcripts and identify themes, both from the list above plus any new themes we find. You can code these as follows: when you see a theme that is covered by the list above, just put its letter next to that section. For any new themes, you should write a descriptive word or phrase. As an example, someone might mention the importance of networking. So next to that section, you could write the word "networking."

Another thing to look for is interesting metaphors. As metaphors are linguistic devices that can reflect an entire mind set or way of looking at the world, interesting metaphors may help us to get an inside picture into members' perceptions about the organization. They can also tell us something about our perceptions, thinking processes and what we believe to be appropriate action. Does the metaphor "We play hard" have anything to do with the way we conduct our events? Or is that an inappropriate expression?

Once the transcripts have been coded, we will meet and share our findings. A new list of themes will emerge. Finally, we can begin to develop some ideas and explanations as to why these themes emerged and what importance they may have for Schoolpower.

Appreciative Inquiry

The following were instructions given to the analysis team for final review of transcripts and the key points highlighted in the literature review. It is at this time that Provocative Propositions are constructed by the team for the purposes of helping the organization as it transforms and grows.

I. The Theory of Appreciative Inquiry

Appreciative Inquiry is a form of organizational study that selectively seeks to highlight what are referred to as the " life-giving forces" (LGF's) of the organization's existence. These are "— the unique structure and processes of (an) organization that makes its very existence possible. (LGF's) may be ideas, beliefs, or values around which the organizing activity takes place — "(Srivastva, S. et al, Wonder and Affirmation, undated)

II. The Appreciative Inquiry Process

AI identifies and values the factors that give life to the organization — by tapping, for example, times when teamwork was at its best.

ENVISIONS WHAT MIGHT BE — New possibilities based on valuing the best of what exists in the situation. It is "passionate thinking"— working to create a blueprint of the ideal which stretches the status quo and inspires collective momentum.

ENGAGES IN DIALOGUE — It is through dialogue that individual appreciation becomes collective appreciation.

CREATES A REALIZABLE VISION FOR THE ORGANIZATION — Innovates with new ways to move the organization closer to collectively imagined ideal.

III. Steps in Appreciative Methodology

1. Affirmative Topic Choice - usually made through a preliminary set of interviews designed to collect information about individual "peak experiences" in organizations The focus is on "peak experiences" and core factors that give life to the organization.

2. Data Collection: Inquiry into Life-Giving Forces around the topics identified. What are the factors and forces of organizing that heighten the "ideal membership situation" for all members of Schoolpower?

3. Articulation of Provocative Propositions: (statements that bridge "the best of what is or has been"and one's speculation about "what might be"). Building Provocative Propositions:

   a. Locate peak examples of cooperation, the best of "what is"

   b. Extrapolate from the "best of what is" to envision "what might be." Challenge the status quo by expanding the realm of the possible — allow for utopian speculation of the ideal!

   c. Construct a proposition about what is possible. State the proposition in affirmative language--as if the proposition were already true and happening at the current time.

d. The Provocative Propositions should be: novel, bringing an element of surprise, challenge and intrigue; ensuring continuity from old to the new; and making sure there is a smooth transition from the familiar to the unfamiliar and that the change is not felt so abruptly that continuity and novelty are lost.

4. Identify obstacles and facilitating forces — and creates innovation in moving toward the ideal imagined by the organization.

5. Experimentation with Provocative Propositions.

IV. The Four Principles of Appreciative Inquiry:

1. Every system works to some degree, so look for those social innovations which give life to the system and active members' competencies and energies- "What is"perspective.

2. Look at what is possible and practical.

3. In looking at what is possible, be provocative basing appreciative knowledge on member's imaginative and moral purposes.

4. Research should be collaborative as there is an inseparable relationship between the process of inquiry and its content.

V. Provocative Propositions

1. A common vision helps give all members a feeling of significance, purpose, pride and unity.

2. In a truly inclusive organization, people feel as if they are owners of the organization.

3. The organization is relationally driven.

4. Ultimate authority is derived from the consent of others.

5. Leadership is inspirational and participative.

6. The organization has a devotion to excellence.

7. Organization dreams are translated into action through a process of consensus mobilization.

8. Failure is not punished as much as success is applauded.

9. There is an organizational and individual commitment to life long learning.

10. Members may initiate change.

11. Though there is an understanding of the formal structure of the organization, it is not seen as constraining.

12. There is a high tolerance for and welcoming of diversity.

13. The organization puts time and resources into an ongoing review and reflection process.

14. There is an alignment between what members value in themselves and what the organization values.

As indicated, AI also assumes that organizations, like people, adapt their behavior and move in the direction of images that are the brightest, boldest, and most compelling — that it is possible to move from individual images of possibility and develop collective images of possibility.

The Synergy of Appreciative Inquiry and Collaborative Inquiry in the Study of Schoolpower

It seems particularly appropriate that the research be conducted by a team of Schoolpower members and not just by this researcher alone. As Reason has so eloquently discussed (1988, 1994), the use of teams is particularly suited to this type of study for the following reasons:

1. As knowledge and understanding are socially constructed (Dallmayr & McCarthy, 1977; Marcus and Fischer, 1986), the capacity of a group with shared cultural values and organizational framework will be greater than an individual in eliciting cultural meaning from a data set. An important part of this is that team members have a sense of equal stake and interest in the project (Reason, 1994).

2. Groups have the capacity to prompt a member's memory and insight, to cross-check one another's knowledge, and to support each other in revealing sensitive information about themselves as well as their culture (Fetterman, 1988 &1989).

3. Collaborative efforts can create synergies from which emerge new knowledge greater than the sum of what individual group members have to offer (Reason, 1994).

4. Multiple perspectives represented in a group can bring a greater richness to the data interpretation (Patton, 1990; Reason, 1994).

5. Experiences and insights gained by the research committee members can be used to the benefit of the organization. The energy generated during the study will help implement actions based on findings in the study. Also, skills learned and practiced during the research and analysis phase can be employed in the future for the benefit of the organization (Reason, 1988). As one Schoolpower member said, "The amount of interest and excitement generated by this study has re-energized and re-motivated people to do better than ever for the organization."

In an organization, the capacity to learn and change is fundamental to its long term success and viability. Engaging members in thoughtful data collection and analysis as part of a formal research process provides the organization with trained and experienced members that can be transformative change agents. That is one of the fundamental goals this researcher has for the conduct of the study.

This study draws upon both the methods of collaborative inquiry and Appreciative Inquiry. As reflected in this chapter, they form a synergistic model that is reinforcing, uplifting and empowering not only for the organization insiders but for all involved in the process of this study.

Appreciative Inquiry focuses on the good, from the present and the past, and inquires into the future by asking "What if?"questions. These questions are referred to as Provocative Propositions (Cooperrider, 1987). They are provocative because they challenge us to create a new future by building on life-giving forces that are the foundation of the organization. By focusing attention on these Provocative Propositions, a momentum is created that can turn them into reality.

Appreciative Inquiry also assumes that organizations, like people, adapt their behavior and move in the direction of images that are the brightest, boldest, and most compelling — that it is possible to move from individual to collective images of possibility.

The process of Appreciative Inquiry identifies and values the factors that give life to the organization by tapping, for example, times when teamwork was at its best. It envisions what might be — new possibilities based on valuing the best of what exists in the situation and encourages"passionate thinking"— working to create a blueprint of the ideal which stretches the status quo and inspires collective momentum.

Srivastva & Cooperrider (1986, p. 690) provide an example of this within their examination of the Cleveland Clinic. "— the general spirit and guiding logic behind the (Cleveland Clinic's) growth was qualitatively different than predominant bureaucratic rationality of efficiency and effectiveness. Consensus about the primary task of organizing went beyond the economizing functional one (to make profits or fulfill a market demand) and centered around a broader, open-ended psycho-social one."

Appreciative Inquiry engages in dialogue, as it is through dialogue that individual appreciation becomes collective appreciation. It also works to create an attainable vision for the organization through innovating new ways to move it closer to a collectively imagined ideal. The questions asked of insiders are therefore uplifting and generative:

1. Can you describe an experience with the organization that was particularly heartwarming?

2. What elements do you believe have been particularly important to the success of your organization?

3. What vision attracted you to joining this organization?

4. Can you share with us what most excites you about the organization?

5. In imagining your organization's future, what vision is most compelling to you?

To engage people in asking questions that lead to visioning and build on feelings of success, they need to focus on the following:

1. We must ask them to dream, to envision, to remember back and appreciate what attracted them to the organization, then to share their stories with one another as both validation and confirmation of the foundational energies.

2. We then look to the future and construct provocative propositions, challenging insights that ask what might be.

3. Grounded in our past and present successes, motivated by our dreams of what might be, we can then build a commitment for what should be that re-grounds and energizes our mission.

Finally, they look to their resources, energy, membership and mission to answer the question, "What will be?" The focus of AI, then, is on the good from the past and present, the intent being to build on the core energy and vision and what has been the best to envision and then act for the future. Topics for research are affirmative, usually developed through a set of preliminary interviews that focus on individual or group "peak experiences" within the organization (Cooperrider, undated).

Our values and vision form the core of who we are. In their implementation, we move the focus of our attention onto the essence of why organizations are created and sustained. For the investigator who wants to approach organizational analysis appreciatively, there is a special focus on the inspirational, the valued, and the loved. The underlying assumption is that if we can help people to identify and touch within themselves the core meanings of why they value their organization, what motivated them to join it initially, and what things have brought joy to them, we can begin to understand the core of the organization and where

its true power resides in attracting, motivating, and inspiring its members.

Appreciative Inquiry is a form of organizational study that selectively seeks to highlight what are referred to as the "life-giving forces"(LGF's) of the organization's existence. These are "...the unique structure and processes of (an) organization that makes its very existence possible. (LGF's) may be ideas, beliefs, or values around which the organizing activity takes place..." (Cooperrider, Wonder and Affirmation).

The process of Appreciative Inquiry identifies and values the factors that give life to the organization — by tapping, for example, times when teamwork is at its best. It envisions what might be — new possibilities based on valuing the best of what exists in the situation. It is "passionate thinking"— working to create a blueprint of the ideal which stretches the status quo and inspires collective momentum. It engages in dialogue — it is through dialogue that individual appreciation becomes collective appreciation and creates a realizable vision for the organization — it innovates with new ways to move the organization closer to its collectively imagined ideal.

The bonding of the new faculty team

was significant and the process signalled

an understanding of the culture and style

of the groups coming together.

STRATEGIC PLANNING

BY LIZ MELLISH

The Situation

A newly appointed Planning Dean had the task of developing one new Faculty from four existing departments; Mathematics and Computing, Information Systems, Communication and Media Studies and Health Informatics. These existing departments were aligned to two different faculties; The Faculty of Engineering and Physics and the Faculty of Business. Within the existing departments there were a plethora of distinct discipline groupings including applied computing, systems analysis and design, multimedia, mathematics, communication and media studies, journalism, cultural studies and so on. The rationale for creating one new Faculty was to provide students with a world-class blend of subject matter, teaching expertise and research opportunities (e.g. a new Multimedia Studies degree). A further need existed to reduce duplication and capture synergies between the existing departments (e.g. Mathematics and Computing and Information Systems). The overarching idea was to put together the "technological" and the "human" aspects of communication in an innovative and complimentary way.

The Planning Dean recognized the opportunity to transform strategy, structure and culture simultaneously. The scope of the change involved 160 academic and general staff who represented multiple sub-cultures and passionate views about the future of their particular areas.

The Approach

The Planning Dean had been exposed to Appreciative Inquiry on a recent *Women in Leadership Program* and saw the potential of the process to provide an inclusive and generative approach to developing the new Faculty. She was committed to building the new Faculty on the "best of" what existed, she wanted a consultative process so as to provide voice and space for all participants and she wanted a deliverable at the end: a New Faculty Plan, to which everyone was committed.

A three-stage process over six weeks was planned based on the 4-D Model of Appreciative Inquiry. In stage one everyone was invited to a two-day celebration which covered the Discover and Dream phases. Self-selected; representative concept teams were formed to pursue Discovery questions, emergent topics and provocative proposals with those unable to attend. Two weeks later, participants returned for a two-day workshop, which addressed the Design phase. Finally, two weeks later a one-day workshop addressed the Deliver phase.

The 4-D Model

Discover

A group of ninety academics and general staff participated in the process. The Planning Dean shared her commitment to an inclusive and consultative process for managing the transition to the new Faculty. She outlined the following:

Principles of Appreciative Inquiry

1. **Appreciate (yourself and other people)**
2. **Apply (our knowledge of what works best)**
3. **Provoke (our imaginations about what's ideal)**
4. **Collaborate (share, affirm and co-ordinate our efforts)**

She proceeded to provide an overview of the 4-D Model and stressed the following desired outputs of the process:
• a compelling vision for the new faculty
• provocative propositions regarding function and form of the new faculty
• an agreed transition plan towards the new faculty
• an agreed set of strategic performance indicators to deliver on the new faculty

Participants proceeded to interview each other, in mixed pairs, using the sample interview protocol provided in Appendix A. The appreciative questions were specifically designed to focus on personal highpoints, co-operative relationships, types of communication, hopes for the future, values and positive images.

People were asked to pair up with someone they didn't know and didn't work with so as to discover cross discipline stories. These were retold in small groups of 8 people who reported back on emergent, compelling topics. Ten topics emerged in the large group plenary session. These were:
• positive working relationships
• small effective teams: partnering between academics and general staff
• opportunity focussed
• respect, appreciation, trust and integrity
• control own futures
• shared information
• transparent financial accountability
• supportive environment for teaching/learning/research
• co-operative management style
• incentive driven teamwork

In order to facilitate the process of developing provocative propositions which were to frame the social and strategic intent of the new faculty, these topics were grouped into five themes;
• **Leadership and Management,**
• **Communication,**
• **Marketing,**
• **Teaching and Learning**
• **Research.**

Dream

The transitional process between Discover and Dream was facilitated by individual self-selecting, based on interest and expertise, where best they would contribute to developing provocative propositions. Five mixed groups were formed. Using the detailed topic data, relevant to their theme, each group developed a compelling provocative proposition which would be used to frame the new Faculty. The whole group discussed and endorsed the following provocative propositions.

Provocative Propositions

Leadership and Management
- Our management style will be participatory, open and result oriented.
- There will be a climate of innovation, flexibility, individual growth and mutual respect.

Communication/Culture and Fun
- We will foster a culture of open communication, mutual trust, respect for difference, inclusiveness, and personal empowerment through the use of a variety of appropriate and timely communication strategies within a multi-campus university.

Learning must be a Valued Fundamental Activity
- We will actively foster learning through innovative, flexible, collaborative professional and effective approaches in a supportive and appropriate resourced environment.

Research
- By March, 1998 we will have identified specialised research directions that capitalize on the unique discipline mix in our Faculty.
- By December, 1998 we will have a general faculty research output above the university average, and will have established at least 2 (two) research groups with a potential for external funding.

Marketing
- To embrace the challenge of marketing the unique identity of the Faculty as an attraction in its own right.

These provocative propositions, grounded as they were in the group's collective positive organisational experiences, reflected the "ideal" shape and practice of the new faculty. There was a shared sense of excitement that the group was in a position to impact the manner in which they organised and the future direction of the emergent faculty. A need was expressed to rise above the five provocative propositions and to dream a vision statement that would represent the new faculty. This suggestion was considered important by the group who felt that an overarching statement of intent could best be used for "external consumption" (e.g. students, industry, other faculties) whilst the provocative propositions were to guide their internal organising dynamics. The large group divided randomly into four groups who proceeded to brainstorm ideal statements, which would capture and define the "spirit" of the new Faculty.

In the final hours of the first two-day workshop, the group worked out how best to include their colleagues in the process. A "concept team" was formed around each of the five provocative propositions. The composition of these teams purposefully included academic, administrative, multiple disciplinary, mullet-campus representatives. Their task was to interview their colleagues on the topics, provocative propositions and proposed vision statement prior to the second workshop. A small transition-monitoring group was also formed to explore and report on any other issues relating to how people felt about the transition towards the new Faculty. A co-ordinating Faculty Advisory Committee was established comprising the Planning Dean and the Chairs of each of the concept teams.

VISION AND MISSION

THE VISION THAT EMERGED WAS:

People and Technology: Communicating in the 21st Century

THE MISSION STATEMENT READ:

To promote and inspire knowledge and learning by linking people and information using the best of ...

- information technology
- contemporary communication and
- mathematical and decision systems

Design

A group of approximately 60 people reconvened for the second workshop. They reported on additional data from their appreciative consultations with colleagues. The focus of the workshop was on the design implications of the agreed provocative propositions i.e. how best to organise the new faculty in terms of its core business, teaching and learning and research and its co-ordinating functions of management, marketing and communication.

The concept teams focussed on their own provocative propositions and developed a list of key operational impact issues. They continued work on these operational impacts by developing a project plan for each provocative proposition including scheduled tasks, accountabilities, resource implications and a timeline. Each concept team reported their implementation proposal to the large group in a lively plenary session. The proposals were refined to maximise synergies across the teams, and to generate collective commitment and excitement around the creation of the new faculty.

The concept teams progressed the application of their revised project plans and proceeded to map a detailed transition plan towards the new faculty. Observable changes in modus operandi were evident in terms of how the concept teams approached their tasks. For example, the Leadership and Management concept team facilitated an appreciative dialogue with the large group on the range of options, which existed for structural change, and development of new decision making forums. After everyone's active participation in the process, a format for broader consultation with colleagues unable to attend the workshop[1] was developed and endorsed by the group.

The excellent output from the second workshop was based on and constantly linked to the topics and provocative propositions from the first workshop. There was exceptional commitment, goodwill, tolerance and willingness to explore the operational impacts of the Discover and the Dream phase outputs.

It was impressive to realise how much work was voluntarily undertaken between the second and third workshop as each of the concept teams consulted with colleagues and established what would work best in their implementation plans.

---

[1] Some people were unable to attend the workshop due to lecturing, leave and other prior commitments.

Deliver

The third workshop was focussed on "tying it all together", making some key decisions and agreeing upon strategic performance indicators that everyone was happy to use as measures of their collective achievement in successfully developing the new Faculty.

The leadership and management concept team presented provocative options for the function and form of the new faculty based on their additional extensive, collegial consultations. It was finally agreed that the new Faculty would have three theme-based schools;

- **Decision Sciences,**
- **Contemporary Communication, and**
- **Technology,** with a team of administrative support staff overlaying the school structure.

The schools would have permeable walls and staff would be able to move between schools for teaching, community service and research purposes.

The final process involved clarifying appropriate and meaningful Faculty performance indicators. These emerged directly from the provocative propositions (or statements of social and strategic intent) in the first workshop. Examples of performance indicators include:

Teaching and learning
- Finalise proposal for rationalised units - Faculty Education Committee (March 1998),
- Academic Board (June 1998)
- Finalise proposal for new courses - Faculty Education Committee (March 1998),
- Academic Board (June 1998)

Leadership and management
Have management structures in place with widespread and active support by December 1997

The result of the process

The Appreciative Inquiry approach to moving a large group of people with multiple agendas towards a collective view of the future and their contribution to that future resulted in a number of positive outputs:

- The Faculty of Informatics and Communication Faculty Restructure Plan was produced and endorsed by the Vice Chancellor
- The strategic performance indicators are understood and will be used by the group to affirm their own progress
- The detailed transition plans are collectively understood, widely supported and happening on a daily basis.
- The Planning Dean has sustainable support for an extremely challenging 18 months ahead.

With respect to the appreciative process and the 4-D Model, some examples of feedback from participants include:

"Very positive, I valued the 'staged' timing of the workshops as there was time to reflect"

"I considered the time investment worthwhile and felt, for the first time in any change we've been through, that there was collective ownership of the outcome"

Facilitator's reflections

The 4-D Model[2] and the appreciative inquiry process provide client organisations with a practical tool and a positive approach to facilitating large-scale change. Whilst the facilitator continually adapts and invents strategies to move the group, the energy and collective goodwill of the group becomes self-sustaining.

The key "value adding" skills that the facilitator brings to the appreciative planning process include:
- acute listening
- positive care
- an insatiable curiosity and
- the ability to spontaneously reframe questions which bring the "best" out of everyone.

Flexible and Pragmatic Process Management

My experience is that clients require ongoing reassurance that the process is leading somewhere. In this respect, the 4-D Model supported by carefully designed worksheets, is a helpful guide and a confidence building tool to organise large group input and interaction with a view to delivering a meaningful "product" at the end. In terms of pace and space for dialogue in the process, I have found that the time spent storytelling at the front end of the process will be directly reflected in the quality of and commitment to the deliverables at the back end of the process. The manner in which topics emerge from small group story reflections and how these are subsequently translated in provocative propositions is a challenge. One lesson to be aware of at this stage relates to the facilitator's "stewardship" of the process. In my case, I am conscious of attempting to creatively ensure that contextual factors such as "strategic givens" are integrated into the development of provocative propositions. Examples of "strategic givens" may be the budgetary allocation available or a key player's perspective, which will influence the planning outcome. Working through the 4-D Model is an iterative process; the group may commence exploration of the design phase, which, in turn, raises further questions about their propositions and their capacity to deliver. The 4-D Model and appreciative inquiry process enables the group to create a new language for planning through appreciating the interrelated components of the process.

A final skill that the facilitator requires is a perceptive and anticipatory knowledge of the contextual issues faced by the client so as to be able to usefully direct energies towards an outcome within which all parties can see themselves operating productively.

---

2 In the Australian context, we have experienced mixed reactions to the terminology used in appreciative inquiry. A typical client response to a proposal to use the appreciative inquiry process would be "the structure looks great but maybe the terminology is a bit *over the top* for some/many of our people", "I think it's a bit academic - are you sure it'll work?" "It sounds highfaluting - what do you mean?" In addition *Dreaming* has particular connotations for Aboriginal Australians, which require acknowledgement. It is particularly important for us to acknowledge the dreaming as a valid way of thinking about creation. The process of dreaming links the past, and stories associated with the past, providing powerful metaphors which guide us foreword. Dreaming enables vital cross cultural meanings to be shared in a legitimate and respectful manner.

Acute Listening

This skill is probably implicit in all sound facilitative processes however; I have experienced a shift in what I listen for! Cooperrider, a leading exponent of appreciative inquiry in organizational life, has applied the notion of an *appreciative eye* to business (Hammond 1996:6). To the appreciative eye, organisations are expressions of beauty and spirit. **I am experiencing the development of an "appreciative ear". Listening for how people create possibilities, listening for their stories and examples of their best experiences and ideas in organisations,** reflecting on these and using them to fuel the appreciative inquiry process in terms of *the best of what is* and *the best of what can be* is key to the facilitative process.

I have found that the energy I commit to listening and reframing with the *appreciative ear* is considerable. As a facilitator, my ears are tuned to positive experiences, how things can work best, and how unexpected synergies have been achieved. Pleasant exhaustion at the end of a day of appreciative inquiry is a positive indicator for me that my *appreciative ear* has been exercised!

Positive Care

I believe the best facilitators acknowledge the context of their life experience, their assumptions and their commitment to assisting the client achieve the best possible outcome from the process. Based on the initial brief by the client, the facilitator makes choices about content and process delivery to achieve an outcome. The values that underpin my approach include "making it easy", facilitating the best out of the client and his/her staff. The end result of the process is almost always unknown — one should never contrive an appreciative inquiry process — hence the stories, topics, propositions, organising methods and deliverables emerge in process. At each step of the way, the facilitator exposes his/her interest and values in terms of the nuances, emphases, and ways of reporting and reflective summarising techniques used. I am more conscious than ever now of the ongoing need to exercise the appreciative philosophy and positive care in every facilitative expression.

An Insatiable Curiosity

I have always enjoyed discovering the ways in which people and organisations "get it together" both at the strategic and operational level. Appreciative Inquiry with its emphasis on exploring what works in organisations provides everyone in the process with opportunities to reflect on those best parts of the past that they want to carry foreword as they imagine an ideal future. The process provides space in organizational life to share stories which otherwise remain untold; for people impacted, but frequently overlooked, by planning and decision making processes, to contribute. In my view, the facilitator needs to demonstrate a genuine interest, a wonder if you will, in the day to day proceedings of organisational life. To some extent, this may be an informed naivete'; for me it occurs in expressions of amazement, delight, and affirming acknowledgement of the creative ways in which people organise and dream of being organised. In addition, because everyone's story counts, the process validates multiple ways of being which is precisely the dynamism so clearly needed in many organisations today.

Ability to spontaneously reframe questions in an attempt to get the best out of everyone.

Wedded to the assumption that organisational effort follows the line of inquiry, the manner in which questions are used at every stage of the appreciative process has assumed paramount importance. The collaborative design of the initial interview protocol, which underpins the discovery phase, works best when tailored to the context of the organisation, people's experiences and hopes for the future. The questions surrounding the generation of topics need to be framed in terms of the best categories, the most representative groupings, the deepest passions, the most valued components etc. The questions which push the boundaries of imagination for generating provocative propositions relate to being "bold enough", interrupting one's thinking, illustrating pride in product or service, affirming commitment to core business or a daring redefinition of core business. Questions relating to design of new and innovative ways of organising relate to who is best at what, who is most interested in what, who has expertise in what and how. Practically, can it all be made to happen in an agreed timeframe, given the resources available? Finally, questions about delivery are designed to link intent to outcomes. How will we know we've achieved the intent of our provocative propositions? How does it all fit together? Is there a stream of passion and logic through the process and the product we've developed? Who's going to benefit and how best can we communicate these achievements?

While the positive thrust of the inquiry described above appears straightforward, the dynamics of every group are, naturally, different. Holding on to the belief that the process is meaningful, worthwhile and productive involves the facilitator in multiple spontaneous reframing, inputting and provocative inquiry processes.

The appreciative inquiry principles of appreciation, application, provocation and collaboration apply as much to the facilitator as they do to the group. The facilitator models, in many respects, the journey, which is undertaken with the group. It is very useful for the facilitator to engage in mini 4-D cycles of appreciative inquiry into his/her own facilitative approach in order to accumulate and keep developing best interventions, process techniques and questions to enhance their own professional practice.

Conclusion

Appreciative consultation is a "way of being" in our management consultancy practice. The theory and approach has enabled us to participate with our clients in the positive social construction of their organisational worlds. We are surprised and delighted at the multiple applications of Appreciative Inquiry in corporate, government, higher education and community organisations. We have found that using the approach involves a true commitment to people and processes in change and this commitment can be shared and can deliver outcomes to clients which exceed traditional planning and evaluation methods.

In conclusion, Appreciative Inquiry offers management consultants and their clients a low cost high impact change process which deals with culture, strategy and structure simultaneously.
© L.MELLISH, 1998

ABOUT THE AUTHOR

DR. LIZ MELLISH founded her national management consulting practice, Mellish & Associates, in 1984. Mellish & Associates consults to government, corporate, community and higher education organisations throughout Australia in the areas of leadership, strategic management, organisational change, executive mentoring, training and development and project management.

Having commenced her journey with Appreciative Inquiry in Taos in 1996, Liz completed her doctoral thesis *Appreciative Inquiry at Work* (Queensland University of Technology) in 2000. *Appreciative Inquiry at Work* is about working with AI in the context of organisational change. Specifically, the knowledge and skills required to use Appreciative Inquiry as a participatory method for engaging people in planning and implementing sustainable organisational change and the lessons learned, for consultants and for organisations, from the multiple case research is covered.

Liz provides coaching, mentoring and mediation services to corporate and government leaders, parliamentarians and community representatives in various fields. Liz is a Director on the Main Roads (Qld) Corporate Governance Board, and a Councillor on the Queensland Children's Council. She is a Fellow of her professional association, the Institute of Management Consultants.

Liz has two children and enjoys travelling, playing tennis, golf and hiking.

For more information, contact:
Mellish & Associates
132 Victoria Ave
Chelmer
Queensland 4068
Australia
phone: 07.3379.1143
fax: 07.3379.6641
e.mail: info@mellish.com.au
web: www.mellish.com.au

References

Hammond, S. (1996) *The Thin Book of Appreciative Inquiry*, Thin Book Publishing Co Plano, TX (972 378 0523)

Mellish, L. and Limerick, B. (1997) *Appreciative consultation: Reclaiming our imaginative competence:* Paper presented at the 1997 Australian Human Resources Institute National Conference: The Journey to Business Partner Brisbane

Limerick, D., Cunnington B, and Crowther F. (1997) *Managing the New Organisation Management: Management Strategies for the Post Corporate Era,* Sydney Woodslane Publishing

Phase 1: Discovery:
APPRECIATING THE BEST OF "WHAT IS"

PAIRED INTERVIEWS
1. Reflect on your time with this university
What have been the high points for you? Select one high point, a time when you felt most alive, most happy; a time when you felt you were making a difference and doing creative, useful, meaningful work. What was it about you that felt good, who else was involved, what were you doing, what did you feel you achieved? Describe the STORY around the moment

2. Co-operative relationships
Identify a scenario which you feel demonstrates the positive aspects of working together, co-operating to get something done. What was the scenario? Who was involved? Why did it work? What were you doing? What were other people doing?

3. Types of communication
What different types of communication occur across the Faculty? What do you value most about effective communication? When does this happen for you? Who and what are involved in the best types of communication? Why is effective communication good for you and the Faculty?

4. Hopes for the future
What does the new Faculty of Informatics and Communication have the capacity to become? How could working together make a difference? What do you see as priorities? What part could you play in making these priorities happen?

5. What do you VALUE most about:
Yourself
The people that work with you (colleagues, students, partners)
The university

6. What are your positive IMAGES of the future function and form of the Faculty of Informatics and Communication?
3 wishes?

Note: Spark the appreciative imagination of the other. Learn from each other. Share key stories that unearth values. Follow what you are sincerely curious about.

*I*n every community something works.

Change can be achieved by identifying

what works and focusing energy on doing

more of what works.

CREATING A

HEALTHY HILLTOP
COMMUNITY

BY PEGGY HOLMAN,
ALLAN PAULSON,
AND LAURE NICHOLS

Introduction

Franciscan Health System (FHS) is a system of hospitals, primary care clinics, and long term care facilities with operations in the South Puget Sound area of Washington State. It is part of the national health system, Catholic Health Initiatives. In 1996, the governing board of FHS recognized the need to more effectively achieve its vision of "being a healing influence in the communities we serve and improving health status." They authorized the formation of Community Health Councils in discrete geographic areas served by the Health System to act as catalysts for long-term, systemic change and to build capacity for improved health. Each Council brings together individuals with extensive community experience and professional expertise in such areas as public health, medicine, education, public and private sectors, religious, public safety, and community activism.

After completing a preliminary community health assessment using data from sources including the Health Department, schools, cities and United Way, members of the St. Joseph Community Health Council in Tacoma decided to pursue a process of direct assessment with residents of the Hilltop area. The Hilltop community has a wide range of ethnicities, including African-Americans, Hispanics and many Asian immigrants for whom English is not an easy language. The area is often characterized as poor and crime ridden. St. Joseph Medical Center has been located in the Hilltop area of Tacoma for over 100 years, yet has had little direct interaction to improve the health of the neighborhood's residents.

Appreciative Inquiry was chosen as the means to do direct assessment because of the experience of a Council member. She had participated in an inquiry at Group Health Cooperative of Puget Sound. The impact she described to the Council got their attention.

WHAT WE DID

Creating a Healthier Hilltop spanned seven months of planning and action. It began with the kernel of an idea — that those in the community were best equipped to set the priorities for a healthy community. While the final project activity took place on a set day, the impact of the effort continues to ripple through the community. What follows is the story of what we did.

Early December, 1996

A call came from a colleague at work, who also happened to be the chair of the St. Joseph Community Health Council. He was looking for someone who knew something about Appreciative Inquiry to participate in this volunteer project.

When we gathered later that month, there were four consultants who received such a call to work with the Community Health Council to accomplish our task. We began by looking at desired outcomes. The discussions reflected the diversity of perspectives among the Council. Some were focused on the people in the community. Others were focused on creating more synergy among the service providers that served the community. What we ultimately concluded was that these goals were quite compatible and that we could accomplish both in our design.

THE GOALS THE COUNCIL SET WERE:

1. To develop relationships and improve connections among a broad variety of constituencies around the values and agenda of being a healing influence in the communities we serve;

2. To enhance individual and organizational visibility and capacities by training a significant group of stakeholders in Appreciative Inquiry;

3. To learn how the health care organizations might more effectively collaborate, align and support existing organizations' healthy community initiatives; and

4. To create a pattern of communication that can be replicated.

So, what were the dimensions of this work? About 85 people were invited to training in Appreciative Inquiry with the expectation that they would do two interviews each. Nearly 70 people from 60 agencies actually participated as *"Listeners"*, completing over 100 interviews with *"Talkers"*.

January, 1997

With some feel for the goals of the effort, we began to put a process in place to make it happen. With four consultants, each with their own views of how best to do this, one of our challenges was to learn to separate our needs to be experts from our conversations with the Community Health Council we were there to serve! The early sessions were very challenging – the agendas of the Council members and the agendas of the consultants made for a messy mix during the formation of the project. With a lot of deep listening to each other, a design emerged that we all felt good about:

THE DESIGN WE OUTLINED WAS:

1. We would invite all of the social service providers serving the Hilltop community to a morning of Listener Training.

2. Each Listener would conduct at least 2 interviews over the next six weeks.

3. A Listener gathering would be held to review what they heard.

4. Finally, we would invite all of the Talkers and the Listeners to participate in a one-day conference to review the interviews, formulate possibility statements and discuss next steps.

January - February

The work began. A letter inviting potential Listeners went to 100 health and social service providers from the Hilltop area on February 21. Meanwhile, the Council grappled with the appreciative interview questions – with much angst over how best to word them. And they struggled with one other challenge: how would they identify the Talkers?

The challenge of identifying Talkers requires some perspective: the members of the Council, while reflecting some racial diversity, were college educated and lived outside the Hilltop area. Given the cultural divide between service providers and the low-income, ethnically diverse residents, how could they link Listeners and Talkers?

The challenge was resolved when, ironically, a group called the Hilltop Action Coalition approached the Council about sponsoring publication of a Block Handbook. The Coalition has been recognized nationally for organizing block groups and they provided the perfect access point into the community. They were quickly engaged and supplied Talkers for the initiative.

Interview questions were also finalized during this time. The questions started by grounding the Talker, then focused on the best of what is, began to shift focus to what might be, allowed the Talker to dream about what was possible and finally, how they might act to create the future they wanted.

INTERVIEW QUESTIONS

1. Tell me a little bit about what it is like to live in this area.

2. Tell me about the best experience you've had living in this community.
> What happened?
> What did you do?
> What were your thoughts and feelings?
> What made it a good experience?
> What made it possible?

3. What are the best things about the Hilltop that you think the community should build on to make this a better place to live?

4. What is your picture of the Hilltop community you want to live in?

5. What are three things you and others need to do to make this neighborhood a healthier place to live?

April 1 - Listener Training

We had three and one-half hours to help Listeners understand what an appreciative interview was and to cover the logistics of doing interviews. It was a day full of anticipation. The members of the Council were there to express their excitement and support for this collaboration among service providers. The consultants were all primed to equip the Listeners with the information and the spirit of the project.

We started by giving them an overview. We then covered the very basics of Appreciative Inquiry. Most of the time was used to practice interviewing each other. We then discussed their interview experience, enabling them to assimilate the concepts of Appreciative Inquiry through their own discussion. We ended the session by covering the logistics of contacting Talkers and collecting interviews. And we sent them off to listen. The morning did its job. The Listeners left excited by their role and the potential value for the community.

April 25 - Interim Review

The desire for this meeting grew out of the Community Health Council's need to know what people were saying before there was a large gathering of Talkers and Listeners. Ironically, once they had done some interviewing, their need for this interim review disappeared. Nonetheless, the date had been set, so an optional gathering of about 25 Listeners came together for a half-day to check-in on the experience to date.

The structure of the session was very simple. We had copies of interviews at each table. People took some time to read them and discuss their impressions of what people said. We then identified common themes among the interviews for use during the Talker-Listener conference in June.

People came with stories to tell. The positive voices and experiences the Talkers described stunned professionals who had served this community for years and had never really ventured into it. This neighborhood was characterized by the media as one of the West Coast's most poverty-ridden, dangerous places. Yet, it was full of people who cared about the same things that the professionals did — a nice place to live, a good place to raise their kids, a community that drew strength from its diversity.

One challenge crept into our process design about this time. The County Public Health Department had volunteered their Office of Community Assessment to analyze the interviews. Their highly skilled community assessment staff was trained to look at data for problem-solving opportunities. The clash between our now tight-knit band of consultants who focused on the appreciative qualities of the interviews and these newly arrived community assessment experts provided a background drama throughout the remainder of the project.

June 7 - Talker-Listener Conference

By this time the goal of the initiative had been much simplified: *To build and sustain a healthier Hilltop community.*

When the 50 Talkers and Listeners gathered on a Saturday morning, the anticipation in the room was palpable. **These were the people who had been most profoundly affected by the stories they had heard or told. They came together to discuss how they could make a difference.**

We began the day using the themes that had come from the April 25 session coupled with the analysis done by the County Health Department. These themes along with participant's experiences became the basis to develop possibility statements about the Hilltop Community they really wanted to live in.

We then put the participants in a circle and used Open Space Technology to focus the dreams expressed through the possibility statements into activities to create what they said they wanted. What we asked them to do was to declare any idea to discuss that they personally felt would move them towards the possibilities they had identified. Because there was no sponsoring agency who would follow up on recommendations, we made it clear that "If it's to be, it's up to me." This refrain was heard frequently through the day as people gathered to discuss project ideas and schedule time to pursue them following the conference.

AMONG THE POSSIBILITIES:

1. In this community – every child grows up in a nurturing home with neighbors and community members valuing and supporting the nurturing home.

2. A model of cultural ethnic engagement where our streets are more like day camps than armed camps and neighborhood mentors emerge.

3. The Hilltop is a peaceful, respectful and connected community that shares, cares and involves everyone.

4. The community thrives because of diversity.

AMONG THE PROJECTS THAT EMERGED:

1. Develop a Police Athletic League for sports activities targeting Hilltop youth;

2. Create a quarterly Hilltop news bulletin delivered to residences and businesses describing opportunities for linking people to community activities and resources; and

3. Enhance resources available through the Hilltop Family Support Center to bring isolated residents of the Hilltop together.

As part of the physical layout, we had posted a mural sized sheet of butcher paper with the title "Picture of a Healthy Hilltop Community." Throughout the day people added to the drawing. By the end of the session, an inspiring mural had been created that gave form to the possibilities stated by these committed people.

We consultants had an interesting learning from this day. The interview summary document compiled by the County Health Department contained some less than appreciative observations, including reference to crime and poor police relations. These observations did not in any way shift the focus from creating a healthy Hilltop community. Participants successfully made the leap from problem solving into the realm of possibilities.

The final role of the St. Joseph's Community Health Council was to send out a summary of what took place to all participants and key community leaders.

Outcomes: What's Happened Since

Six months after the June conference, we interviewed a number of members of the Community Health Council and the Council staff person from the Franciscan Health System. Among the Council members we interviewed were two CEO's of social service organizations based in the Hilltop area.

We asked each what outcomes they had expected. Three desires were consistently identified:

1. To listen to the people of the Hilltop talk about what they see as the community's assets and what constitutes a healthy community;

2. To find collaborative ways that the health system could help advance the community's health agenda;

3. To create a more positive reputation for the Franciscan Health System.

As one Council member put it, " We want to meet the community where they are and be a catalyst to help the community help themselves."

All of those we interviewed reported that their expectations have been met, along with surprises about what they heard from the community. Several specific initiatives are moving forward, and the Community Council itself has a new sense of energy and purpose, as well as an influx of new members from the community. At the same time, some Council members pointed to opportunities to extend the learnings of the inquiry through the community by more provocative sharing of the data.

There have been several tangible initiatives growing out of groups that first convened during the Open Space. One group focused broadly on communication and identified needs for better exchange of information between both the residents and the service agencies in the Hilltop. As a result of that session, a large group of social service providers and funders have met to focus on the objective of building an electronic information network that would facilitate information referral and provide easy access to health information and education. Another initiative is attempting to further identify and showcase the community's assets through developing a "100 year project." The project will identify both buildings and institutions that have existed in the community for 100 years, supporting both the sense of pride and desire for multi-culturalism that was expressed in the appreciative interviews.

It is less clear what happened to a number of other ideas that surfaced in the Open Space sessions. As one person pointed out, "We did not create another movement, but gave more focus to others' ongoing efforts." However, some Council members believe it would be good to have more follow-up to see what else is happening, and perhaps an occasional newsletter to highlight, encourage and recognize people's efforts.

In late fall, the Council presented its efforts to the System's Board of Trustees. In making the presentation, the Council Chair tried to convey his significant learnings from the process: discovering and collaboratively supporting a community agenda is far different from the usual modus operandi of the business world. "What we typically do," he said "is find a problem and solve it, making every effort to control the outcome with goals, timetables, etc. You just can't approach a community in this way."

Most of those we talked with about results spoke enthusiastically about the interview process itself. They described their experience as "exciting," "enlightening," "wonderful." **The positive focus of the interviews helped both the Listeners and the Talkers recognize and affirm the most positive aspects of the community, and this in itself contributed to the feeling of pride that emerged in the interviews.**

All of the Council members felt that the process helped them to understand the community better, and was successful in creating a more positive perception of the Health System's role in the community. Too often, they noted, a person's only contact with a hospital is during an experience of illness, pain and sadness. People don't normally think of what positive influences a health system can bring to the community's well being.

One specific change has been in the membership of the Council. Through natural rotation, the Council has recruited seven new members in the past few months. Every person asked to join the Council accepted the invitation, and the new members as a group are more closely connected to the Hilltop community. Their willingness to commit their time, in the face of a multitude of opportunities and demands, is viewed as a significant endorsement of the Council's relevance and sensitivity to the Hilltop.

Another positive result has been the establishment of stronger relationships between the Health System and several important community organizations such as the County Public Health Department and the City of Tacoma Police Department. The Health Department has been represented on the Council and took on responsibility for processing the interview data. In the course of the project, the hospital and the health department learned much more about how each works and approaches their role in the community. As a result, they have opened a dialogue on new ways they can work together and be resources to each other's efforts. As for the police, a wide spectrum of views of community safety and the role of law enforcement in the Hilltop were expressed in the interviews. Both the fact and the perception of safety were important components of the picture of community health that emerged. Recently, a senior member of the Police Department joined the Council to support continued focus on the connection between community health and safety.

Opportunities remain. While most of the data generated from the interviews and workshops was sent in written form to many social agencies in the broader community, there is still an opportunity to bring the learnings from the inquiry to other community organizations in an interactive fashion, asking them what they might want to do to facilitate the community health agenda. Some Council members noted that the turn to action after the Open Space also seemed to end the generative aspects of

What problems are you having? What is working around here?

These two questions underline the difference between traditional Change Management theory and Appreciative Inquiry. The traditional approach to change is to look for the problem, do a diagnosis, and find a solution. The primary focus is on what is wrong or broken; since we look for problems, we find them. By paying attention to problems, we emphasize and amplify them...

In the mid-seventies, David Cooperrider and his associates at Case Western Reserve University, challenged this approach and introduced the term Appreciative Inquiry. David's artist wife Nancy brought the "appreciative eye" perspective to David's attention. The idea of the appreciative eye assumes that in every piece of art there is beauty. Art is a beautiful idea translated into a concrete form. Cooperrider applied the notion to business: to the appreciative eye, organizations are expressions of beauty and spirit...

Appreciative Inquiry suggests that we look for what works in an organization. The tangible result of the inquiry process is a series of statements that describe where the organization wants to be, based on the high moments of where they have been. Because the statements are grounded in real experience and history, people know how to repeat their success.

Reprinted with permission from *The Thin Book of Appreciative Inquiry*, Sue Annis Hammond

the inquiry and the possibility of engaging and empowering others who had as yet not been involved. As both the outgoing and new Council Chairpersons noted, there is a tension between the need to problem solve and show results and the desire to generate greater levels of involvement and initiative throughout the community. This will provide the challenge as the Council continues its work.

PEGGY HOLMAN is an independent consultant focusing her practice on supporting organizations in becoming who they say they want to be. Productive, fulfilling work is performed by people who bring themselves fully to their work: mind, heart, body and spirit. Her work is about supporting organizations in remembering how to do this.

Since 1990, Peggy has worked with organizations in transforming their cultures using a variety of approaches involving Organizational Learning and Total Quality Management. She entered organizational change work with 20 years of Information Technologies experience because she was seeking better ways to support people in improving their work. She brings the project management skills from her years in Information Technology, a strong customer focus from her Total Quality work and the disciplines of organization development and learning to create a holistic approach to her work. During her career, Peggy has worked with a variety of organizations, including GTE, Rainier Bank, U S WEST NewVector Group and Weyerhaeuser Company. She holds an MBA from Seattle University.

For more information, contact:
Peggy Holman
15347 SE 49th Place
Belleme, WA 98006
phone: 425.746.6274
fax:425.865.8168
e.mail address: peggy@opencirclecompany.com

ABOUT THE AUTHORS

ALLAN PAULSON has an active practice in strategic planning and organization change consulting with non-profit and public service organizations in the Northwest. For 10 years, he was a quality consultant for Weyerhaeuser Company at their corporate offices. His passion is in helping public and social service organizations achieve their objectives for developing authentic collaboration with their communities and other service providers.

For more information, contact:
Allan Paulson
phone: 425.746.6274
fax: 425.865.8168
e.mail: arpconsult@mindspring.com

LAURE NICHOLS is Vice President, Community Health Integration for Franciscan Health System. Laure is responsible for working with other community based organizations in the design, development and implementation of health improvement initiatives focused on primary and secondary prevention for residents in the South Puget Sound area of Washington.

Prior to serving in this capacity, Laure worked for ten years as Senior Vice President for Franciscan Health System-West, overseeing managed care contracting, planning, marketing and communications, real estate development and property management. Laure received her B.A. from Smith College and her Masters in Public Health and Hospital Administration from Yale University.

For more information, contact:
Laure Nichols
phone: 253.591.6700
fax: 253.591.6700
e.mail address: LaureNichols@chiwest.com

COMMUNITY APPLICATION

*Imagination
is more important than knowledge.*

— ALBERT EINSTEIN

COMMUNITY APPLICATION

IMAGINE CHICAGO

BY BLISS W BROWNE

Cities echo creation. They are a living symbol of our ability to imagine and to create, to turn our visions into tangible products. They are an inventory of the possible, an incarnation of human capacity and diversity. Cities concentrate forces of light and darkness, and hold the world in miniature.

Reflecting on one's relationship to the city raises questions of meaning and mystery at the heart of human life and community. What does it mean to share a place with people from all parts of the world? As citizens of a common city, for what and whom are we responsible? What powers govern our common life? How has our own experience shaped what we see as possible and worthwhile? What is our own vision as creators in the city in which we live?

Aristotle said, "A vivid imagination compels the whole body to obey it." What might happen if all of Chicago's citizens were encouraged to give public expression to their imagination about a healthy future for the city as a whole, and were invited to claim their own role in bringing that vision to life? Is it not likely that giving public voice and support to deeply held civic visions will help create Chicago as a more vibrant home for the world's people?

MISSION

IMAGINE CHICAGO is a non-profit organization, created in 1992, and dedicated to cultivating hope and civic commitment. It enlists young people, and others who want to make a difference, to bring to light the experience, hopes, and aspirations of Chicago's citizens and to act on that imagination in ways that benefit individuals, communities, and the city as a whole. This work is done in partnership with local organizations — schools, churches, community groups, cultural institutions — and serves as the catalyst to encourage people to think about themselves as creators of the city's future, and to form communities in which that future can be created and the ownership of that future shared.

IMAGINE CHICAGO is designed as a partnership between community builders, educators, and the city's young people. Visions, values and accountability are shared; collaborative, creative leadership is encouraged. There is little likely to be more motivating to the city's youth than their confidence in a viable future, based on their own direct experience of having a role to play in shaping the city's future as a positive one for themselves and others.

Project History and Background

IMAGINE CHICAGO arose out of Bliss Browne's interest in what would be necessary to create a vision and action plan for the city's future which was owned by the people of Chicago. Working as a Division Head at First Chicago in corporate banking and as an Episcopal priest, with well-established civic interests in community development, Browne began to question how to stimulate civic imagination on behalf of Chicago's future. She convened a group of 65 experienced community builders actively engaged in civic, corporate, religious, and neighborhood activities in Chicago for a 2-day conference, which took place in October of 1991. Together, they explored "Faithful Economic Imagination", or how individuals might collectively steward the city's resources to sustain life for everyone. **The highlight of the conference turned out to be an exercise in which people were challenged to imagine visions of Chicago's future considered to be ultimately worthy of human commitment, and to identify what would be necessary for those dreams to become reality.**

On the strength of the energy and conviction which emerged from this conference for many of its participants, Browne resigned from a sixteen year corporate career to work full-time on discovering what might be an effective process for "faithful economic imagination" to become a way of life in Chicago. Browne dedicated nine months to learning Chicago history, listening to people's

concerns and hopes about what might constitute an effective visioning and economic development process in Chicago, visiting other cities with emerging citywide initiatives (such as Atlanta and Pittsburgh), and working with the Council of Religious Leaders on articulating their vision for Chicago's future. During that time, an informal network of Chicago leaders began to gather around the questions at the heart of Browne's inquiry. In September 1992, twenty of them — educators, corporate and media executives, philanthropists, community organizers, youth developers, economists, religious leaders, social service providers — were convened as a design team for the project, which Browne had already initially conceptualized as "Imagine Chicago". The MacArthur Foundation supported Browne to pursue the work of designing the project's first phase, testing the project's viability, and getting the project organized and institutionalized.

From September 1992 to May 1993, the design team created a process of civic inquiry as the starting point for engaging the city of Chicago in a broad based conversation about its future. **Two ideas emerged from the design phase which shaped the ultimate process design: first, that the pilot should attempt to discover what gives life to the city, and second, that it should provide significant leadership opportunities for youth, who most clearly represent the city's future.**

It was hoped from the outset that positive intergenerational civic conversation could provide a bridge between the experience and wisdom of seasoned community builders, and the energy and commitment of youth searching for purpose, yielding deeper insights into the collective future of the community.

Two types of pilots were designed and implemented in 1993-1994: a citywide "appreciative inquiry" process to gather Chicago stories and commitments, and a series of community-based and led processes. In each case, the intent was to give young adults and community builders in Chicago opportunities to share their hopes and commitments in a setting of mutual respect. The process was designed to use intergenerational teams, led by a young person in the company of an adult mentor, to interview business, civic, and cultural leaders, about the future of their communities and of Chicago, using a process of appreciative inquiry. The youth would then distill the content for public view in ways that would help inspire public action, and reinforce commitment. The premise was that young people could be effective agents of hope and inspiration, if they were released from the negative stereotypes in which they held themselves and were held by others. Each pilot had the following phases:

PHASES	ACTIVITIES	PARTICIPATION SKILLS
ONE	• foundation for the project • developing interview questions • recruiting and training youth and adult volunteers	• planning/organizing • presentation skills • identifying key community resources • interviewing • designing appreciative questions
TWO	• interviews scheduled and accomplished • follow-up process (thank you notes, etc.)	• presentation skills • analyzing data • interpersonal skills • communications skills
THREE	• interviews concluded • compilation of data begun	• synthesizing data • organizing data • planning events
FOUR	• completion/celebration with interviewees, students and adult volunteers	• planning, organizing events • presentation skills
FIVE	• evaluation and feedback	• designing evaluation • sharing learning • accountability to constituencies

Citywide Pilot Implementation and Feedback

The citywide interview process involved approximately 50 young people who interviewed about 140 Chicago citizens who were recognized by members of IMAGINE CHICAGO's design team as "Chicago glue". These included artists, media executives, civic and grassroots leaders, politicians, business and professional leaders, and other young people. The interviewees represented over half of Chicago's neighborhoods. Young people were principally recruited from the Chicago Area Project, the Chicago Cluster Initiative, Public Allies, candidates known to the Urban Teacher Corps, and various local schools. Some young people became involved through the involvement of their friends.

The interviews were conducted between the summer of 1993 and the spring of 1994. A letter of introduction was sent from IMAGINE CHICAGO explaining the process, and requesting an appointment for a young person. Appointments were set up, and travel arranged, through IMAGINE CHICAGO.

Interviewers were given modest coaching in interviewing skills, and equipped with a set of questions created by the IMAGINE CHICAGO design team. They were encouraged to ask other questions that arose for them in the conduct of the interview, and to engage the interviewee in as personal and positive a conversation as possible. They were also required, as part of the interview process, to send a follow up thank you letter to the person interviewed summarizing the conversation, what they had learned, and their appreciation for the work the interviewee was doing in the life of the city.

In the citywide pilot, it became clear that appreciative conversations help broaden the participants' view of what is possible, both within themselves and within the city. **Looking into the face of a young person, adult leaders found themselves thinking hard about the future and what they could do to ensure that it would be a bright one for the coming generation.** Young people learned the power of their own commitment and how to make a difference.

Once the first round of interviews had been completed, a group of ten young adults spent several weeks summarizing the data for public view. This summary was shared in three public events: the anniversary dinner of the Center for Neighborhood Technology on Dec.2, 1993, the Christian Laity of Chicago annual forum in February 1994, and a citywide IMAGINATION CELEBRATION at Preston Bradley Hall on May 7, 1994, to which all interviewers and their interviewees were invited. Ninety people were in attendance at that event. A data summary of the citywide interviews is available.

CITYWIDE INTERVIEW QUESTIONS

IMAGINE CHICAGO *(1993-1994)*

IMAGINE CHICAGO Interview questions

1. How long have you lived in Chicago? in this community?

    A. What first brought your family here?

    B. What's it like for you to live in this community?

2. When you think about the whole city of Chicago, what particular places or people or images represent the city to you?

3. Thinking back over your Chicago memories, what have been real high points for you as a citizen of this city?

4. Why did these experiences mean so much to you?

5. How would you describe the quality of life in Chicago today?

6. What changes in the city would you most like to see?

    A. What do you imagine your own role might be in helping to make this happen?

    B. Who could work with you?

7. Close your eyes and imagine Chicago as you most want it to be a generation from now. What is it like? What do you see and hear? What are you proudest of having accomplished?

8. As you think back over this conversation, what images stand out for you as capturing your hopes for this city's future?

9. What do you think would be an effective process for getting people across the city talking and working together on behalf of Chicago's future? Whom would you want to draw into a Chicago conversation?

Community Pilots

In addition to the citywide pilot which was run by IMAGINE CHICAGO, there were three principal community pilots, in Little Village/Lawndale, Grand Boulevard, and Englewood. In the community pilots, IMAGINE CHICAGO worked as a collaborator with local organizations. In the case of the first two, the local collaborator was the Chicago Cluster Initiative. In the case of the Englewood pilot, the local partner was the African American Leadership Partnership, and its member Englewood churches. IMAGINE CHICAGO was invited in to help develop the capacity and interest of young people in gathering hope and civic commitment in ways which might inspire collaborative action. Intergenerational appreciative inquiry was the tool used to engage the community's values and vision. The intent was both to gather important information and perspective and to build critical relationships which might change what was possible.

The first pilot, done in Lawndale/Little Village in October 1993, with almost no notice or training, involved 20 younger children, in the company of Urban Peace Corps volunteers, in interviews of local community builders. Different ethnic communities were linked in constructive ways. African-American youth learned to respect Latino leaders from a neighboring community which they had held in suspicion. Latino youth learned that African-American neighbors cared about their community. **One of the leaders who was interviewed framed the thank you letter she received from her young interviewer (which summarized her expressed hopes and commitments) and put it on the wall of her office.** IMAGINE CHICAGO learned to design materials

for training, debriefing, and follow-up which could be built upon in other settings. The young mentors involved in Lawndale were sufficiently engaged by the process to volunteer to conduct the training and implementation of a similar process in Grand Boulevard, which they did without IMAGINE CHICAGO's on-site help, except for training support from other young people who had been involved with the IMAGINE CHICAGO citywide process.

In the Grand Boulevard pilot, held in January 1994, a dozen or more elementary children from Robert Taylor Homes were involved in community interview training and visioning exercises. Unfortunately, the disbanding of the staff of the Chicago Cluster Initiative (who were the local implementers of the process) short-circuited the community interview implementation. But the young people who had been trained were sufficiently confident in what they had learned that they were able to serve as facilitators of a suburban Christian Laity of Chicago conference in February entitled "IMAGINE CHICAGO!" with youth from the Chicago Area Project. The event changed the image that many of the adult attendees carried of "inner-city kids from tough neighborhoods" and what they were capable of accomplishing.

IMAGINE CHICAGO was also invited to work with the African American Leadership Partnership, a coalition of 62 black churches on the South and West sides. AALP, and its executive director were captivated by the possibility of using IMAGINE CHICAGO to link young people and appreciative inquiry into community assessment and outreach that might be done by local churches. IMAGINE CHICAGO's training of the community organizing staff of a well-known community organizing organization resulted in their reconfiguring their community outreach programs to include teenagers as organizing partners, and rethinking their organizing strategy to focus on constructive issues.

IMAGINE CHICAGO worked with AALP in Englewood from June to August of 1994. IMAGINE CHICAGO was brought in to teach 90 teenagers and their supervisors, all employees of the Mayor's Employment and Training program, a way of thinking about community capacity building, with young adults as vital leadership resources.

For two months of the summer program, IMAGINE CHICAGO worked closely with one of the 5 church groups, approximately 20 youth from Christian Covenant Outreach Church to develop and create a community organizing process to get a YouthNet for Englewood. To bring local youth organizations and local community leaders together, the Christian Covenant youth organized a presentation for community leaders, so that the youth could share their own vision and action plan for the community and also solicit the support to make the YouthNet a reality. These dedicated youth also developed an appreciative inquiry protocol around the YouthNet. Before and after holding the community organizing meeting,

the youth from Christian Covenant conducted appreciative interviews across their community to gain further support and involvement from residents.

The possibility of applying for and securing a YouthNet center gave focus and energy to the community outreach work the young adults wanted to do. This was the first IMAGINE CHICAGO pilot that had in place a tangible community organizing goal. Under the leadership of the pastor and his wife, from CCOC, the youth recruited a variety of community organizations and individuals to join together to form a youth collaborative. The YouthNet vision brought together scores of community organizations, both public and private under a new youth collaborative, which is itself the designated youth component of the enterprise community application from the city of Chicago. Below are quotes describing the impact of IMAGINE CHICAGO on them personally as well as the broader community.

"IMAGINE CHICAGO has stirred up our neighborhood. It has gotten community people, activists, youth centers, police, churches, all stirred up about something positive that can become a reality. People who have never been together have come together to do something positive...to bridge a gap between young people and adults. It has sparked energy in Englewood. If IMAGINE CHICAGO hadn't told us about YouthNet, we wouldn't have

known...and I wouldn't have gotten such boldness to work on it. It has sparked hope...We have worked together; we have collaborated, young and old. It took all of us to put the program and proposal together. It took all of us. Now everyone is looking forward to getting a YouthNet. We know it's going to happen, because we've become one family, everyone encouraging one another. Now it's going to become a reality. If IMAGINE CHICAGO hadn't come, I don't know if we would have tried. Thanks be to God...This has formed respect for our young people, that they can get an idea and bring it to life."
— Debra Garner, Christian Covenant Outreach Church

"Just when I needed it most, IMAGINE CHICAGO provided a very positive outlook on how to view things in a positive way instead of negative... Through appreciative inquiry, it enabled me to mobilize more effectively and to be able to get the most out of talking and working with people."
—Yvonne Orr, The Woodlawn Organization

Having pioneered an intergenerational Appreciative Inquiry process, IMAGINE CHICAGO found a groundswell of invitations to link appreciative inquiry to community based outreach, using young people as the resource of choice, in a variety of contexts. In addition to its Chicago impacts, IMAGINE CHICAGO's intergenerational interview process was replicated in Dallas, and has been under consideration in Cleveland, Minneapolis, Boston, Baltimore, Seattle, Washington and London. It was featured in the Chicago Mayor's Task Force Report on Youth Development as an exemplary and innovative program. In 1995, 1996, and 1998, IMAGINE CHICAGO received a Eureka Communities Award from Washington for innovative programming for youth, families, and communities.

Summary of Outcomes to Date

In its 1993-1994 intergenerational city interviews, IMAGINE CHICAGO played a generative role in the lives of many Chicago citizens from different ages, cultures, creeds, and socioeconomic backgrounds. In late 1994, a formal evaluation gathered feedback on the effects of IMAGINE CHICAGO's appreciative inquiry process on those involved. Interviews and focus groups were conducted in November, 1994, with participants from the citywide interview process as well as from the least extensive community-based pilot. IMAGINE CHICAGO's Board of Directors also did its own evaluation. The Board noted two distinct levels of impact: visible outcomes and products (concrete), and "subterranean" outcomes (less measurable but perhaps more significant). In both tangible and subtle ways, IMAGINE CHICAGO has inspired hope and a sense of commitment and dedication to a greater Chicago community.

Three outcomes of the interview process are worthy of particular note as being of potential importance in reconstituting a shared sense of civic community:

1. Shared identity:

The conversations facilitated by IMAGINE CHICAGO brought people together across boundaries of age, race, experience, and geography to reflect together on their relationship to the city as a whole. The connections that were made through IMAGINE CHICAGO were extremely positive because the meetings were grounded in mutual respect and appreciation, and solicited positive visions and stories which people were eager to share. Participants found their Chicago citizenship provided common ground. These appreciative intergenerational conversations prompted a mindset shift among many participants. **Participants, who may have expected to feel separated from their conversation partners by age, culture, or background, instead experienced powerful and positive relationship connections. This, in turn, shifted their sense of possibility about their own and their community's future.** They began to understand the commonalities between their visions for the city's future, and be encouraged by their respective commitments. Experiencing an *undivided* "Chicago conversation" seems to have nurtured hope in the possibility of sharing ownership of the city's future. The process itself modeled the hope held by many participants, and expressed by one, of "a new Chicago in which all people can (and would) participate." As another commented, "it was helpful to pull together all of our visions and create understanding for those who had not shared your experiences."

2. Intergenerational Partnership and Accountability:

It was important that the interviews were conducted by intergenerational teams led by young people. The conversation opened lines of communication. Both the young people and the adults involved commented that they gained an appreciative understanding of the other generation. A prominent African American pastor said, "Yes, I gained hope too. The thing we lived for...hopefully will be shared by the young person and enhanced through them". A young person commented "It has made me think about the youth and how much people care about us". The adults talked about their understanding that youth are vital partners in creating a vision of the city's future, and that youth need to be viewed as community organizing partners. In the citywide interview process, a frequent interview response to the question **"What image captures your hopes for the city's future?" was for the adult interviewee to point to the young person and say "You!"**

3. Creating new possibilities and methods of civic conversation:

In addition to gaining a shared hope and identity across a well documented intergenerational divide, many participants benefitted from learning the power of appreciative inquiry. Shifting civic conversation away from problem-solving to collective visioning about a shared future created energy and opened new possibilities. Learning to ask and answer positive questions, and to engage in active listening, was a subtle and welcome shift for many participants. A significant by-product of the process was an obvious collective ease and goodwill among all those who had participated, which was evidenced in the May 7, 1994 gathering of all those who had participated in the citywide interview process. Constructive civic conversation, in a diverse group, seems to create momentum and interest in making commitments to bring the visions to life. A number of people who were involved in the interview process are now using the process of appreciative inquiry within their own organizations. Organizations continue to come to IMAGINE CHICAGO to be trained in the process.

It was suggested that these changes were caused by the contagious mindset of positive question/positive image/positive action that IMAGINE CHICAGO is spreading. This belief brought to the surface deeply held hopes and values, and created connections among people who could band together to bring the hopes to fruition. In some cases, that led to very practical projects in which the hope became focused, as in the formation of an Englewood Youth Collaborative, and its application to be a YouthNet center. In other cases, it led to less immediate results but demonstrably improved communication skills and community interest among those involved.

Other outcomes to date include:

Youth participation results:
- Ownership of greater community
- Empowerment to change conditions in the city, create youth vision for Chicago
- Intimate connections in a broader community
- Successful team work demonstrated through planning and organizing
- More ease in traditional social situations
- Greater self-esteem and self-confidence
- Self-expression and creativity demonstrated in public speaking opportunities
- Appreciative understanding of older generations

Adult participation results:
- Opportunity to express hopes/dreams for the City
- Potential to influence a newly inclusive community
- Renewed commitment to making a difference
- A (re)awakened sense of accountability to one's own possibilities
- Appreciative understanding of the younger generation
- More confidence regarding young people as positive civic resources

Community results:
- Higher visibility for civic issues / civic conversation
- Development of young civic leadership
- Adoption of appreciative inquiry / appreciative listening as powerful methodologies for organizational development by many organizations
- Intergenerational new collaborations
- Shared ownership of Chicago's future
- Identification and connection of people willing to invest in that future
- Reservoir of goodwill and energy that can be tapped in the future

Reflections: Where it all Led

The power of the above process has been summarized. Its limitation was that it proved difficult to move the process from inquiry to action. There was simply no "holding structure" or institution to do that. During 1995, IMAGINE CHICAGO worked in partnership with local organizations to design and test ways to engage Chicago youth in civic projects that challenge their imaginations, enrich their communities, and build their confidence in a viable future. IMAGINE CHICAGO learned that the appreciative intergenerational interview process is more effective if it happens within structures that can move more readily to action.

IMAGINE CHICAGO has therefore created a number of initiatives targeted at community-based and educational institutions which move through all stages of the appreciative inquiry process and accomplish practical outcomes consistent with the institutions' mission.

IMAGINE CHICAGO

encourages individuals and institutions to

focus constructively on their capacities and

opportunities to make a difference as they

*U*NDERSTAND WHAT IS;

*I*MAGINE

WHAT COULD BE, AND

*C*REATE

WHAT WILL BE.

Working in collaborations and consultative partnerships with schools, museums, community and governmental organizations and communities of faith, IMAGINE CHICAGO creates opportunities for dialogue about the city's future which invite creative reflection and stimulate collaborative action. These partnerships take different forms — public school curriculum development, public forums, grassroots leadership development, and coordination of intergenerational collaborations. All reflect three core processes:

Dialogue across generational, geographic, racial, economic and cultural boundaries;

Framework development, structured presentations and blueprints for understanding, imagining and creating Chicago; and

Network formation, to link individuals and organizations to organize creative projects that meet the needs of their communities as they perceive them.

Recent IMAGINE CHICAGO Initiatives Include

Citizen Leaders (1996 — on going)
Funded by the David K. Hardin Generativity Trust, The Surdna Foundation, Barney II and Seabury Foundation

The Citizen Leaders program is designed to increase the leadership capacity of residents in at-risk communities. It enables them to initiate projects that meet the needs of their communities, as they perceive them, and to learn from the experience of citizen leaders in other Chicago neighborhoods. The program trains residents and their sponsoring organizations to prepare proposals, organize and implement imaginative community development projects and evaluate and sustain their projects' impact. Project examples include block clubs, community gardens, intergenerational tutoring programs and a neighborhood crime watch. A training manual is available at www.imaginechicago.org.

Urban Imagination Network
(1996-June 2001)
Funded by the Chicago Annenberg Challenge

Seven public schools and six Chicago museums are working with IMAGINE CHICAGO and the DePaul Center for Urban Education in a network of educators committed to improving student reading comprehension using museums as partners in educational innovation. The program includes a civic literacy program for parents which links reading to city living.

Teacher Renewal (1998— continuing)
Funded by the Fetzer Institute and the Chicago Annenberg Challenge

A personal renewal program for Chicago public school teachers. Using seasonal themes at quarterly overnight retreats at the Chicago Botanic Garden, the program addresses the "heart of the teacher", making use of personal stories, reflections on classroom practice, and insights from storytellers, poets, and wisdom traditions. It explores the connections between attending to the inner life of teachers and the renewal of public education.

British Airways World Sales Conference, "Inspiring People" (April, 1998)

An intergenerational cross-cultural initiative partnered 340 British Airways' top sales executives with 400 members of the Chicago Children's Choir at The Field Museum for a day of music, innovative education, and corporate-community connections. The conference was designed to inspire people through coaching and asking the right questions to increase understanding and promote good decision making. As a lasting legacy, the children and executives created "inspiration exhibits" from objects brought by the executives from their 83 countries of origins. The exhibits tour local schools as a part of The Field Museum's Harris Loan Center.

IMAGINE CHICAGO is eager to identify and expand its partners in this work. For more information, please contact the author.

© B.W. BROWNE, 2001

ABOUT THE AUTHOR

BLISS W. BROWNE is the creator and President of IMAGINE CHICAGO. She is an ordained Episcopal priest, and was formerly a corporate banker and Division Head at the First National Bank of Chicago. She serves as a director of nine non-profit boards. A graduate of Yale, Harvard Divinity School and the Kellogg School of Management at Northwestern, she is the proud mother of three teenagers. IMAGINE CHICAGO's mission is to cultivate hope and civic investment in Chicago by building the capacity of individuals and organizations to work together to envision and create a positive future for their communities and for the city.

For more information, contact:
Bliss W. Browne
IMAGINE CHICAGO
35 E. Wacker Dr. Suite 1545
Chicago, IL 60601
phone: 312.444.1913
fax: 312.444.9243
e.mail: bbrowne@teacher.depaul.edu
www.imaginechicago.org

*Y*our views on individualism and diversity

have inspired me to evaluate

my outlook on life.

After speaking with you and adhering

to your advice, I feel that I too can make a

difference in others' lives.

A PARTICIPANT IN IMAGINE DALLAS

COMMUNITY APPLICATION

IMAGINE DALLAS

BY MARYSUE FOSTER

The Beginnings of IMAGINE DALLAS

In June of 1994, Bliss Browne, Executive Director of Imagine Chicago, spoke to a group of executives and community leaders at EDS. This group of fifty or so prominent citizens had been engaged for nearly a year in a conversation regarding making a difference in the city of Dallas and had focused on youth initiatives as the most potent intervention available. Bliss was one of five speakers from national groups making presentations, leading the group to choose one or more of the initiatives to support.

From this original meeting, a core group of five women met through the summer of '94. The women were particularly intrigued with the idea of creating an AI project with adolescent girls as the interviewers. They called themselves the J-I-T Sisters for their uniform, shared operating style of Just-In-Time. One member paid her way to Chicago to view the Imagine Chicago operations first hand. Late in the fall, John Castle, an executive at EDS, offered his help in kicking off Imagine Dallas. A luncheon was planned for February '95 and about 100 community leaders were invited to the event, held at a private club atop a skyscraper in downtown Dallas. Bliss Browne and Leslie Welch, a young woman who had initially been a youth volunteer with Imagine Chicago and now served on its board, were flown in to speak.

About 60 community people attended the luncheon. Leading up to presentations by Bliss and Leslie, a trained volunteer at each table asked each guest, "What was the time you felt most connected to the city? A time when you felt the most alive and excited?" The energy level of the room raised noticeably and the "listening" of the attendees was prepared for the presentation by the Imagine Chicago team.

Nearly $20,000 was raised at the luncheon — enough to motivate the J-I-T sisters to seek additional funding to meet a projected budget of $30,000, complete incorporation efforts, recruit and install a board of directors, and recruit and hire a one-person staff.

Two board members attended an AI seminar led by David Cooperrider in March of '95 in Dallas. Two other women participants at the course later became volunteers with Imagine Dallas and participated in the design of the project.

During the summer and fall of '95, Imagine Dallas completed incorporation procedures, was certified by the IRS as a 501(c)(3) (not-for-profit) organization, was offered free office space (in a block of restored Victorian homes, endowed by the Meadows Foundation, one of Texas' most revered foundations), recruited a board and an advisory board, hired staff and began to craft the first year of operation. This author became the Executive Director in January '96.

MISSION

Imagine Dallas is a constructive, voluntary process that seeks to enrich the future of Dallas through the collective imagination of its citizens. The forging of appreciative intergenerational connections is at the heart of the enterprise. Imagine Dallas ignites the civic imagination of a broad spectrum of community builders by inviting them to share publicly their Dallas stories and visions, in interviews led by young women. Through this catalytic process, both the young women and community builders of our city will be inspired to shape deeply held hopes into opportunities for action.

Project Design

We plan to use individual girls from several organizations in the city and set up interviews for them with adults in the city who are making a difference in their communities. Because we are dealing with an enormous population, an entire city, we will focus our project almost entirely on the AI process itself. Although we are expecting to uncover some trends and underlying assumptions about life in the city, we are not in a position to implement changes. The role of Imagine Dallas will be to bring people together to begin the conversation and, perhaps, furnish them with a powerful technology to begin their own inquiry. This is not to say that the project is outcome-free, but that, as a practical matter, we will spend our time and effort on setting up numerous cross-cultural, inter-generational interviews.

Girls Groups: We select four girls' organizations: a mostly Hispanic community center in a poor neighborhood; an after-school program for Girls Inc., located in a subsidized housing project, involving primarily African-American girls; the YWCA/Y Teens program at an urban high school; and girls from an exclusive private school. Each group must be separately trained. Then, because adult volunteers will transport each girl to an interview, all adults must be screened by the agency and trained by Imagine Dallas as well.

Adult Volunteers: The original plan called for recruiting 15 to 20 adults to escort the girls. Instead, a local civic group of about 50 members volunteered to escort the girls. An enormous amount of effort was spent coordinating the group, working through legal liability issues with the sponsoring organization, scheduling 14 separate training sessions in order to give all their members a convenient time to attend, etc. The group of 50 yielded 38 trained volunteers and seven interviews in total. An anticipated outcome of ongoing volunteer and financial support from the group never materialized.

Logistics: Four groups are playing: girls, escorts (adults who schedule the interviews and drive the girls to interviews), companions (adults who accompany the girl and the driver on the interview – a security measure demanded by the participating agencies), and subject of interviews (community builders). The girls and escorts must be trained in Appreciative Inquiry principles. The community builders were invited by letter or phone call to participate.

After a girl or an escort receives training, they go on a master list of those available for interviews. The escort is given the name of an interview subject (chosen more or less at random) and the name of a girl. The escort contacts the girl to find out her availability, then contacts the subject to set up an interview. (The girls' schedules tended to be less flexible than the adults'). Then the escort must find a companion to accompany the pair on their interview.

The companion's role is to sit in the back seat of the car and help put the girl at ease. The companion does not go into the room for the interview. We added the companion to the process after some participating agencies would not release their young clients to an individual adult, or an adult of the opposite sex. The sponsoring community group was also concerned about the legal liability of having adults take youngsters individually in their private cars.

At the interview, the escort's job is to sit in the background and take notes. The interview, about 45 minutes or an hour in length, takes place between the youth and the community builder. As soon as the interview is completed, the youth and the escort find a quiet place to do a de-brief. A de-briefing form (see Appendix A) was developed to make the process more uniform.

On the spot, the youth writes a thank you note, coached by the escort, if needed. The thank you note and the interview notes are returned to the Imagine Dallas office. We then write a thank you on our letterhead, enclose it in the youth's card (a greeting card designed to fit a #10 business envelope), drop both in an envelope and mail to the community builder. Interview notes and a photocopy of the youth's thank you note are kept in our files.

INTERVIEW QUESTIONS
IMAGINE DALLAS

1. What brought you to Dallas? How long have you been here? What keeps you here?

2. When you think about the whole city of Dallas, are there particular places or people or images that represent the city to you?

3. When was the time you felt most connected to Dallas or its people? That you felt the most alive, filled with hope? What was happening? Who was with you? Why did it mean so much?

4. Let's focus on you now.
   a. What do you value most about yourself as a citizen?
   b. What do you value most about your work in the city?
   c. What do you value most about Dallas?

5. What gives you the most hope about the city's future? Who do you think will need to be involved in fulfilling that promise?

6. Imagine that Dallas is featured on the cover of *Time* magazine in January 2005, as City of the Decade. What have we done to deserve this recognition? What is featured about your own contribution?

7. What do you think would be an effective process for getting people across the city talking and working together on behalf of Dallas' future? Who would you want to invite into a Dallas conversation?

8. I have really learned something from your replies. What insights can you share about beginning/embarking on my civic path?

Design details

- **Liability insurance for a new agency.**
Insurance costs are prohibitive for the original program design – about $2500 annually. We rely on the sponsoring agencies to cover us.

- **Pilot project.**
We attempt to run a pilot during spring school break to test questions and procedures but are delayed by process of training the civic group and do not succeed.

- **Men's participation.**
Some agencies forbid their girl clients to be transported by men in a private car. We spend a lot of time finding a way to have men participate. To date (March '98) not a single interview has taken place where the escort was a man.

- **Adult volunteer selection process.**
The need for a selection process is side stepped when the civic group comes forward. Many of our early volunteers were board members and personal friends of board and staff. We plan to participate in a criminal and background screening program.

- **Youth selection process.**
After several preliminary plans, we abandon this idea as well. We present the program to the agency/school and interested youth will self-select.

- **Interviewee selection process.**
We collect names from volunteers, board members, members of the civic group, and friends. We are looking for both high profile and little-known people. At the current time we have about 400 people in the data base as interview candidates.

Despite all the obstacles, we ultimately completed 22 one-on-one interviews during early 1996. The labor-to-results ratio was incredibly high and late in '96 we changed our strategy, choosing to conduct two larger, "Community Celebration" days. The first, held in January '97, involved about 35 girls from North Dallas High School (an enthusiastic partner for Imagine Dallas) and about 45 community leaders. The second celebration, held in September, was at the AT&T Wireless workplace and involved 35 North Dallas girls (some repeaters from January) and about four dozen AT&T employees. Both events took the better part of a school day and were inspiring and engaging. Both sparked hours of conversation and helped forge links between the girls and community people. In the case of the day at AT&T the girls were also exposed to important possibilities about careers in technology.

Basic Day Structure

BEFORE

• A briefing for adult volunteers, introducing them to the project, held a few days before the event at the business site, taking about 45 minutes

• A briefing for student volunteers, introducing them to Appreciative Inquiry and giving them a chance to practice on each other, held about two weeks before the event during a class period at the school. Also, the day before we held another session including a preview of adult expectations, what the girls might experience on the day of the event, tips on wardrobe, etc. The youngsters also were given a chance to practice the questions, re-phrase some in more comfortable words for themselves, etc.

DURING

• An overview of the day, introduction of facilitators

• Individual interviews. Girls were paired in various ways with an adult. We found that two adults and one girl meant the youngster could do two interviews, with an adult taking notes at each one. We designed a note taking form to facilitate capturing the stories and quotes for each interview.

• Medium group process. Groups of 10 to 12 adults and youngsters assembled. They shared some of their findings from the interviews, searching for some common themes and experiences. A facilitator led them to create provocative propositions, which were then posted on flip charts to be shared later. A youth speaker for each group was chosen.

• Large group process. The entire group assembled (in a circle) and girls from each group shared the Provocative Propositions their group had created. Much cheering and shouting accompanied the presentations. The facilitator can preface this piece with words about circles and their meaning through time and how this is an event to honor our youth and our elders as a way to add a more spiritual element.

• Girls are transported back to school by bus. On the bus there is more processing of the day with board members and other volunteers who are riding the bus; girls also fill out a "what I learned" form we developed. This form becomes the basis for a thank you note from them.

AFTER

• Girls write individual thank you notes to their adult partner(s). These are photocopied before they're mailed so we have a record of their learnings. Some of our best quotes have come from these documents. (See Appendix A)

What we have learned

Although the beginning of our process has been difficult and the progress has been slow, Imagine Dallas has provided many hopeful and soulful moments for all who are involved. Creating a free-standing non-profit organization is a challenge in any environment; focusing on girls is particularly daunting in this community. Nationally girls-and-women-specific programs receive about 5% of contributions; in Dallas that percentage drops to less than 4%. Recruiting and training a board of directors in Appreciative Inquiry is both humbling and gratifying. Early in our evolution, the board discussed affiliating with another agency and discarded the idea, choosing independence rather than subvert the process. That is still the predominant feeling on the board.

Imagine Dallas was not blessed with a charismatic leader or deep pocketbook or the existing communities of Chicago. We have had a much different environment. We are still struggling with direction and focus. The five founders (masters at the starting phase) have moved on; the second generation of directors is just beginning to mature. As of this writing, the board is considering whether to continue the Community Creation Days with different groups and in different settings or to create something else.

Have we made a difference? Yes, emphatically yes. The girls at North Dallas High School have made connections with people in the community that still remain in place. One young woman is being sponsored with scholarship support at a nearby college; she starts school there in the fall. Several have forged strong bonds with adults in their planned careers. All have gained the confidence and assurance that comes from wading into unfamiliar waters, and returning to tell the tale. **They have learned that adults care about them — even unfamiliar adults — just because they're a part of the community. We won't know the total results for years to come.**

We also know that more than 200 adults and youth in our city have been exposed to the thinking that comprises Appreciative Inquiry. Many of the youth are quite facile at using the approach and report to me that it has transformed relationships in their family. The soulful affirmation of the good in human beings is the richest aspect of this work and the aspect that will last the longest and have the most unpredictable, far-reaching results.

© M. FOSTER, 1998

ABOUT THE AUTHOR

MARYSUE FOSTER has been conducting workshops, classes and in-service programs for individuals and professional groups since 1972. She has an M.Ed. and has designed and delivered programs in management and supervisory training, effective communication and leadership skills, career change and many aspects of Equal Employment Opportunity. In 1976 she co-founded the first Affirmative Action consulting firm in the Southwest. She has authored numerous articles and a business book and is listed in *Who's Who in the South and Southwest*. Recent clients include: the cities of Plano, Duncanville, and Grapevine, Texas, Oryx Energy, Bank One, Texas Instruments, and Frito-Lay. MarySue is a founder of The Virtues Institute, and founding director of Imagine Dallas, Inc. She has two grown children, lives with three cats, a filmmaker husband and loves sailing and the outdoors. She calls her Mom every Sunday.

For more information, contact:
MarySue Foster
The Foster Group
13321 Purple Sage Road
Dallas, TX 75240
phone: 972.458.9481
e.mail: marysue@earthlinknet

Examples of Provocative Propositions

- The school is a safe haven and central focus of a community partnership; school is stimulating, fun, supports growth, and prepares students for careers.

- Youth are the future of tomorrow. Learn from them as they learn from you.

- We have a safe protected environment which allows us to have conversations and to build networks which build communities.

- We improve our city one person at a time with our determination, energy, urgency, and commitment.

- We honor the arts!

A P P E N D I X B

Debriefing form for IMAGINE DALLAS

C O M M U N I T Y B U I L D E R :   **Y O U T H :**

E S C O R T :   **C O M P A N I O N :**

D A T E O F I N T E R V I E W :

1. When you think over the interview what is the most interesting thing that you learned?

2. What positive ideas and images of the city did you hear as being most important to the person you interviewed?

3. What suggestions do you have that might help you and the person you interviewed to work together to help make your community and Dallas a better place to live?

4. What work in your community is the person you interviewed doing that you would like to thank them for?

5. How would you capture the essence of the interview in 12 words or less? You can use the next sheet to draw something or otherwise depict your impressions graphically.

The greatest gift is not being afraid to question.

— RUBY DEE

IMAGINE
SOUTH CAROLINA

BY ALEXSANDRA STEWART
AND CATHY ROYAL

Introduction

In the Fall of 1995 we were contacted by an organization who wanted a consultant team to work with them to facilitate what they anticipated would be a highly charged conference on race. Their intention to have a statewide dialogue was intriguing to us for several reasons. One, the client was not an organization in the conventional sense. They would be a designated hosting organization who would pull together a cross section of a southern state with a history of race bias and policies of exclusion. Two, they wanted something that would reach past this polarization to find new ways to talk about race, and the impact of race on economic and community development. And finally, with our suggestion to use Appreciative Inquiry as the process for the Summit, a relationship developed and they were willing to trust and experiment.

Client Description

The client for the inquiry was a statewide non-profit organization created in 1984 to develop innovative community-based partnerships to address South Carolina's social and economic challenges. In ten years it had initiated more than 75 community-based collaborations. These collaborations ranged from providing free primary, preventative medical care to South Carolinians without health insurance, to a toddlers immunization program, to a Voter project which produced 53,000 new voters and the highest voter turnout in the state's history in 1994. The Board of the non-profit organization had come to believe that the single, most significant stumbling block to addressing the state's social and economic problems was the growing polarization of communities along racial lines. In a press release detailing the background of their organization they said they believed that the lack of trust and simple dialogue is so pervasive that community-based strategies to address problems are often doomed from the very start. In 1993 they initiated a statewide program to create opportunities for improving dialogue and friendship among black and white communities' leaders. This program, known as the Carolina Community Forums, existed in 20 of South Carolina's 46 counties. By 1995, each Forum had a membership list of about 200 persons. The Forums and other initiatives are sustained through partnerships with volunteers, churches, businesses, utilities, banks, newspapers and some foundation support.

Client Objectives

Based on their experience with the Forums, the client wanted a broad statewide initiative which would generate a year of public dialogue. The conversation would focus on how South Carolina's communities could transcend long-standing racial divisions to create grassroots projects. They wanted an initiative in which the practical experiences of everyday South Carolinians would drive a broad re-examination of racial differences and the creation of constructive local strategies to address community issues in which race appeared to be a factor. The Director said they wanted a January 1996 Summit which would lead to a series of dialogues in local communities. A major goal was to bring the races together for discussion, to sit down together and get to know each other, and to develop a new way of communicating which would create dialogue on racial issues. The Director, in collaboration with Summit organizers, had identified 20 persons to serve as facilitators for the Summit. As he described his early thoughts, the facilitators, along with corporate and community leaders, would come to Pre-Summit sessions. The Summit itself would take place in one day, a Saturday. He anticipated that 100 – 200 persons would attend the Summit. His plans included conducting a statewide survey on race relations prior to the Summit for additional data to use at the Summit.

Proposal

After extensive dialogue with the director, we proposed training in Appreciative Inquiry for the facilitators and community leaders. The training, some months prior to the Summit, would do two things: provide a cadre of persons trained in AI and develop themes for them to conduct an Appreciative Inquiry (AI) in several regional and local communities. The agenda for the Pre-Summit would be to process the community interviews, identify the themes and create an Inquiry Protocol for the Summit itself. The Summit would be facilitated by the AI trained facilitators with coaching and input from us. To create an affirming statewide climate we proposed working with the Director and spokespersons for the Summit on language for press releases and descriptions of the AI process, as well as on the questions for the survey on race relations.

Rational For The Use Of Appreciative Inquiry

We feel that AI is a natural process for creating dialogue on race relations and communities. **AI is uniquely designed to focus on creative conversation between people.** Relationships between Blacks and Whites are often not talked about outside an individual's own racial identity group. We saw AI as a way to bridge this reality and an effective and energizing process for conversation about the parallel histories that emerge from historical and structural race bias. It is these parallel histories that lead to the current realities of Black and White South Carolinians.

AI encourages the sharing of stories, invites creative reflection and stimulates ideas for co-constructed action. The AI approach also allows space for people to name how they envision the best race relations. AI calls for a series of conversations, in this case they would be about relationships across race and ethnicity that are positive, energizing and life enhancing. By talking about collaboration, communities that work and successes that benefit all, without denying the parallel realities, we knew that Summit facilitators and attendees would have an experience that would lead to desired dialogues in regions of the state.

Factors Managed

Funds for early facilitator training, community interviews and Pre-Summit themes identification were not available. The Director, working to juggle a variety of agendas, needed to mount a conference that would include some fairly traditional ideas about activities. These ideas included three panel discussions in the Saturday morning agenda. Thursday evening and Friday would be set aside for Pre-Summit training of facilitators and inclusion of corporate and community leaders. The Governor had scheduled a press conference and dialogue on race relations at the Summit site for 5:30 Friday evening. Anticipated attendance at the Summit had grown to above 400. A challenge was to provide a large number of people with an experience of Appreciative Inquiry along with some theory and an opportunity to feel the difference that intentional choice of language can make – all in a short amount of time.

Preparation

Since we know that the first question, the first interventions are fateful, we focused energy in coaching the Director on the language of AI. We worked with him to incorporate the Imagine South Carolina concept into press releases and the wording of a race relations survey they intended to disseminate. A key was to rephrase questions in ways that would help people look forward and not get stuck in the past. Some of the survey questions were in the traditional, problem focused language. Others were more affirming and AI focused, such as: Is there now, or has there ever been a person of another race whom you would describe as having had a *significant positive impact* on your life? Although slightly lower for Blacks responding, still almost 70% of all respondents reported having a person of another race as a *close personal friend*. Questions also gave respondents an opportunity to describe places where their lives intersect with persons of other races, such as work, church, social events and community organizations.

We gave the Director several articles such as, "Positive Image. Positive Action"[1](Cooperrider, 1990), as well as other handouts with information about the AI process. Conversations and coaching were primarily by phone and fax. We provided suggestions for the memos and invitations to the Summit. We wrote a one page description, "Appreciative Inquiry/Imagine South Carolina" [2]

---

[1] From: S. Srivastva, D. Cooperrider & Associates, *Appreciative Management and Leadership.* San Francisco: Jossey-Bass, 1990. Now available at www.thinbook.com
[2] *Appreciative Inquiry/Imagine South Carolina*, Royal, Cathy, L. and Stewart, Alexsandra K., © 1996

(Royal and Stewart, 1996) which wove the Imagine South Carolina concept throughout the text and served as a briefing about both. This description was included in mailings and in the notebook which was distributed at the various sessions of the Summit.

This attention had several positive results. In many instances, Pre-Summit media stories were favorable, open minded and allowing of more hope than Summit organizers had seen in the past. Some were mixed. One article began: "Imagine South Carolina in perfect racial harmony. Idealistic? Unrealistic? Impossible? Maybe not. An upcoming initiative aims to get the state on that track." The Director began a press conference with a release which began "S. C. Survey reveals 'Rare Moment' for Progress in Race Relations."

One result of the positive media coverage was to increase the number of attendees. Originally, organizers thought about 200 persons might be interested. They developed a list of invitees. They wanted to be as inclusive as possible so their list included traditional designated community leaders as well as informal leaders, from a variety of religious organizations, elected officials and membership organizations such as NAACP and Rotary. People had the opportunity to invite themselves as well. Many people, including the Governor, did ask to be invited to the Summit. The final number in attendance on Saturday was over 500 persons.

Highlights

Beginning with the first evening we opened each session by asking people to think about their passion for the South Carolina community they were most connected to, "the South Carolina of their heart." We varied that somewhat as other groups arrived. Additionally the corporate and community leaders were asked to think of a time within the last two years they had felt most connected to a Black (if they were White), or White (if they were Black) person. They also were asked to think about and share an experience where their community has come together to create a positive response to race matters. One large group activity was to list heroes and "sheroes" significant to them personally and to the story of South Carolina. The range and variety of significant actors in South Carolina's story was impressive.

Participants often saw the history of South Carolina through different lenses. When this happened, we asked them to again imagine South Carolina's future and the reasons they had come together in community. Two of the strongest voices of the Friday afternoon large group dialogue belonged to two powerful men, one Black and one White. They were close in age, and their formative years had been those of the generation of segregated South Carolina of the 1940's and 50's. When given a chance to rethink their images of the future, build on the things they valued and loved about South Carolina, both were able to see the future as possible. Neither had to retract his history, each was able to continue the dialogue with a different focus: the new South Carolina. As much as possible we used the frameworks of

DATE	TIMEFRAME	AGENDA
THURSDAY	8:00 to 10:00 P.M.	Community Building
		(20 persons designated as facilitators)
		Appreciative Inquiry South Carolina
FRIDAY	9:00 to 11:30 A.M.	Theory Base Imagine South Carolina
	1:00 to 5:00 P.M.	Inclusion of new community members
		(20 facilitators and 40 community leaders)
		Stories and parallel realities
		Develop questions for Governor
	5:30 P.M.	Governor's press conference
		(200 persons)
	8:00 to 10:00 P.M.	Sense of AI/SC Identify replication focus for Saturday
		(60 persons as above)
SATURDAY	9:00 A.M.	Invocation & opening
	9:30 to 11:30 A.M.	Three panels
		(500 plus persons)
		Brief reframing and iteration of themes heard
		in each panel
	1:30 P.M.	Regional meetings for advancement of
		Imagine S. Carolina into every part of SC through
		regional networks
		(small groups of 15-30 persons)
	3:30 P.M.	Mini reports to the larger community
	4:00 P.M.	Adjourn

pairs conducting interviews with each other and then joining with 2 – 3 other pairs to create small groups for the identification of common themes. These themes were shared with the larger group. We asked participants to use appreciative language. A Friday afternoon task for the 60 persons present was to develop affirmative questions to ask the governor at the press conference on Friday evening.

Saturday morning our role was to summarize, and recast, in appreciative and imaginative language, points made in three panels. Saturday afternoon, the 20 facilitators had the responsibility to provide an AI focus and approach while working in small groups of similar interest or region. The facilitators focused the language appreciatively and put into use what they had learned. They assisted groups to talk about what worked at present in their regions and to make plans for continuing to dialogue after the Summit.

Observations and Conclusions

Persons who attended the Thursday and Friday sessions used language, for the most part, in different ways than those persons who had not had an AI experience. This was particularly evident at the Governor's press conference and dialogue. Pre-Summit attendees posed their questions in a way that invited dialogue and exploration. One Pre-Summit participant said, "Let me think a minute Governor, they told me not to be negative and I want to phrase this question right." Another began his question with, "Governor, I invite you to

imagine with me... Can you do that?" Other attendees asked questions in a manner that fostered polarization.

One of the persons who opened the Summit Saturday morning used imaginative language to evoke images of communities that work in a variety of ways: "I imagine a South Carolina with all students receiving education that prepares them for life. I imagine a South Carolina where all people are actors in the story of South Carolina. I imagine a South Carolina with homes for all people. I imagine people who hope and trust in tomorrow."

Throughout the day on Saturday, people conversed in hallways, South Carolina media conducted interviews with attendees, as well as observed small group meetings and there was a sense of high energy. A wide variety of persons attended, including several groups of persons under 20 years of age. They formed their own group to discuss the areas that mattered to them. Overall, the ambiance was upbeat and infectious. The language of Appreciative Inquiry and affirmation was having an impact on the conversations throughout the Summit. Some persons did express some concern that nothing "would come of all this" and wondered what differences would result. Four months after the Summit we received an announcement for the first regional committee meeting of the Project on Race Relations to be held in June. Quotes from the Summit were an intrinsic part of their announcement. The mission of the Regional Committee was stated as: *"Imagine South Carolina is a commitment to creating and sustaining communities that work."* Their flyer described Imagine South Carolina as *"a starting point in re-focusing civic conversation on the promise of community in our state. Such conversation does not ignore the racial divisions, but seeks to confront and transcend them in ways that heal the fractures of the past and empower a common vision of the future."* These descriptions are straight from the language that was developed for the statewide Summit in January.

One year after the Summit, the Governor engaged people in the question about the Confederate flag by proposing that perhaps the flag might more appropriately be moved from the pinnacle of the State capitol and placed in a nearby location. One phrase which had been posed within his hearing at the press-conference had been: *"I imagine a South Carolina where state symbols inspire hope and pride in all its citizens."*

Our Learnings

The care for language and the energy focused on the images we convey is worth more than can be estimated. The time spent assisting people to clarify the positive image which lies under their criticism, or their complaint, and then to describe how things are when the situation is the "way it should" be is invaluable. **A small number of people trained in the AI process do have a great impact on a larger group.**

People know what they want in their communities. AI is a valuable tool and philosophy that supports "participatory community development." It affirms what is currently present in their surroundings and experiences, and helps citizens see what their community can be. When given the time and opportunity ordinary citizens can create the mechanisms and plans necessary for their communities to thrive and inspire hope in the future. When people share what is in their heart, tell the passion that connects them to each other, community is built. The community desired becomes a co-created future, alive in the present, and extraordinary.

ABOUT THE AUTHORS

ALEXSANDRA STEWART grew up in Oregon, finished high school in South Dakota, married, had children and divorced while passing though Germany, Montana and Minnesota. She has been a working single parent, a mom on welfare, and an undergraduate at the University of Minnesota where she received two degrees in 1979. Her MA from St. Mary's College examined a Multicentric Approach to curriculum development. The ability to be multicentric informs her work in Diversity Based Management and the courses she teaches. In 1993, she attended the first NTL AI training, Bethel, ME and became an interviewer for the AI diversity study for NTL. Since that time she has used AI for a variety of domestic and international clients. Her focus on the language we use and how it shapes the world in which we live, and create, began in her first Spanish class, and has been strongly influenced by attention to inclusive language in her diversity work. In the past eight years, this focus has been sharpened by her work with AI language, and by thinking about the social constructions of 'reality.' In 1988 she chose to live in Washington, DC where she has her own consulting business, Pancultural Associates. She is a member of the NTL Institute for the Applied behavior Sciences. A major emphasis in her work is equity and creative relationships between individuals and among groups. She coaches leaders in creating conditions where people can maximize their potential. Currently she is working on a book that examines historical perspectives of oppression and resistance throughout United States history.

For more information, contact:
Alexsandra K. Stewart
1628 Oak St NW, Washington, DC 20010
phone: 202-667-6855
e.mail address: alexsa@pancultural.com
www.appreciativeinquiry.com

CATHY L. ROYAL, PH.D. is the founding president of The Diversity Institute, a not-for-profit international learning community dedicated to research, training and dialogue to promote social and structural equity. She is an organizational development professional with specialties in diversity management, race and gender relations, appreciative inquiry and organizational transformation. Dr. Royal designs and conducts training in each of these areas for corporations, foundations, educational institutions and international agencies and donors. In 2000 Dr. Royal designed and facilitated the first all department diversity appreciative inquiry for the Department of Health and Human Services (DHHS). This was a large systems change initiative that impacted and reached 56,000 plus employees of the government. She is a member and trainer for the NTL Institute for Applied Behavioral Science (NTL) and she is the NTL Institute Ken Benne Scholaran. She was on the five-member team that facilitated the United Nations/Mountain Institute Rio Earth Summit. Dr. Royal has conducted training in Africa, Latin America and throughout the United States. She is a contributing author on: *Transformational Social Change: Self as Change Agent, Visible Now: Blacks in Private Education,* and *NTL Training Handbook.* Her continuing project is completing her research for her book *The Fractial Initiative: Appreciative Inquiry- Living in the Positive.* Dr. Royal's passion is using Appreciative Inquiry to promote structural equality, honor diversity and social justice. She is the recipient of the Fielding Institute Social Justice award.

Cathy L. Royal, P.h. D.
PO Box 326
Riverdale, MD. 20738-0326
phone: 301.552.3625
e.mail address: catroyal@aol.com

The following description of AI was written for Imagine South Carolina and has become a staple of our Appreciative Inquiry work. Since 1996, we have further changed the language, and adapted it for a variety of clients including organizational capacity building and excellence in schools.

Appreciative Inquiry
Imagine South Carolina

Appreciative Inquiry (AI) is a dynamic dialogue. It is designed to focus on creative conversations between people. AI is a process that seeks to bring all voices into a conversation. It involves all levels of a community who work together to co-create a desired future. AI is uniquely intended to discover, understand and foster innovation.

A basic belief of Appreciative Inquiry is that communities and individuals, like plants, are heliotropic; that is they move toward the light. Results from research (placebo studies, the Pygmalion effect studies, positive imagery for athletes) confirm this: positive images create positive futures.

Appreciative Inquiry asks people to tell their stories about their connections with others when they have been at their best. AI enable people to talk about race relations in South Carolina that are affirming (life giving) and equitable. It assists peo-ple to imagine their communities in more affirming ways. AI assists in envisioning policies, practices and behaviors that promote equity and that enhance the life giving forces in relationships.

AI seeks out the "best of what is" to help ignite the collective imagination of "what might be." The goal is to expand the realm of the possible. People envision a collectively desired future. They carry forth these possibilities in ways that translate intention into reality. Communities create the processes they wish to use in order to put belief into practice.

AI has at its core the belief that communities are affirming and that people in these communities want their neighborhood to thrive and succeed. AI asks people to reflect on selected ideas and dialogue with each other to discover when they and others have been moist satisfied with race relations. People describe the factors that give life to their commitment to South Carolina. The dialogue looks for examples, stories, metaphors and anecdotes. Each person helps the other person hear and understand their passion for and connection to equity and race relations in South Carolina.

Imagine South Carolina is an energizing process for conversation about the present reality and the shared vision for race relations in South Carolina. It helps develop more effective and creative communities that work. The Summit creates space to listen, to engage, and to enhance trust between people of other races. The inquiry encourages the sharing of stories, invites creative reflection and stimulates ideas for co-constructed action. The approach allows space for people to name how they would envision the best race relations and communities.

AI focuses on the generative forces already present in communities. The Imagine South Carolina Summit becomes the seeds for the preferred future. The ideals are grounded in reality. This combination open the status quo to transformation.

Creating the conditions for organizational or

community-wide appreciation is

the single most important measure that can

be taken to ensure the conscious evaluation

of a valued and positive future.

— *DAVID COOPERRIDER,*
Positive Image, Positive Action

COMMUNITY APPLICATION

BANANA KELLY EXPERIENCE

STRENGTH-BASED YOUTH DEVELOPMENT

BY JOE HALL

Background

The Banana Kelly organization began in 1977, when thirty residents gathered to stop the demolition of their homes along the banana-curved block of Kelly Street in the South Bronx. Founded, owned and governed by local people the organization today employs over 100 full-time staff members (90% community residents) and operates programs in housing, economic development, and education. Projects include Youthbuild, Home Instruction Program for Preschool Youngsters (HIPPY), school-based family support in three junior high schools, and a Banana Kelly Community Learning Center public high school. We are also developing the Bronx Community Paper Company (BCPC) which will create 600 onsite permanent jobs while advancing environmentally sound technologies. In 1996, from over 800 nominations worldwide, the United Nations recognized Banana Kelly with one of six Gold Medal Best Practices awards for Improving the Living Environment.

Young people are an integral part of the Banana Kelly community, and some 35% of the organization's full-time employees are under the age of 23 years working in all areas of housing, economic development, education and administration. Historically their contribution is significant in rebuilding the South Bronx. We are in our third generation of youth leadership working side-by-side with adults in a wide variety of projects. One example is Yolanda Rivera, our board chair, who started community development work as an 11 year old girl translating in housing court for her parents, neighbors and other tenants fighting to reverse the destruction of the

neighborhood. Early on in this 30 year rebuilding effort there were limited, if any, funds available for youth programs. This deficiency focused youth activity and attention towards family, schools, and action movements within the systems that affected their own lives and those of their families, friends and neighbors. Youth, like Yolanda, were in the room with adults — listening and participating in conversations — and being an integral part of what would eventually transform this part of New York City.

History has shown us that young people have always been at the forefront of great social change movements. Whether ending apartheid in South Africa, championing human rights in China, or integrating education systems here in the United States, youth have provided the energy, enthusiasm, creativity and courage to see beyond what is, dream, and then create better possibilities for themselves and others. In the South Bronx , the church, schools, tenant associations, and grassroots organizations provide leadership and infrastructure to focus this talent and rebuild an entire community. Along the same path (with the infusion of private, government and local citizen investment) people grew a capacity to sustain this success long-term and across generations. Banana Kelly today balances access to all kinds of resources with the powerful instruction of the self-help movement within an infrastructure that makes for sustainable community building. This sustainability — really an enhanced imaginative capacity that allows us to learn — is perhaps our most important innovation and what keeps us receptive to and in synch with young people.

Appreciative Inquiry

An innovative organizational development intervention called Appreciative Inquiry (AI) is being shared throughout the world by Dr. David Cooperrider and his colleagues at the Weatherhead Graduate School of Management at Case Western Reserve University. Several Banana Kelly people have been through the AI executive certificate training, and we also completed the 1996 Organizational Excellence Program (OEP) with partners in our Americans for Better Communities network. The kinship-based relationships found in our organization create a cloth of network associations that strengthens our community. Given these multiple, interwoven and seemingly invisible layers of relationships within the Banana Kelly, learning community the AI organizational development strategy eventually found its way into our personal, family and neighborhood lives.

Appreciative Inquiry – with its four "D" cycle of Discover, Dream, Design and Delivery — provides us with some important insights and breakthroughs with regard to our youth development work. Reaffirming that the quality of our language — how we talk about ourselves, our work and our relationships with each other — in conversations with youth is important for them as well as a gauge on where we are as an entire community. Much of our work with young people is consistent with the Discovery phase of AI: problem-solving or need identification gives way to conversations that value the best of "what is" working well.

The power of the question and how it is posed (in relation with them, not to them) takes youth in a direction where inquiry and change happen simultaneously. They begin to name the process and pose questions for themselves — where they live and work — which moves them through a continuous learning and growth process. Over time these conversations begin to work with a skill inventory tool and other exercises to surface assets, capacities and most importantly positive images that create a life-long, mutual learner. Much more valuable than the hard skills obtained through traditional Job Training Partnership Act (JTPA) programs, **the enhanced imaginative capacity that flows from this relational process builds engaged, alert, self-aware, conscious young citizens prepared for a 21st century where softer skills like effective team participation and an intimate, informed understanding of one's own learning style is required.**

Most adults will not introduce future hopes, dreams and aspirations into our practice with urban youth, lest we be accused of being so irresponsible by not dealing with the reality at hand such as the violence, drugs, and oppression that plagues their world. Help professionals are trained to work "where the client is at, "through incremental, doable small steps so as not to discourage them from one more devastating failure or setback. I would argue that a caring, mutual learning relationship that is consciously building community, actually encourages that same young person to take more risks and bask in the luxury of their very own special mistakes. Dreams are not necessarily born from or nurtured by our successes, and failure even in its most dramatic form does not necessarily knock a person out. It is how that experience is reflected upon, talked about, defined, and the reality we co-create that ultimately makes it positive or negative. **I have seen young people at Banana Kelly time and time again do amazing work and push everyone's idea of what is possible through great acts of kindness delivered on South Bronx street-corners, meetings with corporate executives and foundation officials, and training sessions with their peers in Mexico, Turkey and Germany. Each and every one of these precious stars could easily be defined by a professional diagnosis as "at-risk." Each and every one.**

Assets-Based Community Development

The work of John McKnight and Jody Kretzman at the Assets-Based Community Development Institute at Northwestern University has been catalytic in galvanizing support around the country for a return to organic, reciprocal relationships that define community as a broad set of people, gifts, skills, capacities and resources. The momentum their work provides is grounded in the lessons of neighborhood success stories, and has important policy implications through cooperative sharing with government, civil society and institutions (e.g. the United Ways and professional training schools). Their inclusion of these "bad guys" is difficult for some, yet critical for all of us given that this paradigm shift is necessary if multiple stakeholders are going to free themselves from the damage brought by the imbalances we are seeing. While not minimizing historic oppression of entire communities, individual social worker burnout is not to be overlooked in terms of the pain it brings everyone. The ruin found on all sides of these deficit-based relationships is both unacceptable and avoidable. To understand assets-based work, as liberation for only one segment of a complicated equation is to ignore the depth and breadth of what is really going on — and the ultimate power this approach holds for youth and their communities.

Banana Kelly's generic assets inventory tool that was highlighted in ABCD's recent workbook publication does not create a data base inventory of skills that can be accessed in our larger community-building strategy. Many groups around the country, however, have used this kind of systematic collection of information as an important resource in rebuilding their neighborhoods.

We use our inventory tool as a prompt for appreciative dialogue with people that formally acknowledge that they are holders of knowledge, skill and capacity. These conversation are probably new for those involved (and the silence one hears after asking anyone "Name five things you value most about yourself" is universal). Surfacing tacit knowledge or awareness blocked by years of socialization, as a problem-waiting-to-be-fixed is not going to happen in one meeting no matter how genuine the interaction.

Assets-based work with youth needs an organizational/community practice that moves the skills into tangible action, given the ever-present influence of problem models, training and methodologies. The fear fueled by media sensationalism (spanning gang violence to day care center scandal) inhibits our ability to connect with youth in a meaningful and loving way, but no more so than naming a young client a "consumer" in an alternative to incarceration program. At Banana Kelly we spend a great deal of time perfecting the conversations, the quality of our language and the quantity of positive images we use with our neighbors and in our own quiet moments. Youth are a part of the dialogue at all levels in this learning community and begin to process their own transformative growth by naming it and then living it out in their daily lives.

The Role of Reflective Evaluation

The loom that weaves together youth engagement, assets-based development and appreciative inquiry on a daily basis is a reflective evaluation practice. While the funding sources of our programs are usually focused singularly on the success of a specific activity, our outcomes also include human, community, and organizational development. Thus, for our learning community, evaluation involves not only program or even organizational effectiveness, but also personal growth and development. In this model of evaluation, we learn how to design and operate good programs with our neighbors and learn how to innovate and excel as leaders by creating new knowledge. This environment of learning, growth and risk-taking by many creates the space where youth thrive.

We work closely with an evaluator who combines Appreciative Inquiry, assets-based assessment, and organizational learning strategies with qualitative and quantitative evaluation methods. She is simultaneously Teacher, Coach and Mentor. She is a member of the Banana Kelly family, and a partner, but remains outside the organization and its day-to-day work. By using evaluation techniques that are learner-centered, she creates natural opportunities for us to learn.

Learner-Centered Evaluation Techniques

• Providing an appreciative entry into a project or program: valuing who we are, what we bring to the program, and what we can learn from each other.

• Establishing an appreciative baseline from which to measure growth and chart change: creating an inventory of assets of the individuals involved; their knowledge, skills, and values; what gives life to the organization; and its work in the community.

• Learning through a developmental cycle of reflection, experimentation and action.

• Learning meetings: including appreciative self-assessment, peer assessment, and program performance assessment.

• Learning inventories: what we know and how we know it and how we can transfer that knowledge to others.

• Focus groups: bringing the whole system of stakeholders into the room.

• Surfacing our tacit operative assumptions: staying close to the "so what" of the project and what we mean by success, as a basis for building program propositions and hypotheses.

• Profiles in practice: case studies of program in action.

• Documentation of practice: capturing the lessons learned "in our own words."

The Role of Storytelling

Youth at Banana Kelly participate in a variety of interactions that are key to our model: focus groups; conversations in the hallway; assets-based program planning; reflection sessions; and the documentation and dissemination of ideas — in their own words, within and outside the community. Through these four they are also introduced to external models and theories, methods, organizations, and practices applicable to their own work and experience. An important cultural aspect that makes this all accessible and easily integrated is storytelling. **Our community uses stories as a powerful medium to impart values, vision and critical information.** Stories are rich sensory tales and, unlike theory or abstract practice models, have a life of their own — they breathe, invoke feeling and emotions, and bring the youth present into the moment. That person then also adds to the story, gives it their flavor, and makes it their own while sharing it with others and becoming one with the community.

The successes we have seen with youth in both their achievements and capacity to dream provide strong evidence that a reflective, learner centered practice can move evaluation from a position of passive objectivity and aggressive accountability toward a much more rewarding, meaningful role in community-building. The artificial limits of traditional project evaluation are such that intended and unintended outcomes cannot be wholly documented, integrated, disseminated, and put to use across the organization or community — especially within the fertile learning areas found in the "life after" program funding.

We have made a large investment in evaluation, an investment that surprises many people. For us this approach not only binds all of the theoretical models and practice methods we use when engaging young people, it also is another example of redefining and leveling critical power relationships that have limited many South Bronx youth. **There is perhaps no gift that makes a larger impact than to give a person control of their learning by teaching them conscious self-assessment and evaluation.** Over time this frees them from past negative experiences with control, bringing them into an invigorated, meaningful sense of interdependence and worth in an expanded world.

We learn by asking, So What?

Once the organizational mission, practice and evaluation functions are aligned in a mutual learning model there is a range of program or intervention possibilities. When designing a program or writing a funding proposal we often times ask: "So what?" This question keeps us close to the ground and true to ourselves. We are not being lulled into applying for anything that is available. We also ask, "How would rich folks do it?" which keeps us out there, reaching and striving for what is outside the box. With an engaged, informed multi-dimensional planning team these questions not only get answered, but people's ideas – sometimes their own personal dreams – get tested out in a supportive environment where we challenge each other. We have declined or

given back millions of dollars in funding over the last five years when the institutional limitations would not allow us to honestly answer these tough questions. **Our true asset is the way we work together and as a result, our dreams get stronger and stronger providing us with more provocative possibilities for the future.**

Travel as Development

One example of how we use the organization to create interesting programs (low cost or free) is travel and presentation. **Naming and declaring the change in our lives and community to an audience outside the community makes it real.** We are blessed with a great many opportunities to travel all over the world and deliver presentations and training to a wide range of audiences. We use these occasions as a vehicle for a very specific piece of our work with youth. Whether here in the South Bronx, Atlanta, Los Angeles, Istanbul or Mexico City, young leaders at Banana Kelly get that "rich kid" exposure to the magic of travel. Travel strips us from the comforts of our everyday normalcy and habits — and because these habits may be holding us back, we can let go of something we don't like and dare to plunge into new ways of being. New food, foreign languages (including business English or foundation-speak), flying on a plane, or getting up to talk in front of 400 people have all been terrifying for most of our young leaders. Having heard about the prior experiences of their peers, our youth are able to embrace each of these trips as learning classes-in-action.

We also find that we can experience being in a new place while we're home by, — for example, hosting a team of Brazilian academics in our neighborhood for an entire day. This gives us the advantage of new insight, perspective and clarity to our daily lives. However it is critical we take the time to reflect on those opportunities, because we learn from our experiences only when we reflect upon them. Youth gain a greater understanding of themselves, their work at Banana Kelly and their community because this new space jolts all of their senses into highly alert conductors of their feelings, thoughts and behaviors. This also places them in the position of teachers — we know we have learned something well when we can share it with others. **The role of travel and presentation in our development model is not to say what has happened, it is what is happening for them now and defines their dreams for the future.**

Travel and presentation creates another opportunity for us to confidently meet and ride some of the inherent tension generated by others and ourselves. How can we put someone in front of an audience, who is clearly not well prepared? Our goal for these presentations is not making sure others "get it" with regard to Banana Kelly (as if that is possible in such limited time) but that the young presenter have that experience and understand it as a learning tool for themselves and for others. We ask that they later share the experience with the community.

It's great to take them away from the community to learn, but what about the violence on their block? One colleague asked me if I thought these "junkets" were respectful given the situation faced by the rest of their family. My response to these kinds of issues is ask the young people themselves and listen, listen carefully as they describe the experience and you will hear the words of those early South Bronx community-builders: We don't know everything, and we are powerful.

Outcomes

We honestly struggle with outcomes, more specifically how to name them and fully capture the broad set of experiences. We can measure basic skills, attendance, and other indicators but young people do not enter the Banana Kelly community always knowing up-front exactly what they will come out with later. Measuring the quality and impact of relationships, and sharing that with others so that they too may learn from the experience, has not been easy. This ambiguity has been very limiting for some and a challenge for all of us. We continue to get help from our friends and work through how to measure outcome. In the meantime, our youth continue to create opportunities for themselves and others. During a 1995 visit to Los Angeles young Banana Kelly leaders formed a vision and created our Community Learning Institute (CLI) which brought five young men from Los Angeles for a four month living/learning experience in our community. The CLI has hosted artists from Mexico and currently two graduate student interns from a university in Hamburg, Germany. While we never anticipated or worked towards these opportunities, we were able to realize the benefits when they became available.

Conclusion

The most profound thing we do for young people at Banana Kelly is show them the high expectations we have for their greatness, while being careful not to be drawn-in to the low-vision reality the rest of their world may hold for them. Young people started Banana Kelly in a very organic way, so that our work today is not an "add-on" or a program initiative. This fact is something that we declare to the world as recognition of their contribution, never taking this for granted. Work with youth occurs by meeting organizational goals, which happens through the youth development agenda. A youth-centered commitment is about them growing and thriving in the process — the ends are the economic and community development outcomes that they deliver for themselves and their neighbors. This is contrary to everything they may have experienced up to this point, since their education has operated from a foundation that sees them as empty vessels to be filled with information. But as with most situations young people bring a curious, gutsy daring to the mix that makes all kinds of success possible. Leaders in their early twenties run Banana Kelly projects that have enormous impact, accounting for hundreds of thousands of dollars.

Development for an individual or community never plays out in a linear process, though the organizations we have inherited from the industrial revolution continue to perpetuate assembly line mental models. The Banana Kelly experience draws a developmental model that is much more free-flowing. There is constant movement in our young leaders' daily lives all over a continuum of developmental success and setbacks that challenge all of us in profound ways. The organizational metaphor of the hammock — with its strength, ability to swing back and forth, and flexible supportive structure that wraps around the person — allows us to see this movement through a more receptive lens. Since our organizational design is not structured around rigid bureaucratic accountability and control, or looking for outcomes grounded in the prevention of something bad, we can see the person. Building quality people builds quality solutions to everything we need — the strength-based approaches give a practice and supportive infrastructure that makes this happen.

Given the dynamic acceleration of change present in the world today, and if our work with young people is to be successful in preparing them for that demanding environment, a dramatic overhaul of our organizational, institutional, and community structures is required. We believe that assets-based development and Appreciative Inquiry ultimately hold great promise for people, as well as their organizations and communities. We know that the true power of AI and the assets based movement has yet to fully emerge, and that the potential these concepts hold will be unleashed when informed by the personal, spiritual and communal places found within ourselves — places that do not separate work from family, professionals from community or practice from values.

A recent discussion here focused on the movie *Good Will Hunting*. What began to form during the conversations were two distinct schools of thought about what was the defining moment that moved Will to positive change. The visiting professionals thought that Will's emotional breakthrough with his therapist finally allowed him to heal his past and eventually move to make major changes in his behavior. Local folks here thought it was really cool when Will's best friend tells him how great he is, wonderfully talented and better than settling for less in their neighborhood. Their relationship allowed Will to hear this loud and clear, giving him the courage to move from his confining existence and on to California. Perhaps the real shift is when Robin Williams (as Will's therapist) shares with him that Will has made a huge impact on him, affecting him deeply, and thereby redefining the power relationship between professional and client. This makes the tearful breakthrough possible because young Will has felt someone's unfettered care in a relationship that values his

input, knowledge and contribution. But in our imagined *Good Will Hunting* Part II we now see the therapist as part of a learning community using strength-based approaches, their organization bringing possibilities and literally the whole world to that neighborhood. Will is back home finding everything he needs to grow and thrive, and making that available for his neighbors. Fiction? Our young heroes here at Banana Kelly live that script every day.

© J. HALL, 1998

Resources

For more information of Asset Based Community Development Institute for Policy Research contact:
Northwestern University
2040 Sheridan Road
Evanston, IL 60208-4100
phone: 847.491.3214
fax: 847.491.9916

ABOUT THE AUTHOR

JOE HALL has been helping build the Banana Kelly community development model for the last six years . A resident of the South Bronx, he and his neighbors travel throughout the world sharing their experiences, providing training and the stories that highlight possibilities for others. He is President of Banana Kelly, lecturer at Columbia University and holds an executive certificate in Appreciative Inquiry from Case Western Reserve University.

For more information, contact:
Joe Hall, Founder
The Ghetto Film School, Inc.
P.O. Box 1580
Bronx, NY 10459
phone: 917.270.5731
e.mail: boogiedownjoe@hotmail.com

The important thing is not to stop questioning.

Curiosity has its own reason for existing.

One cannot help but be in awe when one

contemplates the mysteries of eternity, of life

of the marvelous structure of reality.

— ALBERT EINSTEIN

APPRECIATIVE PLANNING AND ACTION

EXPERIENCE FROM THE FIELD

BY MAC ODELL

Introduction

Drawing on the relatively new organizational development methodology known as Appreciative Inquiry, The Mountain Institute (TMI) has developed and piloted in Nepal, Sikkim, Tibet, and the United States an innovative approach to grass-roots village planning and mobilization. It's a participatory process that builds on the global practice of Participatory Rural Appraisal (PRA), using visual tools that do not require literacy. The approach is known as Appreciative Planning and Action (APA). Unlike problem-focused planning and development strategies, APA, like Appreciative Inquiry, is built on searching for the positive, for what works. The technique shows considerable promise as a mechanism for helping empower groups and communities to take positive action for their own development.

This chapter focuses largely on the development and application of appreciative planning and action in The Mountain Institute's Makalu-Barun Conservation Project (MBCP) in Nepal, in which virtually all 100 project staff have now received training. This evolutionary action-research approach has seen APA programs conducted with more than 1,000 villagers in more than two dozen settlements, from tropical lowlands to mountain highlands.

Practical exercises in Nepal's villages have shown that APA

Empowers — helps groups celebrate, embrace, and learn from their successes instead of focusing on their problems

Mobilizes — gives groups concrete actions they can start immediately,

Energizes — provides a future focus that encourages groups to create a vision, to select steps that help move them toward fulfilling their vision, and to take the first step toward achieving it.

And best of all, Appreciative Planning and Action is quick, easy, and replicable.

My own experiences in Africa, the Middle East, Pakistan, India, and Nepal, and fieldwork with Robert Chambers, the architect of PRA, have caused me to become concerned about the fact that while many of those involved in international rural development are committed to participation and empowerment, I rarely see real, living examples of empowerment that go beyond the anecdotal level of individual case studies. Empowerment must involve people feeling a sense of power, not just participation. Empowerment involves self-confidence and/or self-generated initiatives. Yet, after decades of commitment to participation and programs promising empowerment, many villages and villagers remain ashamed of their lack of education, their poverty, their powerlessness. **What involvement they have had with development programs, including PRA and Village Planning Training exercises, appears not to have empowered them so much as to have encouraged them to focus on their problems and to have trained them to become little more than professional beggars.**

APA offers an alternative to the low self-esteem and dependency which seem to pervade Nepal's villages. It goes beyond the "power of positive thinking" by giving specific tools and techniques for generating and keeping up the positive thinking and for encouraging self-reliance and local initiative. Coupled with future mapping, commitments, and its "Action NOW" components, APA has the potential to sustain the energy it generates. APA also gives rural people a tool to turn to when inevitable problems crop up again. It's a marvelously simple concept, but it is built on a very sophisticated foundation, one which looks at the world through positive glasses rather than the negative ones worn by problem-solvers, dedicated to problem analysis, problem identification, problem ranking, and critical thinking.

Background of the Makalu-Barun Project

Appreciative Planning and Action is being developed and used by The Mountain Institute in mountain villages along Nepal's border with Tibet, and more recently in reversing negative relations between villages and Nepal's newest and largest hydropower development project. It has proven effective as a tool to help promote sustainable and participatory conservation and community development in remote rural communities.

The mission statement of APA is as follows:
• To empower communities and individuals to take pride in what and who they are and what they have achieved, to dream of what might be, to plan for what can be, and to feel the energy that comes from making commitments and completing the first step
• To be simple enough that anyone can do it; profound enough that it can change people's lives

The Mountain Institute's basic global commitment is to advancing mountain people and protecting mountain environments. The goal of The Mountain Institute's Makalu-Barun Conservation Project (MBCP) in Nepal is to protect the biodiversity of the Makalu-Barun National Park and Conservation Area by establishing an innovative management system that integrates national park management with participatory conservation area management. The project's purpose is for local communities and Makalu-Barun National Park to develop a greater stake in biodiversity protection through the use of traditional and new technologies and management capabilities for improved community development, biodiversity protection, and natural-resource management.

From its outset, Makalu-Barun Conservation Project has been built on participatory planning with local communities and support of community initiatives, including the initiation and implementation of community forests, village development, income generation, culture conservation, and eco-tourism. Participatory Rural Appraisal has been the basic tool for engaging communities in analysis, problem identification, and priority setting. Village Planning Training has been conducted with leaders from all 100 settlements (Wards) and twelve Village Development Committees (VDCs) to give them the tools for the ongoing planning and implementation of local projects, which have frequently focused on the development of drinking water supplies. Other projects have included trail and bridge improvement, irrigation, school building/roofing, and construction of latrines and grain mills. Income-generation activities have focused on the production, weaving, and marketing of allo fiber products from the giant stinging nettle; development and marketing of traditional bamboo craft products; and vegetable, horticulture, poultry, and small animal production. Community Forestry programs involve the formation of community user groups, development of improved management plans, and the hand-over of forests to communities for protection and sustainable management, which provides communities with fuel, fodder, timber, and incomes from both timber and non-timber forest products such as allo, lokta (traditional Nepali handmade paper), bamboo, medicinal and aromatic herbs, and spices like cardamom.

Appreciative Inquiry – A new Approach

In 1993, The Mountain Institute, as part of a long-term organizational development (OD) and team-building program, began using a relatively new OD technique that was proving extremely effective. This process, Appreciative Inquiry, was being developed by David Cooperrider and others at Case Western Reserve University in Cleveland, Ohio. Through facilitated workshops with The Mountain Institute staff, AI had begun to improve interpersonal and institutional communications and effectiveness. In 1994, Bob Davis from The Mountain Institute, who had started intensive study of Appreciative Inquiry at Case Western and American University, introduced some AI exercises into Makalu-Barun Conservation Project's semi-annual planning workshops; **the staff found the exercises stimulating and enjoyable, infusing positive energy into what might otherwise have been a relatively dry and sometimes negative process of reviewing progress and problems and mapping out plans for overcoming obstacles during the year ahead.** Later in 1994, I joined a facilitated AI retreat with The Mountain Institute staff in the United States and brought back some additional tools to introduce into our Makalu-Barun Conservation Project workshops during 1995 and 1996.

Meanwhile, David Cooperrider, S. Srivastava, Diana Whitney, Barbara Sloan, and others associated with the development and practice of AI with multinational corporations had begun tailoring the approach to international NGOs, including The

Mountain Institute in Peru and the United States, and USAID through the GEM program in Eastern Europe and India. Under the GEM program, AI was introduced at a workshop in India during 1996, attracting attention among organizational development specialists in Nepal, who found that the method resonated with traditional Eastern religion and philosophy and had potential application for local and international organizations working in Nepal.

Appreciative Planning and Action

During mid-1996, Bob Davis took the organizational development process a new step forward: With Lamu Sherpa, a Participatory Rural Appraisal facilitator who had been in charge of Makalu-Barun Conservation Project's community-development program from 1993 to 1995, Davis introduced some AI exercises into a Participatory Rural Appraisal village consultation and planning program for ecotourism in Sikkim, as part of The Mountain Institute's Sikkim Biodiversity Conservation and Ecotourism project. **These exercises asked local people to examine what they valued in their culture and community, what they would like to share with others, and what they might do to get started in developing ecotourism activities in their community.** The results were very encouraging and resulted in participants' starting a village clean-up campaign on the spot, at the end of their Participatory Rural Appraisal program.

It was in reviewing this experience that I saw the potential for developing what could become a breakthrough process in mobilizing self-reliant communities, a challenge that has eluded development practitioners for generations. In late 1996, after an intensive training and personal-development program under the tutelage of Barbara Sloan, an advanced AI facilitator based in Washington, DC, I joined Bob Davis, Wendy Lama, and Lamu Sherpa in developing and presenting a series of staff development workshops for selected Mountain Institute/Makalu-Barun Conservation Project staff in Kathmandu, reviewing the theory and practice of Appreciative Inquiry and sharing experiences from The Mountain Institute's Langtang and Sikkim programs and our Makalu-Barun Conservation Project workshops.

From these exchanges, we decided to reorient our 1997 Participatory Rural Appraisal program to introduce a full range of AI techniques into our village consultations and staff training. In January 1997, we began with a team of Makalu-Barun Conservation Project staff members who were involved in community development, including Chandi Chapagain, who shared our vision of a new way of relating to rural communities. We initiated staff training and village practicums in the villages of Bung, Khiraule, Pelmung, and Chheskam in the western project area, two days' walk from a remote mountain airstrip and five days' walk from the nearest road. Despite rugged terrain, snow, and unseasonable rain, we completed a two-week program with a very enthusiastic local team of MBCP staff and local leaders that resulted in, among other things, the resurrection of an old plan to open new trekking routes to an attractive peak in the area. During February, a program was implemented in another half-dozen sites.

From these two months of field implementation, trial and error, and training and assessment, an entirely new approach to community planning and mobilization has evolved: one based largely on the Appreciative Inquiry framework, but also drawing on the grass-roots participatory strategies for involving nonliterate people that characterize Participatory Rural Appraisal; the forward-looking future-mapping techniques from Future Search; and the commitment-oriented concepts used in personal-development programs such as The Forum.

In February 1996, MBCP staff finished their second extended field program out in the villages, involving over a month of total time training local field staff, leaders, and grass-roots NGOs/PVO members in the appreciative process and how to apply it to community development and participatory natural-resource management — together with several weeks of hiking from village to village. Our staff tested a number of models, adapting to conditions in the field, and found that they had moved toward a process that stood on its own. A sense of ownership had developed among staff since they felt actively part of the design, evolution, improvement, and application.

MBCP staff are convinced that the process is unique and relevant in its own right; thus, they sought a title would include the three integral ingredients: appreciation, planning, action. Although these elements stand out as critical, staff recognize the heavy debt to the underlying participatory approach that derives from Participatory Rural Appraisal. The process goes beyond the tools that rural-development staff have generally been exposed to. Participatory Rural Appraisal exercises and techniques — such as the use of participant generated social and resource maps and trend analysis — have been and will continue to be woven into the application of Appreciative Planning and Action, but the core framework of our development work in Nepal is now built on the appreciative model. This new process promises to be especially useful, even powerful, in the village context.

Efficiency and Time Management

The basic elements of Appreciative Planning and Action include simplification, codification, and adaptation to make it possible to complete an entire process with a village in as little as two to four hours, ending up with a basic action plan for the year ahead, plus a set of actions steps to start immediately. In some circumstances the process has been completed in as little as a quarter to half an hour.

This means "right now," while the group is still together, as part of the wrap-up of the meeting/workshop. This action step is combined with empowering personal promises that draw their inspiration from other OD sources, as well as from AI's own "provocative proposition" concept. For field personnel, this means they have a tool that they can use in virtually every meeting and/or village consultation, one they can understand, apply, and use efficiently when their own or villagers' time does not permit the type of in-depth two to four day process often allotted for a typical Participatory Rural Appraisal or Village Planning Training exercise.

This "short and sweet" process, however, does not need to be limited to a few hours. Where appropriate and needed, APA can be augmented with a full range of PRA tools and activities, such as trend analysis, social and resource maps, pair-wise ranking, and/or other exercises directly relevant to needs and circumstances. Several of these classic PRA tools, such as seasonal calendar and Venn diagram, also lend themselves particularly well to modifications drawing on the appreciative approach.

The APA Process

The APA process as it has evolved in Makalu-Barun villages follows a framework of four basic elements, including a modified "4-D" planning-and-action process, making it compatible with most standard project cycles, but, more important, making it relatively easy to understand and replicate for field staff and villagers since it is easily remembered and requires no literacy to implement.

The Makalu Model

One Goal:
"Seeking the root cause of success"
(not the root cause of failure)

Two Laws:
• "What you look for is what you find." (The questions you ask determine the answers you get.)

• "Where you think you are going is where you end up."

Three Principles:
• "If you look for problems, you find more problems."

• "If you look for success, you find more success."

• "If you have faith in your dreams, you can accomplish miracles."

Four Ds

1. Discovery: *Asking empowering, positive questions about the best, about what gives life to this community or group — seeking and understanding successes, analyzing successes for what they teach us — "The answers you get depend on the questions you ask."*

Discovery is tailored to the group and/or situation. It often starts with personal introductions, usually going around the circle of participants. Stimulating, leading questions seeking successes and feelings of empowerment are then used to help one or more small groups get down on the ground or around a table to create their own "Success Map" or symbolic diagram of their village or group as it is now, highlighting their achievements. When asking questions, don't rush or push for answers; wait 30 seconds before rephrasing a question; then if there's no response, ask a new question.

Very important for village development efforts, Discovery typically reveals that the favorite, most empowering projects have been those the community has done on its own, self-help, as opposed to those donated and supported by outsiders. Facilitators must take the time necessary for this discovery to become evident to the group because subsequent planning for self-help initiatives is greatly enhanced when groups understand the power they derive from things they have done on their own.

2. Dream: *Creating a positive vision of what might be, what we would like to achieve ?*
- *Close our eyes for one minute; imagine what we would like to find here in five or 10 or 20 years or so … Think of what is needed to help make our dream come true.*
- *In our group prepare a "Future Map" or diagram that illustrates our dream of the future. Dreams are shared briefly in the full group and then discussed in their small groups to achieve a reasonable consensus on an exciting yet achievable vision for the future that can be illustrated by the group in map or diagram form, using symbols and pictures, not words.*

3. Design: *Turning our picture of the future into an action plan to realize it.*
- *Prepare medium and short-term (five-year, one-year,) action plan for what we will do ourselves to start implementing the dream — to turn wishes into action steps, requests, promises. Plans can be made starting with tasks to be done now and working toward tasks to be done over one year, then five years … or they can start with the longer-term and work toward what is to be done now. Be flexible.*
- *Develop a program to start implementing that plan this month or this season, including "who, what, when, where, why, how" as appropriate to time and complexity of tasks.*
- *Make personal commitments on tasks from these plans that each one of us is to take as part of implementation of the action plan.*

This design step can be done verbally and/or symbolically on the Future Map. Each group member makes a personal, public commitment of one action step s/he is going to make and by when (be sure to clap vigorously as each person states his/her commitment).

Facilitators can make their own commitments, and, where appropriate, commitments for their organization as "topping up" for local action; but the focus should first be on what local people are ready and willing to do for themselves.

4. Delivery: *"Action Now!" — starting now on the path to achieve the vision:*
• *What are we going to do to start this process? Near-term actions we can start now!*

This is the classic implementation phase of the standard project-planning cycle, except that with APA, one or more simple, symbolic, practical steps are selected by the group for immediate action, as part of the meeting process. Action generates energy. It provides a real sense of achievement, is fun, and crystallizes the meaning and lessons of the entire APA process.

"Action Now!" should be a task(s) that can be done immediately, the same day, same place, and within 10 to thirty minutes. These should end with an enjoyable, fun, recreational activity. Relax! Enjoy!

Concluding Discussion: *Participatory Monitoring and Evaluation of what we have just done:*
• *Share impressions, learnings; informal evaluation, accompanied by some speeches by local people in which they share the meaning of the meeting to them personally and talk about the next steps they plan to take on their own.*
• *Enjoy! Finish up with a light touch — a relaxing and fun activity, and/or sharing of food, snacks.*

Participants form a circle, near or around their mini-project, and are encouraged, one by one, to share a thought or two on the process — what was learned, what was the best, what might have been even better? This should be informal, light, and fun — well-sprinkled with laughter and concluded with some relaxing enjoyment, such as dancing, singing, tea, snacks, local brew, storytelling, and/or jokes.

The APA team should not rush off but should join in if possible for an evening of informal relaxation and discussion. Important and unexpected insights, plans, or information can be shared and potential problems turned into opportunities for more success.

Some Basic Principles for APA Practitioners

Appreciative Planning and Action activities and training programs are normally woven in with key principles from Participatory Rural Appraisal and other relevant programs. Here are some key principles:

• "Put the last first, put the first last."

— Empower those usually left out, including illiterates. No exercise should require, expect, or even suggest the need for literacy. All activities and materials should be visual, using pictures, maps, and/or diagrams drawn by the participants themselves.

— APA must involve women and disadvantaged groups directly and ensure they have prominent roles in meetings and/or are involved through separate meetings or groups within meetings. Never miss the chance to work with those who just turn up; rather, follow up by seeking "those who are not here" and attempt to understand why.

•"Hand over the stick." (marker, or maps)

— Average people should be at the front of the meeting, showing and explaining; facilitators, staff, and local leaders should be at the back, listening and learning.

— All Success Maps, Future Maps, and Action Plans must be left with the people who created them. They are their planning tools to be kept and referred to by them, not to be carried away by facilitators (who are welcome to make copies, of course).

•"They are the experts; we are here to learn."

— Facilitators use APA not to teach but to learn, as a tool to understand the richness, value, and utility of indigenous knowledge systems; to help local people appreciate, acknowledge, and honor who they are; to recognize their wisdom and know-how, and the contributions they have made and can continue to make for their own advancement.

• "Whoever is here are the right people, wherever we are is the right place, whatever time it is, is the right time." [1]

— APA should be flexible and responsive, taking advantage of opportunities for being proactive; doing first things first; working with those who step forward to start with; making arrangements for additional meetings with those who aren't involved in the first contacts. Build in follow-up to ensure that balance is achieved over time.

•"Turn problems into opportunities."

— APA does not avoid or ignore problems but instead recognizes and embraces problems by seeking positive ways of looking at them and turning them into constructive action steps.

• "Enjoy!"

— A successful APA program should contribute to "joy in work."

---

[1] Editor's note: These are also rules from Harrison Owen's Open Space Technology.

Scenes from the Field:
Vignettes from Recent APA Exercises

Scene 1: Sisuwatar market, Tamku Sector; several days' walk up in the mountains from our headquarters in Khandbari and/or the nearest mountain airstrip, a week's walk from the nearest road … a dusty, dirty little collection of tawdry bamboo shelters that comes alive once a week as a local market/bazaar (near the allo production center where village women weave the lovely natural hand-loomed material from the giant stinging nettle plant); wrap-up meeting with local staff and representatives from villages, including illiterate, near-literate, and a few tenth-grade completers:

• Discovery: Most exciting moments from the week's training and village exercises: "Hey, I really get this! I can do this … and it really will make a difference in my work! And, besides, it's fun!" This came from first one then another participant, and clearly emerged as a consensus. It is working as a tool to work with people and villages, and, more important, the people appear confident they can use it themselves, without outside "experts" or senior staff.

• Hearing that, we replied: "OK, look at this group of villagers who have gathered here in this little marketplace … . Are you ready to pull together a quick APA with them and see where you can take it, remembering that we have to be on the trail ourselves in an hour or two to get to Bumlingtar by dark? We have to meet the UNDP evaluation tomorrow night twenty miles from here." Answer: "No problem. We'll get right to it!"

• Less than an hour later: A group of villagers comes up to our senior training/ facilitation team (we've left the new trainees, scouts, and villagers to do this one completely on their own; we just wander around and listen in occasionally). An elderly villager, with a bamboo stick and Khukri knife in his hand, approaches us. "We just finished our meeting, made a plan for the development of this marketplace for the year ahead, and have all decided to start right now by cleaning up this place. Will you join us? We're making these bamboo brooms now and everyone is pitching in. We've all made further personal pledges to keep this process going and hope to host a big festival of local songs, dances, handicrafts, and weaving demonstrations here next year as part of the government's 'Visit Nepal 1998' tourism promotion program."

• In minutes, brooms are busy, piles of trash are mounting up, and fires have started to consume the refuse. Within thirty minutes, the place looks better than any of us have seen it look since we did the first surveys here in 1989. Everyone is grinning, and the villagers have called everyone together around a big tree for mutual congratulations, more promises, and speeches.

Scene 2: Small village of Bala, winding up an three-hour APA meeting with three sub-groups, one working on cultural-conservation issues, a second on community-development activities, and a third on income generation. The have finished their appreciative review, shared their dreams and wishes, and drawn up a Future Map for their village, around these main themes. They are now sharing their action plans for the year ahead and their commitments, starting now.

• *Group one, cultural conservation,* commits to the resurrection of an ancient traditional dance representing local cultural links with the environment. Amid cheers, howls of friendly laughter, and great clapping, singing, and simulated drumming, one man from the group jumps into the center of the circle and starts dancing, imitating a whole range of wild animals in a side-splitting rendition of the ancient dance. The group promises that a first-class rendition of the dance will be ready for presentation at a proposed fair in Khandbari, the district capital, in the fall, and for wider presentation at local fairs in the area during "Visit Nepal 1998."

• *Group two, community development,* outlines self-help plans to finish construction of the clubhouse they are building for the allo group, and roofing for their adult study center, plus fund-raising plans to support these. Amid cheers and chuckles, out comes a cash box with a slot in the top and a big lock on the latch. Donations are solicited on the spot from all villagers and visitors at the meeting. The group has set a follow-up meeting date, and each member has made a personal pledge supporting some aspect of the efforts. All members promise that they will each build a latrine at their own homes during the coming week.

• *Group three, income generation,* pledges a new poultry project. One woman, in a gesture both real and symbolic, pledges to purchase her first chicken today as a starter, crosses the circle, and makes a deal on the spot with another member of the group who agrees to sell her a spare chicken. The others make similar commit-

ments to support the allo club, vegetable/kitchen gardens, and, collectively, they all make a commitment to contribute self-help labor to the construction of a new trail connecting this area with our Bung sector to the west, thus opening what we hope will be the first in a series of circle trekking routes, making Makalu a more attractive trekking destination.

Scene 3: Bung Sector, far to the west, Chheskam village; five days' walk from Bala, above, a Rai village that is known for its traditional allo industry but has no organizational structure yet, like the women of Tamku Sector, due to poor communication links and lack of access to markets:

• At the end of the meeting there are commitments among all members to start the repair and rehabilitation of an old and now seldom-used trek route to Mera Peak, several days to the north, to provide another important circle route and bring trekkers into the area ... plus plans to start a self-help trail to join Chheskam and Bung Sector with Tamku, Bala village, and Sisuwatar several days to the east, linking Chheskam to the expertise and market network developed in Tamku: (Bingo, the pieces are coming together!)

Scene 4: Navagaon, Seduwa Sector, four days' walk from Khandbari Headquarters, a Sherpa village, where traditional values are of great importance to the local people. The APA meeting had discussed the diversity of their wildlife, tourist potential, and richness of their culture and turned to what they could do now to start implementing the action plan they had developed for their village:

• A sacred water source was being polluted by

livestock, which was a threat to both local health and their serpent deity. Villagers decided to protect the source with large stones and to provide a way for livestock to pass without polluting the spring.

• Leaping up with great enthusiasm, the group rushed off to start work. The energy of the group, mobilized by the APA process and the opportunity to act now, was visible in the high level of enthusiasm with which this mini-project was completed by about thirty to forty people, including many children, in only fifteen to twenty minutes.

Scene 5: After completing the APA process in a three-hour morning meeting in Chepuwa village, Hatiya Sector, five or six days from MBCP Headquarters, where the people had taken immediate action to build a toilet as a first step, the APA team packed up and left to return to Hatiya. At about noon, the team passed by a house along the way and saw a couple busy in their yard. When the team asked what they were doing, the couple responded by inviting them for a cup of tea. Going to the courtyard, the team found them building a new toilet.

• "What development!" the team remarked. The woman, a quiet participant in the earlier meeting who had made a personal commitment to build her own latrine, brought out a large thermos of traditional butter tea. Helped by her husband and two boys who had not been in the meeting, the woman was busy working on the toilet.

• She explained that this had been her personal commitment at the meeting. "But this was just part of your one-year plan," said the team leader.

"How excellent that you took this up today!"

• The woman and her husband explained that they had decided to honor their commitment right away or else it might be left and never be undertaken. "Through this meeting, we have learned how much we can do if we make commitments and take small steps to fulfill them. Just imagine all the development we could bring to this village if we worked together always in this way."

Trade-offs: Time Constraints and the Use of Other PRA Techniques

Makalu-Barun Conservation Project has used several Participatory Rural Appraisal tools during village consultations. The most valuable among these seem to be Trend Analysis, Social and Resource Mapping, Pair-wise Problem Ranking, and Seasonal Calendars. In the interest of simplicity and time, and to maintain the focus on empowerment and action, we used such PRA exercises only on a "need-to-know" basis. Where time and purpose permit the use of such techniques, however, they can be extremely helpful to get a detailed overall picture of issues of concern for specific planning purposes.

In response to staff concerns about their own and villagers' time constraints, we focused during these APA trials on finding rapid yet effective tools, with the understanding that more time would be taken where a clear need was indicated. **We thus have done a full APA cycle in as little as a fifteen-minute discussion, a training program on the concepts with a practice session of the full**

4-D cycle in an hour, and village meetings in anywhere from two to four hours, rarely longer. This attention to efficiency works well for local people who have busy agricultural schedules, survival demands, and some jaundiced views about outsiders' coming to consult them once more about their "problems" then leaving and seldom or never coming back with solutions to the agreed problems.

APA also responds to staff concerns that traditional village PRAs are difficult to fit into their regular schedules and that follow-up PRAs are seldom conducted. By contrast, the staff in all sectors report that APA is something they can work into everything they do — and they have the confidence to go ahead and do it. They find APA energizing, especially when they see what comes out of it in terms of actions and commitments. Besides, they found APA can be lots of fun!

Raising Expectations and Mobilizing Local Initiative

Appreciative Planning and Action celebrates success. And since successes — best moments — almost always come from things the local people have done themselves, self-help, on their own, this leads to planning for more of the same, avoiding the old trap of village meetings turning into a long list of problems, needs, and requests, which just ends up contributing directly or indirectly to the promotion of dependency on outside support.

When communities are asked to summarize, analyze, rank their problems, and indicate what they can do themselves and what needs outside help, the tendency is to focus on what help might be forthcoming and from whom, rather than on what the community can do for itself. This does not yet appear to be a problem with APA, given its focus on discovering the empowerment inherent in activities undertaken by the people themselves and the short-term action plan built around self-help initiatives.

There is a potential risk, however, in the Dream step, which might be seen as encouraging unrealistic visions of the future and which can be discouraging if no movement toward the achievement of the dreams is evident or likely. Thus the Dream step of APA should be emphasized for what it is — a dream; it should also be emphasized that the achievement of dreams demands real commitments coupled with real belief. Dreams that the group doesn't really believe in should not be painted. APA practice should focus on long-term dreams (10 or twenty years), where the future is far enough away so as not to raise near-term expectations. Allow participants to articulate dreams that energize, preferably based on achievements of other communities of which they may be aware. For example, many dreams in the MBCP area include electricity, often thought by MBCP staff to be totally unrealistic.

In spite of such risks, however, dreams should not be unnecessarily curtailed. For example, several micro-hydro operations have been started successfully in communities within and not far from MBCP's conservation area. During early 1997, one community in Seduwa Sector installed a small power plant that has electrified the area's first village. Another cluster of communities in and around Bung have also begun to pool their government grants and are seeking additional funding for a micro-hydro plant to be built on or near the Hongu River. Current prospects for the success of this initiative are promising. While APA should not raise false expectations, neither should it squelch hope. The power of dreams in which people place real faith is often both surprising and empowering. Rather than raising expectations, APA sessions conducted in Kali Gandaki communities adjoining the construction of a major hydropower dam have proven effective in reducing conflict, reawakening the self-help commitments of villagers, and helping reverse an emerging pattern of dependency and demands by local people for charity from project managers.

Summary and Conclusions

Experience in developing, testing, and utilizing Appreciative Planning and Action in the Makalu-Barun Conservation Project and among communities adjoining a major dam construction initiative suggests that the technique might offer a breakthrough in community development and empowerment in rural areas. Although we must be cautious not to become caught up in the strengths while overlooking the potential pitfalls of APA, when one takes an "appreciative" look at the process as it has evolved in Nepal, the following attributes are worth exploring further:

- *It's empowering* — During a time when there is so much talk about empowerment but we have trouble seeing real empowerment — except in individual "exceptions which prove the rule" cases — APA seems to generate power, energy, enthusiasm, and positive action, on the spot.

- *It's positive* — During times when so many focus on the negative — on problems, problem identification, problem analysis, problem solving, critical thinking, even "embracing error" — APA instead looks for the root cause of success, not the root cause of failure.

- *It's quick* — We've shaved PRA down from a week or more to one or two long days and can now do a full APA cycle — ending up with a concrete action plan, steps to start now, commitments of key people, and implementation of first action step(s) — in two to four hours, and even less. Demonstration training sessions — including theory, methodology, and a full practice session — have been completed in one to two hours, "soup to nuts." Although it is best to arrive in a village the day before an APA meeting is planned, we have also hiked across a mountain to a village, had daal bhaat (the main meal of the day), organized a meeting/training session, conducted same, wrapped up, evaluated the day, and hiked on to another village across another mountain to spend the night in a second community all in a single day — and not a particularly long or stressful day at that. Time should be taken wherever necessary and appropriate, but efficiency has merits, as well, including the ability to make follow-up easier and more frequent.

- *It's easy* — Scouts and village leaders with little or no formal education have run these sessions on their own after as little as one day of training. After an APA introduction, scouts who had lacked the courage to undertake other programs have said, "We can do this! We can understand and practice this." And then they have demonstrated that very confidence, on the spot, rounding up twenty to thirty villagers around a grubby marketplace, going through the full APA cycle, and ending up with an enthusiastic group cleaning up the entire marketplace — all this within an hour and a half, from first kernel of an idea to completion, including closing speeches and the lot.

• *It's replicable* — Training of trainers is not particularly difficult; the concepts are relatively easy to get across (even if they are at heart extremely profound). APA is relatively easy to practice in almost any setting and can be implemented in the field without elaborate preparation. We have already trained virtually all local staff in all four of our sectors in less than four months, all carried out in the field in difficult and remote areas. Approximately 100 MBCP staff have been trained, and most of them have practiced the process in communities. Over fifty APA meetings have now been held, including almost thirty in villages involving over 1,000 people. APA will require continuing follow-up to become fully operational in different settings, but it is hoped that its relative simplicity and efficiency will make such follow-up a replicable reality.

• *It's flexible* — We started with ecotourism; now we've used it for community development, community forestry, cultural conservation, income generation, marketplace development, team building for staff, and organizational development for The Mountain Institute and the Makalu-Barun Conservation Project, and villages along the Kali Gandaki River facing the invasion of a major construction project. Modifications are relatively easy and straightforward (no PhDs required!).

In conclusion, Appreciative Planning and Action has sound roots and has shown itself to be a valuable tool with a promising beginning in The Mountain Institute's programs in Nepal, Sikkim, Tibet, Peru, and the United States. The Makalu-Barun Conservation Project and its 100 villages and 32,000 people are proving receptive to the approach. APA offers a potential breakthrough for mobilizing and empowering rural communities that is worthy of further development, testing, utilization, and assessment.

It is the simplicity of Appreciative Planning and Action that gives it important advantages over some other approaches. On the other hand, it is a profound concept that will be a big challenge to implement in an ongoing manner because of the immensity of and momentum behind our cultural and educational patterns, habits, and professional commitment to institutionalized negativism. But it is always worth the effort to effect positive change, and the potential of Appreciative Planning and Action is too great not to be developed fully.

ABOUT THE AUTHOR

MALCOLM ODELL is a development sociologist who has lived and worked for about nine years in Nepal, where he currently is heading up environment and community programs for a major hydropower construction project in the mountains. For several years before that, he served as senior community-development officer and co-manager for The Mountain Institute, helping oversee the development of a new national park on the Tibetan border; he also developed and tested the application of an appreciative approach to involving the area's 30,000 local people.

He began his career in international rural development and community-based natural-resource management with service in the first Peace Corps group to Nepal from 1962 to 1967. After working in the northern Appalachian Mountains with the rural poor and Native Americans, he spent five years in Africa, helping to establish a national applied-research and rural-development planning program in Botswana. This program sought to address the growing problem of desertification in the Kalahari region under competitive pressures from livestock and wildlife. From 1980 to 1994, he was based in the United States, where he helped generate support for the restoration and operation of America's oldest wooden-boat-building workshop as a living museum. At the same time, he continued his international work as a consultant. His activities included serving as leader or member of more than a dozen evaluation, training, and project-design missions to Zimbabwe, Malawi, Botswana, Egypt, Palestine, Pakistan, and India. He also served as director of international programs at Boston's Education Development Center and executive director of Common Ground, The Center for Policy Negotiation, where he pursued his longstanding interests in education and environmental-conflict resolution. He received his BA from Princeton and holds MS and PhD degrees from Cornell.

For more information, contact:
Malcolm J. Odell, Jr., PhD
Habitat for Humanity International
G.P.O. Box 5367, Kathmandu, Nepal
e.mail: macodell@wlink.com.np
USA Mail: Mac Odell
7 RiverWoods Dr. C-119
Exeter, NH 03833

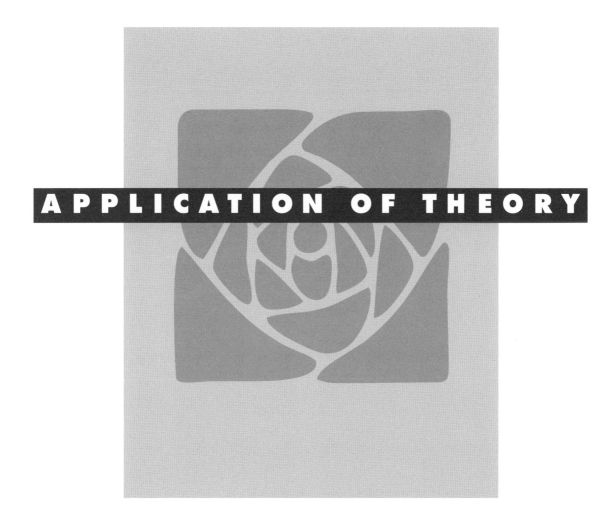

APPLICATION OF THEORY

*B*efore you know it,

the system is in place

and the stories are lost.

DAVID WHYTE,
author of *The Heart Aroused*,
speaking at the Heart of Business Conference
in Austin, Texas, May 9, 1998

APPLICATION OF THEORY

GETTING STARTED

BY DAVID COOPERRIDER

Introduction

This article appeared in the <u>OD Practitioner</u>, (Vol. 28, Nos. 1&2, 1996) and is reprinted with permission of the Organizational Development Network. 76 South Orange Avenue, Suite 101, South Orange, NJ 07079-1923. For more information call (201) 763 7337.

Over the past several years people have been asking more and more for practical tools that will help them transform their OD consulting practice away from the diagnostic problem-solving approaches toward more appreciative inquiry methods. One of the most common requests (when I do workshops on Appreciative Inquiry) is for examples of proposals – proposals that set the stage for OD contracting. This article presents a "composite picture" of several actual proposals that have led to major OD work. The "AMX" proposal represents the best of several projects that combine Appreciative Inquiry and Future Search. The corporate names used in this composite proposal are fictitious.

What I like most about the "whole system" change process spelled out here is that it completely lets go of problem solving. In my view, the problem-solving paradigm, while once incredibly effective, is simply out of sync with the realities of today's virtual worlds. **Problem solving is painfully slow (always asking people to look backwards historically to yesterday's causes), it rarely results in new vision (by definition we say something is a problem because we already implicitly assume some idea, so we are not searching to create new knowledge of better ideals**, we are searching how to close gaps); and, in human terms, problem solving approaches are notorious for generating defensiveness (it is not my problem but yours).

Organizations are centers of human relatedness, first and foremost, and relationships thrive where there is an appreciative eye – when people see the best in one another, when they can share their dreams and ultimate concerns in affirming ways, and when they are connected in full voice to create not just new worlds but better worlds. The AMX proposal is an example of an OD proposal that, in practical ways, mobilizes the appreciative process to the fullest extent I know. The proposal was written the week Congress passed legislation that would deregulate the telecommunications industry, changing the rules that guided the industry for over 60 years. AMX, one of the industry's giants, was literally in chaos with thousands being laid off. Facing the largest whole system transformation in the company's history, the CEO asked, "How can we connect everyone to the adventure of creating the new century telecommunication organization?"

The AMX Connects!

PROPOSAL: ACCELERATING ORGANIZATIONAL LEARNING FOR WINNING THE NEW CENTURY

Background

During the past several years, AMX has positioned itself to take advantage of what may prove to be the greatest single business opportunity in history: the creation and management of the Information Superhighway. Part of this positioning has been the clear articulation of the new strategic "ABC" vision and reaffirmation of the goal of being the most customer responsive business in the industry. Along with the vision has come action. There are literally hundreds of successful new initiatives — reengineering, product innovations, new alliances, public relations campaigns, employee empowerment strategies, etc. — all combining to give birth to the new AMX. The entire system is in the thick of fundamental organizational transformation, and exists in a world where the economic, technological, and regulatory foundations of the business have radically changed. It simply is not the same business it used to be.

Important questions, therefore, are many: How can leaders accelerate positive transformation where the process of corporate change is revolutionary in result and evolutionary in execution? How can people reduce the time lag between exciting organizational innovations (initiatives, large and small, that illustrate what the new-century AMX organization can and should look like) and organizational storytelling, sharing, advocacy, and mass learning from those innovations? How will employees sustain, over a period of years, corporate confidence and faith in AMX's abilities to make fundamental change even in the midst of inevitable setbacks? How can AMX complement its problem-solving culture with an appreciative mindset that selectively sees, studies, and learns from every positive new development? **Can AMX develop and reclaim an oral tradition of storytelling that connects people across corporate generations and that propels the speed and spread of good news?** How can AMX leaders decisively connect people throughout the system to the Future Search, and engage everyone in a "can do" way as social architects of the new century organization — a transformed organizational entity that lives its vision in all its structures, systems, strategies, management behaviors, job designs, partnerships, everything that the company does.

Purpose

The mission of AMX Connects! is to accelerate positive whole system transformation by actively connecting people to the "ABC" vision through the practice of Appreciative Inquiry.

Objectives

• To bring the "ABC" vision alive for 67,000 people at AMX by engaging a critical mass of people in an Appreciative Inquiry into the most positive and compelling organizational innovations, practices, and traditions that (1) best illustrate the translation of the "ABC" vision into transformational action and (2) provide an anticipatory glimpse into the kind of organization AMX should and might become in the new century.

• To deliver tangible follow-up to the 1995 Leadership Workshop (which builds on the momentum of the Aspen, Colorado success where 140 regional and corporate executives were introduced to the theory of Appreciative Inquiry), and tie together executive education with real-time organization transformation. By co-leading the Appreciative Inquiry/Future Search process at the regional and corporate levels, the "action learning" design will contribute as much to leadership development as it does to organizational development.

• To augment AMX's problem solving culture with an appreciative mind set that provides a paradigm shift in ways of looking at managerial analysis of all kinds — e.g., new options for approaching organization analysis, customer focus groups, strategic planning methods, reengineering studies, employee surveys, performance appraisal processes, public affairs methodologies, diversity initiatives, benchmarking approaches, merger integration methods, and many others.

• To build an affirmative atmosphere of hope and confidence necessary to sustain, over the next several years, the largest whole-system transformation in the company's history.

• To discover and pioneer connections between Appreciative Inquiry/Future Search Conference methodologies (often involving hundreds of people interactively) and the voice, video, and data capabilities of AMX's advanced teleconferencing technologies. **The potential for building connection and commitment to the future directions of the company are enormous; corporate visioning, advocacy, and good news telling will not be isolated to a few technical gurus, senior visionaries, or communication messengers, but will engage potentially thousands.** When it comes to bringing vision alive, process is just as important as product. People want to be listened to and to be heard. The large group conference methodologies discussed below are truly impressive in their ability to cultivate the thrill of being a valued member in the creation of new and exciting futures.

Leadership

AMX Connects! will be led by:
President Sheldon Abrahms;
Susan Taft, Vice President Public Affairs;
John Williams, Vice President of Organizational
Development, and the 140 individuals involved
with the recent Leadership Conference. David L.
Cooperrider and Associates from Case Western
Reserve University's Weatherhead School of
Management will provide outside guidance.

Timing

The appreciative organizational inquiry and
learning process will be formally inaugurated in
1996 with a workshop on Appreciative Inquiry.
Participants will be the leadership group of 140
through 1996 and 1997. Appreciative Inquiry
will be introduced and Future Search Conference
completed in every region of Operations. Results
from each of these will form the basis of a synthesizing corporate-wide Future Search in the spring
of 1998 and will culminate with a future report –
to be issued by the think tank group of 140.

The ABC's of Appreciative Inquiry

In a typical Appreciative Inquiry, the process will
lead up to a major Future Search Conference, two
or three days in length, where organization
representatives of the whole (anywhere from 100
to 1,000 people) will come together to both construct images of the system's most desired future
and to formulate creative strategies to bring that
future about. Often, an organizational model like

the 7-S framework will serve as a template for building
"possibility propositions" in each of the key organizational design areas - for example, what will the ideal
organizational structures or systems look like in the
future (the conference organizers will specify how far
into the future to think... usually 3-5 years out.)
The stages for bringing the whole thing off productively
typically follow the ABC sequence:

A **Appreciative** understanding of your
organization (from the past to present);

B **Benchmarked** understanding of
other organizations
(exemplary models to learn from); and

C **Creative** construction of the future
(sometimes called the Future Search Conference).

One possible design would be to launch, in each of
the regions, a broad-based set of Appreciative Inquiry
interviews leading to a regional Future Search conference. The design of the interviews would stress storytelling and study into the "ABC" vision in action —
examples of being "the easiest company to do business with"; times when people feel truly "empowered";
examples of new forms of "servant leadership"; illustrations of how AMX is "winning in the new world", etc.
AMX managers and employees within the region
would do all of these interviews face-to-face. All the
best quotes, stories, and illustrations would be compiled
into a regional report and used to inspire a regionally
based Future Search Conference into "AMX In the

New Century: Images of Organizational Possibility". At the Future Search Conference, with 100 to 2,000 people, participants meet for two or three days to design the organization's most desired future and formulate creative strategies to bring that future about.

The key product is a planning document made of "possibility propositions" describing the collective hopes and dreams people feel inspired to bring about. **In the search conference mode, people learn to think of the future as a condition that can be impacted and created intentionally out of values, visions, and what's technically and socially feasible.** Such purposeful planning greatly increases the probability of making the desired future come alive. What is unique about the Future Search Conference method as described here is (1) its Appreciative Inquiry foundation (often experienced as a liberating personal paradigm shift for people); and (2) the broad base of authentic participation that is demanded.

We live in a world of relentless economic and social change, based on 21st century technologies. Now we struggle to discover management methods equal to the complexity. The power of Appreciative Inquiry and the whole system focus of Future Search combine, our experience shows, to both accelerate and sustain change. **Transformation happens faster, at lower cost, and with more inspired collective follow-up than older, more piecemeal or fragmented approaches.** Studies show that one well facilitated

Future Search with "everybody" — a metaphor for a broad cross-section of stakeholders — will produce more whole systems learning, empowerment, and feelings of connection around business vision than hundreds of fragmenting small group meetings.

The Future Search Conferences, held in each of the regions, would then be capped off with a corporate-wide Future Search of the top 140, the leadership group and key stakeholders representing the whole. If held concurrently in each of the ten regions, the potential for linking up via teleconference for positive story telling across regions might add a creative and powerful integrative dimension. Literally thousands could be involved in real-time inquiry and transformational planning around the "ABC" vision. Each Future Search would involve something like the following:

1. A conference-coordinating committee at the regional level of 4-6 people would meet to plan dates, time, location, meals, group-meeting tasks, and who should attend. **The goal is to get "the whole system" in the room, or at least strong representation of all those that have a clear stake in the future of the organization.** Often then, this includes people "outside" of the organization like customers, community members, partner organizations, etc. The ground rule is that whomever comes to the Future Search must be there for the whole meeting and has the opportunity for full voice in the deliberation.

2. Participants (from 100 to 1,000 people) sit in groups of eight to ten, with flip chart papers or a chalkboard available. Depending on the focus and assigned tasks, groupings may vary during the conference. All output from small group agreement is not required to get ideas recorded.

3. The conference has four or five segments, each lasting up to a half day. Each segment requires that people (a) look at or build a database; (b) interpret it together; (c) draw conclusions for action.

4. The first major activity focuses on macro-trends likely to affect the organization in the future. **Each group is asked to make notes on significant events, changes, and trends they see merging by looking at each of the past three decades from three perspectives: significant changes and events that happened at the world, personal, and institutional/industry levels over each of the past three decades.** Each table reports to the total group, and a facilitator notes trends. The total conference then interprets the most positive macro-trends – those trends that indicate opportunities for building a better organization, society or industry. Even the macro trends that appear negative or threatening often generate creative thinking on hidden opportunities or possibilities for creating the future people want.

5. The second major activity focuses on the appreciative analysis of the organization. Each

group has a copy of the Appreciative Inquiry report that was compiled earlier, with quotes, stories, and comments from all the appreciative interviews. Three questions are then passed to each group: (a) What are the most outstanding moments/stories from this organization's past that make you most proud to be a member of this organization? (b) What are the things that give life to the organization when it is most alive, most effective, most in tune with it's over-arching vision, etc. (make a list of up to ten factors)? and (c) Continuity: What should we try to preserve about our organization — even as we change into the future? Again, consensus is not needed as the results are displayed and discussed by the whole conference.

6. The third major activity focuses on the benchmark understanding of the best practices of other organizations. Each group is given the report from benchmarking studies and is asked to make a list of the most interesting or novel things being done in other organizations. The list should include things that are interesting, novel, or even controversial and provocative. The list is not an endorsement of any of the practices — it is simply a compilation of interesting or new ideas and practices. There is to be no discussion of whether or not to adopt the practices in the present organization. If benchmark studies have not been done as part of the pre-conference Appreciative Inquiry process then group members should generate the list from things they have seen in other organizations have heard or read about. Reports are made to the whole conference and people are asked to comment on the most interesting or novel ideas.

7. The fourth major activity focuses on the future; especially its creative construction. New groups are formed and are given a half day to develop a draft of a preferred, possible future. The focus is on translating the business vision into inspired organizational vision. The focus is on the organizational dimensions of the future. Using a model like the 7-S model or a homegrown model of organization design elements, groups develop a set of "possibility propositions" of the ideal or preferred future organization (3-5 years into the future).

8. The fifth major activity focuses on the next action steps. Groups are then asked to reflect on what has surfaced and depending on the nature of the groupings, to make three lists of suggested action steps: commitments they want to make as individuals to move the vision forward; action steps their region and work unit might take; and things the organization as a whole might do. Action proposals are shared in a total group session and a steering committee is formed to discuss proposals for the total organization, prioritize themes, and prepare a report to be presented at the capstone Future Search.

Whole System Involvement

In a comprehensive study of successful habits of visionary companies, Stanford University researchers Jerry Porras and James Collins point out in their book *Built to Last,* (1994) **that a company may have an elegant vision statement, or a published list of values but that does not mean the company is visionary.** Translating core vision into everything the company does requires ways of connecting everyone — evoking ownership, commitment, understanding, involvement, and confidence in the vision's promise. This proposal provides a do-able way to proceed: it is logistically possible and financially feasible to design a process where all of operations (67,000 people) are involved. Everyone, at a minimum, would be a participant in the Appreciative Inquiry as an interviewer, interviewee, or both. And up to 10,000 would participate in at least three other engaging activities of learning and doing: workshops on Appreciative Inquiry (one day long); conducting the interviews (doing 5-10 interviews); and one or more Future Search Conferences (three days in length). The working assumption, at the regional level, is that approximately 1,000 people would participate in a daylong introduction to Appreciative Inquiry. They would subsequently be charged with completing 5-10 interviews a piece, and then would serve as delegates to the regional Future Search Conference.

Measuring for Results

AMX Connects! will measure its results by asking how each step, and the whole process, achieves discrete, agreed upon objectives. **This is a demanding approach that will force everyone involved to focus on how the method of Appreciative Inquiry actually affects the way people think, communicate, and act in relation to the process of whole system transformation.** Some of the areas of expected impact include:

• Reduction in the time lag between organization innovations (innovations that are consistent with the "ABC" vision) and their spread throughout the corporation.

• The strengthening of a "can do" climate of hope and confidence in the corporation's ability to manage the transition and realize its transformational goals.

• Significant increase in the corporation's positive internal dialogue about the future (e.g., less cynical and deficit oriented discourse; less fear, less negativity; more vocabularies of positive possibility; more rapid spread of good news developments).

• Development of a more appreciative leadership mindset and culture which provides managers with new options for dealing with corporate and customer surveys, re-engineering, strategic planning analysis, team-building, merger integration, performance appraisal and others.

• Significant increase in the feeling of connection to the corporation's "ABC" vision at all levels and regions of AMX Operations.

Sustainability

The telecommunications industry is going through a profound change that involves reassessment of economic foundations, technological infrastructures, organizational forms and processes, and managerial mindsets. The whole system transformation being called for is both comprehensive in scope and fundamental in nature. There are a number of things, therefore, that must not be overlooked. First, we must not overlook the reality of people's resistance to such profound change — to even thinking about it — since it involves challenge to the inner assumptions which have become an inherent part of the culture and individual ways of constructing the "way things ought to be". **Nor should we fail to note that the coming changes will bring about a great deal of fear and uncertainty; in fact, keeping down the fear is probably the greatest challenge of all, since only with low levels of fear can people see clearly and take the right actions.** But perhaps most important is the need to address questions of sustainability. What will make the appreciative inquiry/future search methodologies as outlined earlier more than just a one-time high? What will be done to sustain learnings at regional, corporate, and individual levels? Our own evaluations of Appreciative Inquiry and the evaluation studies of large group Future Search Conferences suggest the following five strategies for long term sustainability (see Wilmot, 1995).

1. Skillbuilding. The Process of Organizational Transformation is a School for Leadership Development. In many respects, there is really no such thing as organizational transformation; there is only individual transformation. Because of this, especially with the leadership group of 140, every major session will involve both organizational analysis and personal planning as well as skill-building modules around all the phases of appreciative inquiry and the methods of facilitating interactive, large group meetings. In GE's recent whole system "Workout Program", for example, it was found that the most important outcome of the initial large group Workouts was managerial skill development — the Workout conference method-ologies have become a way of life for almost two-thirds of the work units. Of course, Chairman and CEO John F. Welch played a major role in mak-ing the new participatory methods a priority. He was notorious in his surprise appearance at local Workout sessions and was consistent in his mes-sage: "building a revitalized *human engine* to animate GE's formidable *business engine.*"

2. Extending Appreciative Inquiry Into Change Efforts Where There will be High Value-Added. Already there are plans being made by various AMX staff to use the appreciative methodologies to re-think and revitalize organization develop-ment practices like corporate surveys, customer focus groups, public affairs projects, etc. These efforts at extending Appreciative Inquiry should be made more systematic and priority driven. Our suggestion is that we should prioritize no more than five major extensions of Appreciative Inquiry — for example AI's contributions to merger integration methods, organizational surveys, process re-engineering, and diversity initiatives. Each of these efforts should be carefully documented and written up later in the form of a practitioner manual (e.g., a merger integration manual, or a customer focus group manual). Appreciative Inquiry involves a paradigm shift that will vitally transform, for example, how mergers or diversity initiatives are approached. The key, early on, is to prioritize several areas where there will be a high value-added contribution and, in those areas, take the appreciative approach to the hilt.

3. Customized Regional Follow-up Consultation. In preparation for the Future Search Conferences, and in response to needed follow-up at the regional level, there will be a consultant/facilitator team made up of internal AMX professionals (e.g., OD, HR, PA) and a specialist from Cooperrider and Associates. This consultant team will commit, up front, to ten days of consulting follow-up at the regional level to tailor-make a response to the initiatives generated at the Future Search Conferences. **By definition, the customized response is unknown at this time, but our experience shows that the commitment to ten days of follow-up consultation is the single most important thing that can be done to ensure sustainability.** In a recent study of Appreciative Inquiry with 25 organizations, it has been found that ninety percent of the organizations are continuing with the appreciative methodologies, some two years after the start (see Wilmot, 1995). An essential attribute of the sustainability was that in each case, all ten days of promised follow-up consultations were in fact used. Likewise, the follow-up was completely at the initiative and request of the organizations themselves. Each organization had to "apply" in writing for the follow-up, define the goals, and the kind of support they needed (e.g., facilitation, training, outside evaluation, retreat design, organization analysis, one-on-one personal counseling). The lesson is simple: we must plan for sustainability from the beginning, and the commitment to the customized follow-up opportunity is critical.

4. Advanced "Internal Consultant" Learning Partnership. Each year there will be two special sessions among all internal AMX change agents that are involved with Appreciative Inquiry and the Future Search Conferences. The learning partnership will deal with advanced theoretical and practice issues, and will use clinical/field-based modes of learning. The purpose will be to build internal skills and competencies, to build a support network among AMX units and regions, and to make good use of the program's evaluation studies for advanced professional development.

5. Appreciative Inquiry "On-Line." Already there have been discussions with specialists at AMX about how to accelerate the spread of innovations and good news storytelling by adding an Appreciative Inquiry protocol to the new AMX on-line suggestion program. An analogy here is useful: an ongoing Appreciative Inquiry will be to the "whole system transformation" what time-lapse photography is to the visible blossoming of an otherwise imperceptible flower. Putting Appreciative Inquiry on-line is a very exciting venture that has yet to be done anywhere. There is no question the time is ripe for this to happen; and it makes sense that it would be inaugurated at AMX, where leadership in the positive human impact of advanced technology lies at the forefront of the corporate mission. One way to introduce the on-line approach would be to conceive of the 67,000 interviews as mini-training sessions in Appreciative Inquiry. After each interview, people would be given a short booklet with simple instructions on how to use the internal on-line "web page". Stories and new images would be made available on a continuous basis. An award could even be established for the stories that best anticipate and give a glimpse of the new AMX, living its vision today. The implications of Appreciative Inquiry on-line are far-reaching and exciting indeed. We are infants when it comes to our understanding of the power of this kind of non-hierarchical information sharing and whole system dialogue. The results could be revolutionary.

In the course of developing the ideas described above, it has become clear that people at AMX have this hope that there's a little window of opportunity for really responding to a radically changed business environment. That window of opportunity, and the current season of hope being expressed, is going to last about as long as Sheldon Abrahms, in the early days of his new presidency, uses this occasion to boldly enroll everyone in the positive transformation. To make it all work we (as an internal/external team) will not only need to work collaboratively, responsively, and flexibly as a "learning organization," but we also will need to be united around a shared revolutionary intent.

Conclusion

The relational, large group, participatory methods, outlined here fly in the face of old hierarchical, piecemeal problem-analytic approaches to change. **Likewise the appreciative paradigm, for many, is culturally at odds with the popular negativism and professional vocabularies of deficit that permeate our corporations and society at large.** Most important, however, there are people, many people throughout AMX, that feel the time has come to make the "positive revolution" happen. These are the individuals that are just waiting to step forward and lead. The constructive, creative, and indispensable voices of the new AMX already exist. But their critical mass has yet to be legitimized. AMX Connects! is about mass mobilization; it is about the systematic creation of an organization that is in full voice. It is about transformation of the corporation's internal dialogue. It is about creating, over the next several years of discovery and transition, a center stage for the positive revolutionaries.

© D. COOPERRIDER, 1998

References

Collins, James, C. Porras, Jerry, I. (1994).
Built to Last. *Harper Business.*

Wilmot, Tim (1995) *"The Global Excellence in Management Program: A Two Year Evaluation of 25 Organizations Using Appreciative Inquiry"* Case Western Reserve University.

For detailed analysis of large group methods and outcomes - from Ford Motor Company, First Nationwide Bank, SAS, Marriott, and Boeing - see Jacobs, R. (1994) *Real Time Strategic Change: How to Involve an Entire Organization in Fast and Far Reaching Change, San Francisco*: Berrett-Koehler Publishers.

For ten case studies of the Future Search methods see Weisbord, M. (1992) *Discovering Common Ground: How Future Search Methods Bring People Together To Achieve Breakthrough Innovation, Empowerment, Shared Vision, and Collaborative Action, San Francisco*: Berrett-Koehler

ABOUT THE AUTHOR

DAVID L. COOPERRIDER Ph.D is Chairman of the SIGMA Program for Global Change and Associate Professor of Organizational Behavior, and at Case Western Reserve University's Weatherhead School of Management.
David is past President at the National Academy of Management's Division of Organization Development — and he is a co-founder of The Taos Institute. He has also taught at Stanford University, Katholieke University in Belgium, MIT, Benedictine University, Pepperdine University, and others. Currently he serves as the Principle Investigator of a multi-million dollar grant working with international organizations dealing with global issues of human health, environment, peace, and sustainable economic development, funded through USAID. David's most recent books include: *Appreciative Inquiry, A Positive Revolution In Change; No Limits to Cooperation: The Organization Dimensions of Global Change* (with Jane Dutton); *International and Global OD* (with Peter Sorenson); *Organizational Wisdom and Executive Courage;* and *Appreciative Leadership and Management* (both with Suresh Srivastva). David has just been named editor of a new Sage Publication Book Series — *Human Dimensions of Global Change.*

For more information, contact:
David L. Cooperrider
phone and fax: 440.338.1546
e.mail: dlc6@po.cwru.edu

*W*e can easily forgive a child who

is afraid of the dark. The real tragedy

of life is when men are afraid of the light.

— PLATO

APPLICATION OF THEORY

INTRODUCING THE

AI PHILOSOPHY

BY JACKIE KELM

Introduction

The purpose of this article is to look at practical ways of presenting the Appreciative Inquiry (AI) philosophy with first-time clients in a formal or structured manner. These ideas are just a starting point for formulating your own ideas about how to introduce the AI philosophy. In the true spirit of Appreciative Inquiry, you will want to begin with these concepts and let the process evolve organically.

If you have worked with AI before, you know that it is a living process and thus sometimes difficult to pin down. Practitioners grow with the practice of AI, and AI continues to reveal itself in new and different ways. Currently, I see it as a way of engaging people in a system to reveal and examine common strengths and desires. It is a way to discover those things they can and should be proud of, things that provide a foundation for building greater effectiveness and satisfaction as a community of people. It is a shared awakening of hope and desire for a future possibility that did not exist or had not been shared before.

Quite simply, the inquiry is the process of joining together in common cause to find these hidden hopes and strengths. Our role as consultants is to initially provide leadership in this process to sow the seed, and then to encourage leadership to emerge within the group so that the philosophy takes root.

Preparing For The A.I. Discussion

When we think of introducing Appreciative Inquiry to a client for the first time, we are really thinking about collaborative learning. The client is learning about AI while we are simultaneously learning more about AI and the client. Ultimately, we are trying to create an ideal learning environment in which all parties feel safe enough to explore new possibilities.

It is important to remember that like the inquiry, the introduction of AI is also part of the change process. What we choose to say, who we say it to, and how we choose to act affects the ultimate changes that will occur within the client system. Several things are helpful in preparing for that first A.I. discussion:

- **DETERMINE YOUR OBJECTIVES**

- **LEARN ABOUT THE PEOPLE**

- **LEARN ABOUT THE ORGANIZATION**

- **GET IN THE RIGHT FRAME OF MIND**

Determine Your Objectives

First of all, determine your objectives. The anticipatory principle of AI as articulated by David Cooperrider suggests that what we anticipate and think about influences what actually happens. It is therefore important to think through ahead of time what you hope to accomplish as a consultant. For example, if your primary objective is to establish credibility and build a relationship, you will behave and speak differently than if your objective is to "close the sale". A lot has been written about the importance of determining objectives prior to a meeting, and these principles apply when introducing AI.

Learn About the People

Once you know your objectives, think about the people with whom you are going to speak. This helps structure the conversation and guide your choice of the types of examples and stories you might use to enhance learning. It may be difficult to gather some of this information ahead of time, but if you are able to do some research up front consider exploring the following:

• What are the major issues or concerns facing them now?

• Where do these individuals fit in the organization and what are the various levels of personal and positional power?

• What are their general educational and experience backgrounds?

• Do they tend toward a certain learning or personality style?

• Are there any cultural differences that might be important to consider?

• In what ways are they most comfortable receiving information?

Some of the information may be gathered during preliminary conversations and site visits, or by checking with others who have worked with these clients in the past. One or two of these considerations will likely be most relevant, and thinking them through will allow you to adjust your approach in ways that will make the audience most comfortable. For example, if you know an audience is highly technical, you might emphasize the principles, and use charts or matrices as a format for presenting information. Using an approach that is familiar enhances people's sense of security and provides a common context for new ideas. This helps to facilitate learning, assuming you too, are comfortable with the approach. Don't forget that the client will also be learning about you simultaneously.

Learn About the Organization

To be of greatest service, it helps to reflect on the unique needs and characteristics of the organization. The following list of attributes will help you think through this:

• Strategy, mission, values - clarity, acceptance, alignment...

• History — formative events...

• Location — local, dispersed, international...

• Structure — hierarchy, matrix, team-based...

• Financial situation — profitable, declining margins...

• Market position — leader, niche player...

• Nature of the industry(ies) — consolidating, mature, monopoly...

• Leadership style — empowering, authoritarian...

• Work environment — individual, competitive, supportive...

• Frequency of and comfort with change — constant, adaptable...

• Urgency for change/improvement — competitive pressure, impending bankruptcy...

• Definition of power and where power sources are located — profit centers, VP level...

• Decision making — consensus, mandates...

• Actions/behaviors/results rewarded — profit, sales growth...

• History with consultants or similar undertakings — positive, skeptical...

Again, it is not necessary to research all these items; two or three will probably have the most impact and relevance. The top portion of the list can be researched through client questioning and public sources, but the bottom of the list is more subtle. The bottom information is best obtained by listening and watching carefully in preliminary conversations and interactions with the organization. You will see patterns of behavior emerge in day-to-day interactions with the system.

Get in the Right Frame of Mind

The final aspect of readying yourself for the AI discussion is mental preparation. **I find it helpful to get in the right frame of mind just prior to the meeting by consciously focusing on affirming thoughts about myself and the organization.** This helps me act more consistently with the principles and often reminds me of the necessity of living AI more fully. The "real" person is always present and is sensed by the audience, which is why it is important to practice what you preach. Here are some examples of the types of affirmations I might use:

- *I believe in these people and I'm honored to be with them.*

- *I believe in what I am doing.*

- *There is possibility everywhere I look.*

- *I believe that the principles of AI have real value for these people.*

- *I am excited about this meeting.*

Engaging In The A.I. Discussion

Now let's explore actually delivering the message. At this point you know what you want to accomplish, you know something about the nature of the client and the organization, and you're mentally prepared. So where do you begin? Here's one approach that I find useful.

- Practice the principles of AI.

- Build trust.

- Establish common ground.

- Build momentum through the content.

- Prepare to answer the standard questions.

Practice the Principles of AI

The first thing to remember is to simply practice the principles of AI. **Remember that everything you do is part of the change process from the first time you speak to the client. The questions you ask will ignite thoughts in the client's mind that may trigger new ideas, behaviors, or actions.** The importance of acting consistently with the philosophy cannot be overemphasized. In the words of Jane Watkins, a consultant and teacher of AI, "the best way to teach it, is to be it." Seen another way, you teach who you are.

There are five principles of AI that I will describe at a very high level. They include the constructionist principle, the simultaneity principle, the poetic principle, the anticipatory principle, and the positive principle.

- **The constructionist principle suggests that every analysis we make is informed by what we know from the past.** We construct our realities based on our previous experience, and hence our knowledge and the destiny of the organization are interwoven.
- **The principle of simultaneity proposes that the inquiry and change are simultaneous.** The questions we ask determine what we find and are part of the change process. Our inquiry into an organization is therefore not objective or neutral.
- **The poetic principle postulates that we can find whatever we want in an organization, because organizations and human systems are like open books or poetry; they are open to infinite interpretations.**
- **The anticipatory principle suggests that what people anticipate determines what they will find.**

Altering the way people look at the future can result in major shifts in human behavior.

- **Finally, the positive principle highlights the importance of viewing organizations and people from a positive perspective.** As an individual's or organization's image of itself is enhanced, the organization or individual begins to act in ways consistent with the positive image. As people feel more valued and affirmed, they become less defensive and more open to change.

Actually practicing these principles means acting as a role model in all your interactions:

- Generate interactive dialogue. Provide space for questions and discussion.

- Tell and solicit stories. Share passion, feelings, and meaning.

- Ask provocative questions. Probe for excitement and possibility.

- Focus on the positive. Look for the budding flower amid the gray backdrop.

- Set aside judgment. Be open and really listen.

- Affirm yourself and everyone around you.

- Look for the value in others and help them see it.

- Care with all your heart. Sincerely want to help.

- Believe in yourself and AI.

- Respect the past, live in the present, and look to the future.

These are just some examples of how to practice the principles of AI. People will learn from you as you act on these principles, and they will hopefully begin to emulate them as well. Encourage your clients to practice the principles as they begin to take ownership of the process down the road.

Build Trust

Trust is important in learning as well as in building strong client relationships. Trust is the safety net that allows us to be ignorant or fail in the process of learning. It is the foundation on which client relationships are built and sustained. There are several theories about the different levels of trust and how that trust is built, but the following list from Robert Rogers offers some concrete examples of how to build trust[1]:

1. Be positive.
2. Seek others' ideas.
3. Listen.
4. Disclose.
5. Don't shoot the messenger.

It is interesting how these factors align with AI. Rogers also lists ways to build trust among team members, which is helpful in group situations[1]:

1. Maintain each other's self-esteem.
2. Support and praise each other.
3. Keep sensitive information confidential.
4. Stand up for each other.
5. Avoid gossip or unfair criticism of others.
6. Appreciate each other's skills and differences.

I see trust as the single most important factor in the successful sharing and use of AI because it is at the heart of building relationships and creating a positive learning environment.

Establish Common Ground

A good way to start the actual presentation is to establish common ground. Basically this means finding a similar base or common area of understanding that creates a sense of connection between everyone in the room. The idea is to get the group talking about something everyone relates to in order to establish a common bond and sense of safety. Sharing our common experiences and meaning also helps build trust.

When David Cooperrider gives presentations on AI he often begins by talking about macro trends in our world. This is a form of establishing common ground, in that the trends have a common meaning shared by everyone in the world. This creates a sense of connectedness and interdependence in the room. Macro trends are an excellent way of establishing common ground because there is literally no one in the world who is excluded! Examples of macro trends Cooperrider uses include global cooperation with such events as the elimination of smallpox, and the end of apartheid.

---

[1] Rogers, Robert, *Psychological Contract of Trust*, Development Dimensions International, 1225 Washington Pike, Bridgeville PA 15017-2838, pg. 29,40.

Build Momentum
Through The Content

Once basic levels of trust and common ground have been established I work into the content of AI. I find it best to start with simple overviews, little detail, low emotional intensity, and work up from there. It's important to keep a pulse on the group and ramp up the discussion as you sense they can handle more. Start with simple ideas so that people don't shut down. If you lead off with something they can't understand, they may feel too threatened to continue trying to learn. Additionally, when people are lost or confused they sometimes rationalize it as inadequacy on your part, which will reduce their perception of your competence.

I usually start out by explaining how I see AI at the highest level, which is a philosophy. I view it as a way of perceiving and interacting with others that transforms the way we think of human systems and organizing. I liken it to a leadership style in that it is a way of being, of thinking, and of believing. It pervades what we do and how we do it.

I then go into the principles as well as the Pygmalion and placebo effects. The Pygmalion effect was first discovered by studying how students respond to their teachers' image of them. In an experiment, teachers were told that certain students selected at random were "good" students, and others were "bad." By the end of the year, these randomly selected students were actually behaving accordingly, demonstrating the power that our perceptions of others have on their behavior.

The placebo effect is the term used to describe how some patients improve when given "sugar pills," or false medication. This shows the power that our thinking and belief systems have on our life experiences.

After explaining the Pygmalion and placebo effects I often talk about other AI concepts from *Positive Image, Positive Action: The Affirmative Basis of Organizing* by David Cooperrider and Suresh Srivastva[2]. I typically include the concept of imbalanced inner dialogue – where it was documented that psychologically healthy people use an approximate two-to-one ratio of positive to negative "self-talk." I also discuss how the image of the future held by society is key in determining the evolution of that culture. At some point I always tell the "bowling story," which people will usually remember even if they forget everything else.

The bowling story basically involves an experiment that was conducted in teaching people how to bowl. Two groups of people were given bowling lessons with different approaches to follow-up

---

2 Cooperrider, David, Srivastva, S. Appreciative Inquiry in Organizational Life in Woodman, Pasmore (eds.), *Research on Organizational Change and Development*, Vol. 1, JAI Press, 1987. ISBN 0-89232-749-9.

over several weeks. In one group the follow-up consisted of reviewing and correcting mistakes, while the other group was coached and encouraged on what they did well. In the end, the group with the positive reinforcement performed substantially better than the other, though both groups did improve.

I then work into the details of AI, talking about the phases and so forth. David Cooperrider also includes mini AI interviews at this point, done by participants in pairs with three to four appreciative questions. The questions are structured around a topic relevant to the group, such as the organization to which they all belong. Abbreviated examples of some interview questions include the following:

1. *What is it that you value most about yourself and/or the organization?*

2. *What is the core life-giving force of this organization?*

3. *If you were granted three wishes for the future of this organization, what would they be?*

When I set the stage for these interviews, I explain how the participants need to try to listen nonjudgmentally, and to look for excitement and inquire into it further. After the interviews I do a quick debriefing, asking open-ended questions such as, "What was it like to do this exercise?"

Another story I always work in is the Omni Hotel story. This a classic story of how David Cooperrider used AI to dramatically change the effectiveness and attitudes of the hotel staff at the Omni Hotel in Cleveland. The Omni Hotel was a one-star hotel with significant management and customer service problems at the time David was called in. He basically took the entire management team to a five star hotel for a week and had them observe the staff and ask appreciative questions. The management team came back highly motivated to change, and succeeded in shifting the hotel rating to four-stars over the next several years. It is a good example of the power of AI. If you are not familiar with the story, it was captured during an AI conference in Taos, New Mexico, in October 1996 on tape #8. (Contact the Taos Institute at 505-751-1232 for information on the tapes.)

I usually end the presentation with some type of open-ended question-and-answer session or dialogue with the entire group. I rarely have to initiate this dialogue — usually people are so fired up that they are blurting out ideas and applications faster than I can respond. It is exhilarating to see the enthusiasm of the group evolve as new possibilities are entertained.

Prepare to Answer
The Standard Questions

During the exciting process of questioning at the end of an AI presentation, some standard questions come up time and again. If you have had any experience in trying to explain AI you will probably be familiar with them. It is important to be clear about how you will answer these questions ahead of time, because they will almost certainly be asked. There are many ways to answer them, and I find that my answers change as I learn more about AI. For this reason I hesitate to list responses, because I will probably modify my responses down the road! With this disclaimer in mind, here are some commonly asked questions and my current thinking in approaching an answer.

1. *What is AI?*
Refer to the second and third paragraphs in the introduction of this chapter.

2. *How do you get people to look at the positive when everything is so negative?*
Negative venting often occurs naturally in the process of looking at the positive. I listen to the negative comments, but try not to feed into them or inquire into them in. I let them be, and continue to inquire into the life-giving forces. Eventually, people will find something positive to talk about, however brief or seemingly insignificant it might be.

3. *How can we fix the problems if we don't talk about them?*
This is the most highly debated question in AI and this brief response will not be satisfactory if you don't already know where you personally stand on it.

Basically, the question itself arises from a problem-solving mentality in which we are all immersed which assumes that looking for and solving problems is the only path to improvement. AI suggests that looking at opportunities and strengths and drawing on the hopes and inspiration of people is another path to improvement. With AI we essentially don't need to outline the problems to address them, because they are essentially addressed as we work the situation from a totally different perspective.

4. *Isn't this a bit like wearing rose-colored glasses?*
No. With AI we use the analogy that the glass is half full rather than half empty. We are not saying that the glass is full, we are saying it is half full. Saying this to an organization that cannot see it any way but half empty may initially appear rose-colored or Pollyanna-like.

5. *What are the steps? Or is there a process?*
There is no process to AI because it is fundamentally an inquiry into human systems and there are numerous ways to conduct an inquiry. The only given is that it requires dialogue, and so there is usually some type of interviewing and sharing of learnings. If I have an idea about a process that might work at the time the question is asked I might share it.

6. *What are the downsides to AI?*
This is like asking, "What are the down sides to leadership?" AI is a philosophy. **The down side is similar to the down side of any philosophy — misapplication and poor execution.**
For example, applying the philosophy of problem solving is a better approach when trying to

address a linear or mechanical situation such as fixing your car. At the same time you might apply AI while talking to the mechanic who will fix your car by engaging in a collaborative discussion of the possibilities for better performance. The proper application can still be problematic if poorly executed. An example of poor execution in AI is not acting consistent with the principles, such as focusing on the weaknesses within the system while using appreciative questions to try and "fix" them.

7. *Where else has this been used?*
Lots of places. David Cooperrider has used it in many places including for-profit companies like GTE and non-profit organizations such as the United Worlds Religions. I have used it within a "big six" consulting firm as well as at a local college and small manufacturing company. Others have used it in their churches, homes, schools, and anywhere else people come together in common purpose.

8. *Where are the places AI works best? Where does it not work?*
As with any initiative, I find that AI works best with strong leadership support. Without this support, people come up with ideas that they may not be able to act on. This creates frustration and cynicism. Key leaders need to be on board with the AI approach and believe in the fundamental principles. I have found that some leaders cannot let go of control enough to trust a group of people to come up with ideas and solutions. This is usually evident in up-front discussions – some leaders want to control the interview data and not involve the rest of the group in processing the information. In these situations I find AI does not work well.

9. *Do you have any information on AI?*
I have some standard materials I pass along which are further referenced in the footnotes. One is a great couple page write-up of a speech given by the president of GTE in which he talks about the value of AI. You can find it in the May 1996 edition of *Vital Speeches*[3]. Another good reference is *The Thin Book of Appreciative Inquiry* by Sue Hammond, which runs about $8 US and is a good little overview book. Finally, there are several articles that speak to the theory of AI. The paper that outlines the fundamental concepts is *Appreciative Inquiry in Organizational Life* by Cooperrider and Srivastva[5]. The second is *Positive Image, Positive Action: The Affirmative Basis of Organizing* by Cooperrider. There are other good articles and references, but these are the ones I tend to use most.

Once the questions have been answered and the presentation has ended, the final thing I often do is put up a quote. I have several favorites, but the one I've been using lately is in a number of Cooperrider's materials:
We can easily forgive a child who is afraid of the dark. The real tragedy of life is when men are afraid of the light — Plato

---

[3] White T.W. Working in Interesting Times. *Vital Speeches of the Day.* May 15, 1996. Vol.LXII, No. 15.
[4] Hammond S.A. *The Thin Book of Appreciative Inquiry.* Thin Book Publishing Co. Plano, TX, 1996.
[5] Cooperrider, David, Srivastva, S. "*Appreciative Inquiry in Organizational Life*" in Woodman, Pasmore (eds.), Research on Organizational Change and Development, Vol. 1, JAI Press, 1987. ISBN 0-89232-749-9.
[6] Cooperrider, David. "*Positive Image, Positive Action: The Affirmative Basis of Organizing. Appreciative Management and Leadership: The Power of Positive Thought and Action in Organizations.* Now available at www.thinbook.com

Conclusion

Introducing a client to the philosophy of AI is really about collaborative learning. The quality of the learning environment is as important as the content of the discussion. Being clear about your objectives and learning about the organization ahead of time helps to prepare for the discussion. Building trust and establishing common ground helps to further facilitate learning, and also feeds into the most critical success factor of all: acting consistently with the principles of Appreciative Inquiry.

It is exhilarating to hear the excitement in people's voices as they begin to embrace these concepts. When I watch clients create possibilities that did not exist before, I feel the hope and enthusiasm that are at the heart of what I love about this work.

© J. KELM, 1998

ABOUT THE AUTHOR

JACKIE KELM is a change management consultant who works with organizations in designing, planning, and implementing strategic changes. She has special expertise in communication processes and technologies which help move the organization forward more quickly and effectively. Prior to her current work, Jackie was a manager in the Leadership and Organization Development Group of Ernst & Young LLP. Jackie holds a BS degree in mechanical engineering from General Motors Institute, and an MBA from Case Western Reserve University.

For more information, contact:
Jackie Kelm
8678 Scenicview Dr.
Broadview Heights, OH 44147
phone: 440.582.6472
e.mail: jkelm@mindspring.com

*I*magine! The beauty and creations

we see around us are all the

manifestation of someone's dream…

everything, including us is

the manifestation of someone's dream.

—CATHY ROYAL

APPLICATION OF THEORY

FREQUENTLY
ASKED QUESTIONS

BY CATHY ROYAL AND
SUE ANNIS HAMMOND

We have both had the privilege of talking to many people who are learning about Appreciative Inquiry: Cathy as a teacher of AI at NTL[1], and Sue as the author of *The Thin Book of Appreciative Inquiry*. Those conversations have led us to compile in this chapter some of the most commonly asked questions, along with our current answers. In addition, we have reviewed some of the mail shared on the Appreciative Inquiry list-serve[2], which made its debut in June 1997. The purpose of the listserve is to provide experienced practitioners a place to seek answers to their immediate questions about using AI and to share their ideas and experience.

What should be emphasized?

The most important step in the process is the analysis of the data gathered through sharing the stories. It is through the analysis of the stories that the group discovers what conditions made success possible and how to replicate those conditions. This is an important point to emphasize when attempting to define AI to a client. Data analysis is a process clients are familiar and comfortable with, so it is a good place for them to make a connection between what they are used to, analyzing data, and what is new, *focusing on what works through the sharing of stories about when we are at our best.*

What is a "real" appreciative inquiry?

A real Appreciative Inquiry is a large system change effort that *gets the whole system in the room* and requires a significant investment of time. Most of the research about AI published in academic journals describes large-scale efforts. This is the way we would all like to do AI because this is where we have the best chance to create large-scale, sustainable change. However, as consultants, we find many, many more opportunities other than large-scale change initiatives to do work within an appreciative frame. We start where the client is and view it as an opportunity to educate the client on this philosophy. This is what we label applying appreciative theory, rather than a full system Appreciative Inquiry.

Which frame are you in?

We suggest that you keep this question in front of you as you work. Are you in the diagnostic, problem-solving frame or the appreciative frame? Asking appreciative questions or positively worded questions within the problem-solving frame is different from appreciative inquiry. We have talked to many people who try to apply appreciative theory simply by inserting positively worded questions into a *deficit framework*. In the deficit frame, you define *what not to do or what to do less of.* **The appreciative frame looks for ways to do more of what already works.** Using appreciative questions within the deficit model creates very different results from using appreciative questions in an appreciative frame. Since most of our profession is built on the deficit model, it is necessary to shift frames, both for ourselves and especially in our client's heads. The shift also begins to create a shift in philosophy about what can be present in organizations and in our thinking about organizing.

What do you do when the client keeps focusing on the "problem"?

We find that eventually the question of "what do we do about our problems?" surfaces. One school of thought within the AI community is to rise above the problem language and immediately convert it to the appreciative approach. Another school of thought is to acknowledge the "problem" so the client feels heard at his or her comfort level (see the question above). We do what we think best for our client depending on their unique situation.

When Cathy is working with a client or teaching the AI course, the question is often raised "what to do with the negative?" Cathy reminds them that language is key to shifting our thinking. **She asks the client to remember that if people hold in their mind what is wrong, they also hold in their mind what should be present to make it right.** It is a powerful point and often a turning point in peoples' minds when asked to focus or shift their frame of reference. She continues her discussion of the negative with information about the power of the negative. Her classes often include a segment on how what we say to the client and how we language these statements permits new thinking or direction. Each time we co-construct or revisit the "problem" the energy shifts within the system and the individual. **Clients come to realize that we are not ignoring the negative, but seeking new ways to illuminate what is beneath the "problem", what it is that the client or the system wishes to create for its future.**

In another example, a woman approached Sue at a break and wondered how AI was going to deal with her perception that "certain people in management had been promoted because of favoritism and did not have good leadership skills." Sue explained that because they were in the process of defining what conditions were present during peak performance the group would ultimately have a "list" of how to create those favorable conditions. That "list" gives everyone (including the managers) clear information on how to behave to create those conditions. Everyone would be conscious of the behaviors necessary to create the conditions and could then monitor group behavior. By concentrating on creating those conditions, the old behaviors begin to fade away, replaced by the new.

Like this woman, most people have not experienced change through appreciation. It is a bit of a leap of faith to accept the facilitator's assurance that AI will produce results. That is why the detailed analysis and conversation on "what worked" and "what will be" is extremely important. The detail and stories connect each person to the reality of past success and how that will be enhanced in the future.

---

[1] Contact Cathy for workshops, conducted four times a year.
[2] To subscribe to the listserve, visit
http://lists.business.utah.edu/mailman/listinfo/ailist

How do you manage continuity?

We think that in general, people approach change with caution and some reluctance to shift their behavior toward the new goals. We believe that Ron Fry and Suresh Survastra[i] did the world a huge favor by coining the phrase "managing continuity." We use this phrase a lot with clients to comfort them and explain what we are going to do. We emphasize that they have done many things right or they wouldn't be where they are. Our job is to surface what has worked, and what conditions created the climate for things to work. Then we help the client determine how to replicate those conditions. There is always a sigh of relief when clients realize and appreciate that they have done something right. **This positive affirmation depends on data collection and theme analysis, not on feel-good talk, and that is the difference that creates results.**

How do you pick the topics and create questions?

When Sue was writing *The Thin Book*, she circulated drafts among colleagues for comments. She had written about how "fun" it was to create questions. One astute editor reminded her that what she thought was fun was not necessarily fun for anyone else. We have learned through conversation and observation, that writing questions from the chosen topics is truly an art. We believe that you have to think about each proposed topic a great deal to get inside of it to understand what it is about. This is one of the reasons topic choice requires a significant investment of time and people. Since topic choice is fateful, we take this step very seriously.

Inquiry is a fateful act; the simple positive question is directional and motivational because "The energy follows the inquiry".

When Cathy trains consultants in AI, she addresses the topic of questions in some detail. "The first question is fateful" because it begins to initiate the thread of collective memory between members of the organization. If this memory is to be a part of what motivates and energizes the people or system it should highlight the best aspects of the organization. Ask the questions of what is working and begin the memory stream on the note of what people are doing well. Remember that in human development theory, it is documented that humans want to do well, they want their organizations to thrive (Cooperrider, 1992) and they respond to recognition. When we structure our inquiry around the aspects that help people recall their capabilities and competencies, we meet fundamental human motivation criteria and position our work as that of coach and collaborator. We highlight how the organization can continue based on what the members have identified as good and worthwhile for their future.

Sue has an example of how to discover the question that is often embedded in the proposed topic. One group wanted to explore the topic of the "us vs. them" mentality between the two sides of their profession, academics and practitioners. By scanning their newsletters and publications and talking to a couple of members, the real concern behind that general topic was about whom was contributing to expanding the knowledge base of the profession.

The theorists thought they were doing all the work while the practitioners thought they weren't getting enough credit for their contribution.

How did we know that sharing knowledge was the issue? By analyzing information from several sources, and then checking the analysis with the client contact. This is really the action research model: Gather the information, analyze it and check it out with the client. In writing questions we now add another two steps. First, we try to write an answer to the proposed question; then we ask a colleague or two to also try to answer the question. **Invariably, we find that other people catch nuances that one set of eyes misses.**

Here's the question we crafted: Describe a time when you participated in or observed information sharing between members of this organization? Notice the question does not ask for a time when knowledge was shared between the academic and practitioner. It stops at the time when information was shared within the organization. That is because the idea is to find when information was shared and how that happened. If we narrow the question to the time it was shared between "us vs. them", we spotlight the tension between the two groups. It is not important to know how information was shared between the two groups, it is only important to know how information is shared within the entire group. By determining how information sharing occurs, we can help the group discover ways to enhance and highlight sharing in the future.

Is there a step between imagining "what will be" and creating the provocative propositions?

Because the purpose of the appreciative interviews is to generate data, there is a lot of data to share and analyze for themes. We find a point during the imagining of the future (through the sharing of the data) when there is an overwhelming number of subjects and ideas. It is important that the facilitator have a process for grouping data into common themes and for voting for the top priorities. The themes should theoretically fall into the categories of the topics chosen for the Appreciative Inquiry (since that is what you asked about), but sometimes, new themes emerge. The themes should be named and data grouped under the appropriate theme. It is useful to have lots of wall space to do this. It is a messy process so good facilitation is a must. It is also helpful to connect the stories to the raw data through the writing of the "quotable quotes" on the flipcharts.

Once categorization is complete, convene the entire group to review the themes. Time constraints may make it necessary to choose which themes will be carried into provocative propositions. As a facilitator, you may have to float a number to the group, but we have found that five to seven [ii] themes are more than enough to work with. You can determine the top five by giving everyone five colored dots. They then can validate their priorities in anyway they want, walking around the groupings (on the wall) and placing their dots on what is most important to them. The result is an instant scatter graph of what is most important.

There are various ways to move people into the provocative proposition stage but we found that letting people go stand by the theme group that they wish to work on, gives you one more check on the priority of the theme. In one instance, the theme of "international presence" received a lot of dot votes, but only one person wanted to work on the next step. The facilitator then challenged the group on how important that theme was in reality. The group did not want to give it up because it seemed important and also a politically correct topic. But as only one person in a group of fifty had chosen to stand by the topic, there clearly was not enough energy to work it through to a provocative proposition. The facilitator suggested that the group put it aside for the moment and re-visit the theme in another year. After some dialogue, they agreed that the other themes had more urgency.

How do you keep focus and bring meaning?

Sometimes the compelling stories get lost in the flipcharts or report-outs. There is a fine line in keeping report-outs brief and losing the power of the stories. The meaning is created for the group through the stories. **The more you can encourage the group to "story" the more meaning you will help them create.**

Does everyone have to buy into the provocative propositions?

There are two levels to this question. First: *Does everyone have to agree on the language of the provocative proposition during the creation of it?*

And second: *Does everyone in the organization have to buy into the proposition once it is "proposed"?* The first question, does everyone have to buy into the provocative propositions sets up people to begin to doubt that the future is possible. Everyone does not have to work on each proposition at once — all members of the team have different strengths and passions — but in any change initiative the level of commitment will determine the outcome. **Remember, one of the first points of an Appreciative Inquiry is to assess the level of commitment of the participants or the team, or the community.** Once commitment is confirmed, the work of creating the provocative proposition statements is the work of the total community, team, or group. Because the entire group may have split up into sub-groups, we recommend that the sub-group "present" the proposition to the larger group. It is then possible to review and dialogue on the images and wording of each provocative possibility statement so individuals can support the statements and work for their completion.

Whether all people in the organization need to buy into the statements if they are not a part of the creation of these statements is a different issue. There needs to be a clear and consistent method for keeping people informed about the work of the change initiative. Training and coaching in the appreciative model of communication about change should be provided for the steward of this part of the change process. This is fairly simple, but it does require intention and careful thought. The people who entrust their proxy to the change-makers should be clear and current with the work of the Appreciative Inquiry process. When this is done and the dialogue is open and fluid, hesitation on the part of organizational members is minimal. If the coaching is in place the hesitation can be easily attended to and the process moves forward.

How does strategic planning work with AI?

AI is a natural for the strategic planning process because it focuses the organization on what it does well and how it does that. However, it is important for a dialogue to first take place in order to define what strategic planning means to the client. We have both watched too many organizations use the term strategic planning to mean preparing budgets and revenue forecasts. Crunching numbers is different from determining the conditions and relationships it takes for people to work together in productive and energizing ways. **An Appreciative Inquiry is an exploration into the relationships of how people actually produce superior results.** Nonetheless, it is important to be well grounded in the language of business and economics in order to bridge the gap between the numbers and the behaviors.

It might even be novel to consider calling this process of planning within the AI paradigm, "Intentional Planning." It implies that there will be deliberate thought to the process and moves the client towards a new language that allows different possibilities to come forward. The more we can provide opportunities for our systems to inquire

into the impact of how language creates meaning for our systems, the more opportunities we have to shift energy toward best practices. Implying that the planning is intentional also asks the client to think about how the energy of the organization is directed toward the future. We can help by reconnecting the planning initiative with the stories and data generated during appreciative interviews. **Each time the stories and wishes for the organization are repeated and used, the participants in the Inquiry are more likely to be re-engaged with the process and the changes they co-created.**

We can always begin an intentional planning process by asking everyone to answer this question: What are the top two trends affecting your business today (economic, resource, global, environmental, competitive)? This is similar to that favorite CEO interview question, "What keeps you awake at night?", but it is framed in a neutral manner. It also creates a great counterpoint to the last question of many AI interviews, "What are your three concrete wishes for the future of your organization, profession, or industry?" And it signals the participants that while the AI interview focuses on individual perceptions, intentional planning by its very nature, means ultimately analyzing what the group believes about not only what the organization can do but also what customers and competitors will do. **Toggling between individual and group behavior and beliefs is the true challenge to culling meaning out of the data gathered first, through individual perception and then from the combined perceptions of the group.**

What does the language convey within the appreciative inquiry protocol and change process?

The language that is most compatible with Appreciative Inquiry processes and protocol should be written in the affirmative, first person, and in the active voice. This language creates images that convey the inclusive, participatory commitment of AI. It is helpful to screen for negative images, phrases and cliches. When there is a commitment to re-thinking the language that is used in the AI and in all documents emanating from the process it allows the system to begin to work towards its preferred future. The shift in language signals the paradigm shift to begin to move into the behavior of the people in the institution. This creates the change we envision and is a significant step in the change initiative.

What is the behavior that is compatible and corresponds to a paradigm shift, at all levels of a system?

When an Appreciative Inquiry is followed by consistent behavior of affirming the individuals in the organization or communities, it further instills in the policies and rituals of the institution those things that people have discovered as their best behaviors and characteristics. Behavior should follow the language discoveries in the initial inquiry.
The information that is gained and shared in the personal questions is vital to defining the new/continued behaviors in the organization.
Behavior also should follow the guidelines of the AI protocol, creating open and inclusive systems,

sharing information, and remaining open to new possibilities. It is helpful to have executives and leadership prepared for information sharing that shifts from "need to know" to collaborative sharing.

Can appreciative interviews be conducted in focus groups?

The telling of one's personal story is an act of trust and intimacy. The power of Appreciative Inquiry is the capturing of each organization's stories and the personal aspects of what each person feels is their excitement and best as a part of the organization. It is best captured as a one-to-one experience. When the appreciative inquiry protocol is structured as part of a focus group session it shifts the emphasis from the individual and her/his contributions. **The dynamics of group disclosure are different than the dynamics that come into play when one is engaged in telling her/his story to one other individual who is focused on hearing that story and capturing it as part of the history and accomplishments of the corporation.**
Remember that when we conduct a full Appreciative Inquiry or when we seek to assist systems with inclusive dialogue we are highlighting the value of every member in the organization regardless of status or position. The focus group changes the emphasis from the personal story.
The behavior in a focus group is often around the prescribed or perceived role behaviors specific to title and status within the system. Members of the group are tempted to respond out of their role within the system instead of their personal sharing.
There is always value in gaining information from

organizational members and the focus group will help gather data however, the information will be different and more general in the focus group. **The one-on-one personal interview is an opportunity to communicate to many members of the organization or community that their voice is significant to any change efforts.** The way we demonstrate commitment is through the allocation of the resources of time or money thus, it is an excellent opportunity to demonstrate commitment to valuing each employee. Providing time for individual sharing also enhances your chances of getting novel and personal data from each interviewee.

What are the groundbreaking applications of AI?

Two important questions from clients and communities around the globe are: *How can Appreciative Inquiry be used to bring about systems change concerning diversity?* And second: *Is AI a process that can promote social justice in communities and countries?* Cathy's dissertation research was a new application[3]; using appreciative inquiry to rethink socially constructed identity. The use of AI for this process is groundbreaking for communities and individuals in various phases of transition. Cathy found that while AI and identity reconstruction is not a substitute for therapy or individual counseling it is very useful for people who are working to understand the stereotypes and socially constructed expectations placed on individuals and members of their identity groups. Her work

began with Black women and has expanded to include adolescents and Black men. She is also working with a team of women and men to create a protocol that addresses positive aspects of relationships between men and women.

She has had significant success with her theory of using AI as a process that helps People of Color examine the stereotypes that impact their lives and how they are viewed in the world. Her work is beginning to create the path forward around understanding the impact of systemic and structural oppression. She is working with change agents and diversity specialists around the world to rethink the changes that should be present when communities inquire about structural equality and the presence of reliable relationships between People of Color and Whites.

Cathy has used AI to begin to help communities think about peace and healing in Africa with her work in Uganda. She has coached other consultants on using this process with teams that are engaged in peace initiatives in Uganda and East Africa. The success of this application for AI is exciting. It indicates that while we often think of AI as a large system change process we can begin to apply it in various arenas. **When Appreciative Inquiry is presented as a process and a philosophy that creates hope in people and**

---

[3]Cathy coined the term The Fractal Initiative in her dissertation. Watch for her forthcoming book, *The Fractal Initiative: Appreciative Inquiry — Living in the Positive!*

systems, it becomes a powerful force for change and the new future of communities and people who are seeking a way to heal the wounds of conflict and reconstruct their communities and lives. Each time Cathy has presented this process and her theories on the use of AI, she has found community citizens excited about the opportunity to begin to heal and rebuild. The possibilities are infinite!

© C. L. ROYAL AND S.A. HAMMOND, 1998

Resources

[i] See their marvelous book, *Executive and Organizational Continuity* (1992), Jossey-Bass Publishers. San Francisco.

[ii] Cooperrider recommends limiting any AI to five topics for this reason. He also recommends allowing 2 full days of work by a representative group in the organization to choose the topics for an Inquiry.

ABOUT THE AUTHORS

SUE ANNIS HAMMOND is a change management consultant who has been focusing on publishing for the last few years. With the unexpected success of *The Thin Book of Appreciative Inquiry*, and commitment to producing a book about AI for practitioners, she limited her consulting work to start The Thin Book Publishing Co and the Practical Press Inc. Both dovetail her early Master's degree in English and her later Master's of Organizational Development. Her goal is to continue to publish high quality, cutting-edge thin books that help all levels of organizational members learn about how change happens within organizations. She also takes her parenting responsibility very seriously and therefore tries to balance her passion for organizations with home-life and has found that both inform the other.

For more information, contact:
Sue Hammond
PO Box 260608
Plano, TX 75026-0608
phone: 972-378-0523
fax: 972.403.0065
e.mail: Suehammond@thinbook.com

CATHY L. ROYAL, PH.D. is the founding president of The Diversity Institute, a not-for-profit international learning community dedicated to research, training and dialogue to promote social and structural equity. She is an organizational development professional with specialties in diversity management, race and gender relations, appreciative inquiry and organizational transformation. Dr. Royal designs and conducts training in each of these areas for corporations, foundations, educational institutions and international agencies and donors. In 2000 Dr. Royal designed and facilitated the first all department diversity appreciative inquiry for the Department of Health and Human Services (DHHS). This was a large systems change initiative that impacted and reached 56,000 plus employees of the government. She is a member and trainer for the NTL Institute for Applied Behavioral Science (NTL) and she is the NTL Institute Ken Benne Scholar. She was on the five-member team that facilitated the United Nations/Mountain Institute Rio Earth Summit. Dr. Royal has conducted training in Africa, Latin America and throughout the United States. She is a contributing author on: *Transformational Social Change: Self as Change Agent, Visible Now: Blacks in Private Education,* and *NTL Training Handbook.* Her continuing project is completing her research for her book *The Fractial Initiative: Appreciative Inquiry-Living in the Positive.* Dr. Royal's passion is using Appreciative Inquiry to promote structural equality, honor diversity and social justice. She is the recipient of the Fielding Institute Social Justice award. She is the mother of three delightful adult children (gorgeous).

Cathy L. Royal, P.h. D.
PO Box 326
Riverdale, MD. 20738-0326
phone: 301.552.3625
e.mail address: catroyal@aol.com

We are some time truly going to see

our life as positive, not negative,

as made up of continuous willing,

not of constraints and prohibition.

— MARY PARKER FOLLETT

APPLICATION OF THEORY

LESSONS USING AI IN A

PLANNING EXERCISE

BY MADELYN BLAIR

Introduction

Communications Development Incorporated (CDI) offers distinct products to a sophisticated and demanding client base. This chapter describes an exercise based on Appreciative Inquiry principles to help this company take stock and create a set of possibilities for itself. The approach was new to the client and had to be first sold to him and then adapted to include looking at negative issues. Managing the negative information presented a valuable challenge. Several lessons came out of this exercise:

• Explanation of Appreciative Inquiry theory must begin from personal experience and conviction. Nothing beats talking from personal experience when describing Appreciative Inquiry to those who have never heard of it before.

• A group can define a common ground quickly through Appreciative Inquiry. Even the staff of a company that had never formally defined its image quickly came to consensus on what energizes them.

• People whose work centers on the use of language find the vocabulary of Appreciative Inquiry to be off-putting. Those who use language with high precision demand more clarity in the language of Appreciative Inquiry.

• The characteristics of the group directly contribute to the product. The group's facility with language contributed to quick, clear articulation of their ideas.

• Watching the energy levels in the room during the process is a means to gauge the effect of the process. When negative information is being used consciously, watching the group carefully is a must.

• Negative comments are not needed but can serve a creative purpose if managed. Negative information can be used to reinforce or test the work of the group if it is conveyed at the right time and the group is given time to process it.

This chapter documents the entire process, from selling the approach to the final set of actions. Client interviews to gather the context for the work started the process. The work of the staff was done in two retreat days separated by a month to allow staff to interview each other. Interviews with clients and staff after the planning activity round out the process and provide insights into the impact of the process and its results.

Background

Communications Development Incorporated (CDI) offers distinct products to a sophisticated and demanding client base. The company has been growing for several years, and its growth seems only to be accelerating. Quality is important to them, and Bruce Ross-Larson, president of the company, sees a danger that the company could suffer if this growth leads to diminished quality. This concern led to a review of where the company is and how it could improve quality as it continues to grow.

BOX 1:
Communications Development

Communications Development Incorporated provides planning, editing, writing, desktop publishing, Internet publishing, and communications management services to clients in the domestic and international policy arenas. With 20 employees and 20 regular consultants, the company put together teams to meet the needs of its clients' projects. Among the company's clients are the Benton Foundation, the United Nations Development Program, the Millennium Group, and the World Bank.

Bruce enjoys talking with his staff about their ideas and concerns, but the day-to-day work doesn't allow this kind of discussion at the depth he would like. He called on me to help design an approach that would help him and his staff have a discussion on quality as they grew. When I

talked with him a bit further, I learned that he loved to help his staff do more, develop more skills, and generally feel better about themselves. Here was the best of all worlds – a group that wanted to talk before it had problems. **The question for me was how could I help a great group become better without jeopardizing its enthusiasm and high morale and help the staff learn something new in the process.**

I was fortunate. Bruce and I have worked together for years and there is a deep level of trust between us. So I didn't have to prove that I was trustworthy, but I did have to deliver. He was confident that I would meet his needs and objectives. And the trust allowed him to deal with any initial discomfort with the different approach I had in mind — Appreciative Inquiry.

I had been introduced to Appreciative Inquiry several years before, when I had a planning session for my own company. The facilitator who conducted the session based the design on Appreciative Inquiry principles, and we found the approach enjoyable, effective, and powerful in guiding our actions for about 18 months afterward. I watched it energize an already highly charged group. I also knew that the theory behind Appreciative Inquiry was something that I had been committed to in my business from the beginning. So much so that when I described the "new" theory to a colleague, she said, "But that is just how you do things!" So Appreciative Inquiry not only proved effective, but was natural for me.

As I learned about Appreciative Inquiry more formally, I began experimenting with the techniques in my own work, for example, by reframing interview questions into positively oriented ones. The approach allowed me to gain all the information I needed without the usual negative impact of an intervention designed to "fix a problem." I liked what I saw with the approach and knew that it never dampens enthusiasm.

I presented the approach to Bruce, relating the benefits to what he wanted to accomplish and contrasting them with the results of a traditional approach (box 2). I also noted that the risk of using Appreciative Inquiry is higher than the risk with traditional approaches, since Appreciative Inquiry opens up the discussion to the staff in a way that makes it impossible to put their ideas "back into the box" once they are out. For some managers, this might seem too risky. Bruce embraced the idea as consistent with his philosophy of helping his staff grow in every way. We agreed that Appreciative Inquiry would be used, and I had only to shoehorn a long process into two days of group work – a schedule required by the work load in the company. I decided that the process could be completed usefully in less time than usual if we set our expectations right from the start.

Following are descriptions of the two approaches. Both involve my interviewing the clients and both use appreciative inquiry.

BOX 2:

PROPOSAL:
Helping CDI Keep Quality as They Grow

TRADITIONAL APPROACH

I conduct all the interviews, synthesize the findings, and present them to the staff in a retreat setting. I facilitate discussion of the findings and development of actions. With this approach:

• The staff's interviewing experience is uniform.

• Staff are interrupted in their work for only an initial hour and a half (for the interview) plus the retreat day.

• Staff learn less about themselves and the process.

• Easier of the two options: I do the synthesizing; I control the process.

• Results: Some new perspectives and an action list that will serve you and your team well.

Approach

In the rest of this chapter, I refer to CDI as "the company." While the company is successful and growing, it is also relatively small and depends on every minute being productive. The budget had to be smaller than usual. This immediately affected how much I could do and how much staff time could be put into the work. But it also challenged me to create an effective way to work within this constraint.

You and your staff participate in the interviewing and the development of the new perceptions as well as the actions desired. The approach gives you and your staff experience in conducting interviews, synthesizing the findings in a group process, and creating together a new perspective or perspectives that the actions will achieve. With this approach:

- There is more interruption: two retreat days (one at the beginning of interviewing and one at the end) as well as time for the staff to conduct interviews of one another (they will spend at least three hours interviewing).

- It is harder, it is more fun, and it creates a learning environment. It is a richer experience for you and your team. It is riskier because control is much more in the hands of your team than in the traditional option.

- Results: An action list that is enhanced by an internal understanding of the why and greater ownership by the team.

I wanted to do the project entirely from the appreciative perspective, but Bruce asked that I also explore the concerns of clients.
I had some reservations about this. On the positive side, asking clients about problems told them that the company was interested in their concerns. On the negative side, I was concerned about how to share with the staff the negative information that I was bound to receive from the clients. Incorporating potential negative information into the design was a diversion from Appreciative Inquiry theory. I had to design into the retreat a way to share the negative information that added to the process and would not disturb the positive energy I hoped to engender through the retreat. I will describe later how I did this.

The interviews proved more effective than I could have guessed. The clients were open and willing to share fully with a third party. I quickly found a new language about the company's products and how they are delivered. I discovered what the clients valued most about the company and why –

a rare look at a company. And I gained something to offer the staff in the retreat that went beyond process. (See appendix 1 for the questions used in interviewing clients.) **Had the staff conducted these interviews, they would certainly have benefited from exposure to the clients in the role of listeners even though the clients may not have been as open. This option just didn't work for the company.**

I summarized the information from the clients in two short briefings. The first reported what the clients believed the company did very well and what they valued most about the company. This positive feedback from clients would serve as a test of how well the staff know their own strengths and the forces that energize them. The second briefing reported the clients' concerns and wishes. I held onto the second briefing material until after the staff had fully defined the possibilities for their future. Given at this time, the information acted as a test of how robust the possibilities were. As an example of what came out of this, when asked to describe how the company was or could be working with the client in a totally satisfactory manner; the clients said that communication between the company and them was a comfortable give and take, the deadlines were met, and the company showed real leadership. (See appendix 2 for actual quotations of client feedback.)

The real work was done in a two-day retreat.

The retreat was designed as a two-day event, with the second day separated from the first by a month to allow the staff time to interview one another, including those who would not be participating in the retreat. Both sessions were held outside the office, although not out of town. The setting was comfortable, the food was good, the supplies were adequate, and the work was hard.

Day 1: Discovering and understanding what energizes them

Day 1 began with eight pairs of the staff (16 staff in all attended the retreat) interviewing each other using a set of questions typical for learning Appreciative Inquiry (see box 3 for the interview questions). For some, it was the first formal interview that they had conducted. So before sending them out to do this task, I gave them simple guidance on how to conduct the interview – keep to the subject, ask more questions rather than comment on what is said, etc. After the interviews, I made a brief presentation on the basics of Appreciative Inquiry. My focus was on the benefits of exploring the positive as described in Chapter 4 of *Appreciative Management and Leadership* by Srivastva, Cooperrider and Associates. I chose to do this after the interviews so that the experience of the interviews would help them understand the explanation.

Then the staff shared the results of the interviews with the group. Although the staff are young and normally vibrant, they found it hard to share from these interviews. They seemed uncertain about why they were talking about themselves and not their work. And they were wondering why they were only talking about what was good. They asked, why have a retreat if you don't have problems? Perhaps as editors, proofreaders, and desktoppers, they are so used to looking for errors that they couldn't help but bring this habit to the retreat.

To help them, I suggested that they share what they had learned in single words that could be explained if someone wanted more detail. This broke the logjam. A long list of words quickly appeared on the flip chart, and the energy in the room began to grow – they were beginning to see the picture. (Appendix 3 lists these words.) **As they continued this exchange, they began to see trends in what was being said. And suddenly the forces that energize this group to high levels of excellence came right off the page.** The staff narrowed the list down to six factors. They began to feel more comfortable as they recognized words that they had said, saw that no one was going to edit their choices, and saw their choices confirmed by repetition of the words on the list. Light bulbs went on as the exercise began to seem meaningful to them.

BOX 3:

INTERVIEW QUESTIONS
Retreat: Day 1

1. What attracted you to your work and to CDI? What excitements? What initial impressions?

2. Describe a specific time, a specific situation, when you felt most alive, involved, and excited about your involvement in this work?

What made this situation or time a peak experience?
Who were the others significant to that situation or time, and what made them so?
How were they working with you?
What was happening at that time in your life?
What kind of project was it?
What kind of time frame were you working in?
How did you learn what to do for this situation or time?
In general, what factors in your work make for peak experiences?

3. What do you value deeply about yourself? When feeling best about work? About the tasks you undertake in your work? What is the single most important thing your work has contributed to your life?

4. What is the core factor that gives vitality to your existence?

5. If you could transform your life in any way, what three things would you wish for to enhance its vitality and strength?

I then briefed the group on the positive things that the clients had said about them. I reminded them that this was the positive day – no negatives on day 1. But we did use the positive feedback to check whether the clients saw the staff as they saw themselves: did clients see the energizing forces that the staff felt? The staff discovered that there was a remarkable convergence of impressions. They were relieved (although they had growing curiosity about the negatives). (See appendix 3 for the energizing forces identified and the descriptive words that define them.)

"It was more enjoyable than I expected because it was thought-engaging."
(Staff member about the process)

As the staff heard the comments from their clients, they began to see new dimensions and new meanings in the words they had chosen. When I presented the client feedback to them, I used full sentence quotations and even small stories, as I had hoped they would do in their initial sharing. **They began questioning, "But what do we really mean by quality?" They were beginning to see the complexity of meaning behind each word they had chosen.** The staff's recognition of this complexity was a good lead-in for the next activity, in which they were asked to design questions they wanted to ask each other about the words they had selected for use in a second round of interviews. This task was harder, and they broke into small groups to do it. Some struggled with how to ask a question in an appre-ciative way. Remember, they had had only about three hours of working with Appreciative Inquiry on which to build. But even though they were unsure about what it all meant, they willingly gave it a try.

BOX 4:

Steps of this Approach

Day 1

1. Staff interview each other (dyads)

2. Presentation on AI (plenary)

3. Share from the interviews (plenary)

4. Find the energizing forces (plenary)

5. Briefing of client's positive comments and check for convergence (plenary)

6. Design questions for second round of interviews (3 small groups, each taking 2 energizing forces)

7. Refine the questions (plenary)

Between Sessions

8. Each person interviews 3 others

Day 2

9. Report out on interviews (plenary)

10. Define possibilities (small groups)

11. Present and refine possibilities (plenary)

12. Brief on negative comments from clients and check against possibilities (plenary)

13. Develop list of actions (plenary)

At the end of the exercise, the three groups brought their questions to the full group, which refined them. The time limits (the day began at 9:30 and had to end at 4:30) again constrained the discussion of the questions. With more time, the questions would have improved. In the end, they tended to be repetitious because people didn't have enough time to develop alternative wording — despite their facility with language. (See appendix 4 for the questions developed by the group.)

After the group had broken up to go back to tasks still waiting at the office, all the work done during the retreat – from the long list of words to the questions to be asked – was captured electronically and delivered to the company by 5:30 that afternoon. I didn't want the staff to lose any momentum.

If there was one thing that limited what the project achieved, it was the lack of time to refine these questions. **If I were to do this step over, I would ensure more time to develop the questions for the second round of interviews. Developing questions for an interview protocol is hard to do at best.** Since these questions were developed by several small groups using a single set of example questions, though each worked with a different set of words, the questions contained overlapping content and approach. Making the questions more effective by refining them into an integrated set of questions, dealing with different content and challenging in presentation was not possible in the time allowed. With more time, a smaller sub-group could have worked on the final protocol.

What I liked about the approach taken was that it allowed the staff to use the questions they had developed and therefore reinforced the trust in their ability to learn the concept of Appreciative Inquiry. In addition, interviewing skills were among the things I was trying to help them learn, and designing an interview protocol and then using it is an important opportunity for learning about interviewing.

All this said, at the end of the session, some staff grumbled very quietly that they still didn't feel they could see the link between what they had just done with developing a plan. The staff still had not accepted the concept of Appreciative Inquiry, nor did they feel fully comfortable with the process. But they all agreed that they were tired.

Between day 1 and day 2 of the retreat, each staff member interviewed three others, using the questions developed during day 1. This ensured that all staff members (including those not at the retreat) would be interviewed and therefore become a part of the activity. A month was set aside between the two days of the retreat, the first of which was in December and the second in January. This schedule allowed time for the holidays as well as for interviewing. But one staff member remarked that one month was too long between. We lost resonance. Staff were allowed to spend whatever time they needed to conduct the interviews and were asked to write up the responses to aid their memories during day 2 of the retreat. Some of the staff immediately took to this exercise. Others were less enthusiastic. As employees of a company for which editing and writing are key products, they performed the task of writing with ease and alacrity. But not all of the interviews were done.

According to one member who interviewed others, those who did not participate in the first day of the retreat were a little uncertain about the meaning of the questions. But those conducting the interviews began to gain some excitement about what they were learning and became curious about what others had learned.

Day 2: Creating the possibilities of their future

Day 2 was a different session altogether. We were to use the day to create the possibilities for the future. The staff were beginning to see that they were in control of what was done in the work sessions and that my job was only to give them a structure in which to do it. They were more relaxed.

The first activity of day 2, reporting out from their interviews, started slowly. They rarely questioned one another during the report-out, and they did not appear curious about what was said. Perhaps they all assumed that they understood perfectly, or they thought they had to appear to be united. But they dived into the task of defining the energizing forces with real enthusiasm once the report-out time was over. And even though a month had elapsed between the two sessions, it didn't take long for them to be up to speed and running at high energy. As one participant said, "This gave me a forum to say some things that couldn't be said otherwise. And it hasn't created a problem subsequent to it."

The discussion after the report-out showed that the staff had lots of ideas about what those energizing factors meant to them as a group. (Energizing forces can be found in appendix 3) **They learned that they had remarkably consistent definitions of what energizes them even though they had never talked about them before. They were naming the common ground on which they were standing and working, and were feeling very comfortable.**

"Yes, (after the retreat) we bandied about the six words (the life-giving forces), but it was in humor."
(Staff member after Day 1.)

After we completed the information exchange, I assigned them the task of defining some possibilities for themselves. I asked them to consider what they might learn (or want to learn) if they were to do these same interviews again one year later. What would they hear in those interviews? I described the exercise on a handout to make it easier to understand and remember what they had been asked to do (box 5). And I gave them a short list of possibility statements from organizations that seemed similar to the company. This time, they grasped the idea quickly. Again, they were divided into three small groups with two energizing forces each.

BOX 4:

Developing Possibility Statements – Instructions and Examples

Imagine that it is 1997 and that you have been given a special assignment in your organization. The assignment is to do an analysis of company performance, operations, morale, communications, management, and the like. You are now putting together a snapshot of what you have heard in interviews with employees and managers at all levels. You know that we have six life-giving forces here, and you decide to give your report to management in these terms. Sum up what you have found about each of the energizing forces in three to four sentences. What do you anticipate reality will look like then? Write in the present tense as if it already exists.

EXAMPLES OF POSSIBILITY STATEMENTS

The structure of ABC International is based on the image of organization as a circle rather than a series of links in a chain of command hierarchy. In operational terms, the circular structure involves a project-based system of temporary networks and project teams. There are no superiors and subordinates. Instead, there are those who convene, chairpersons, colleagues, and partners.

ABC is known around the world for being a learning organization. We continue to dare to experiment with advanced techniques. ABC is an organization that shows the capacity to transform itself and is constantly open to the newer and better things that come along. We seek opportunities to see new approaches, and we demonstrate ours at appropriate opportunities.

ABC's dedication to quality is reflected in its exceeding the expectations of its clients on timeliness, error rate, responsiveness, and leadership. We achieve high standards in these areas by ensuring that client representatives help the client understand our minimum standards of quality for ourselves and the responsibilities we expect the client to pick up. And we achieve high standards by challenging the client to do more than he or she would have done alone.

They worked hard in developing their possibility statements. Despite their ease with language, they struggled to say the right thing without losing important nuances, though clearly the task was easier for them than for people who don't work with language as a profession. In this group, I was struck by their immediate access to many, many synonyms that allowed them to express an idea with subtlety. A quick and energetic start of discussion signaled that they understood much better what they were supposed to do, and so needed less help. Again, each group presented its ideas in plenary, and the full group (still at 16) refined them. **The possibility statements were gems of clarity and filled with purpose** (see appendix 5). More time would have made them even better and maybe a bit more provocative, but not more powerful.

At last, I briefed them on the negative comments from their clients. They were on the edges of their chairs while waiting to hear them, hoping they were perfect. The news that they were not hit them visibly. I almost wanted to say, "But you don't need to hear this! You are going in the right direction to answer all of these. Why do you want to torture yourselves?" But they felt that they needed to hear this negative feedback. They wanted to know that they had turned over every stone in their search for excellence.

What I saw was a group of highly motivated people who were running a superb race hit a wall and almost stop. It took about 20 minutes of explaining to one another that the client just didn't understand before they realized that the client perhaps understood very well, but from another perspective.

At this point, I asked one question: "Would you change any of these possibility statements now that you have heard from your clients?" They re-read their work and thought about it and realized that they didn't need to change a thing. If they achieved the propositions they had laid out for themselves, they would address all their clients' concerns and desires. Now, they only had to make those possibilities happen! As they realized this, the energy in the room began to recover. By the end of their discussion, they were sailing again. Suddenly, the group was back where it had been about an hour before.

Armed with the knowledge that the possibilities they had defined would address the clients' concerns, the group developed a list of actions needed to make the possibilities happen. In about an hour, they had developed a set of actions that were all practical and achievable and would directly affect quality (see appendix 6). And the actions are all based on the propositions that support those things that energize them as a company. That means that they are sustainable. They had seen the truth about themselves and had defined a successful way of achieving not only excellence, but also client satisfaction. Day 2 left them exhausted from the creative process but very satisfied.

Several products were produced after the retreat.

When the day was done, the staff expressed how effective their discussion had been. We gathered up the flip charts and took a day or two to write them up, putting them into a notebook along with the other products from the project: the client feedback, the interview protocol used, the list of words, the final definitions of the energizing factors and the possibilities for their future, and, finally, the action plan. This notebook was to serve as a tool for the staff to refresh their memories on what had happened. The few staff who for one reason or another had never been interviewed would easily be able to see all that was produced, and discuss it with those who had shared in the process.

There were several products from this work. The first was the list of words that describe the common forces that energize their work — their desire for personal freedom, the drive to produce only the best quality, the need to retain perspective while knowing that their work has some impact. The second was the list of possibilities they had defined for their company that gave them direction. The third was the list of actions they would use to achieve those possibilities. In addition to these products that the staff created, there was the client feedback that had been captured in writing. Finally, there was the experience of seeing the world through an appreciative lens that legitimized and valued something other than problems.

Reactions after the retreat

Clients valued having an information broker in the process.

Some of the clients who had been interviewed as a part of the project were interviewed again two months after the retreat. They were asked to remember their interview and comment on it and to think about how they had been served since the retreat (see appendix 7 for the interview protocol for the clients).

"There has been absolutely no deterioration of service."
(Client interviewed two months after the project)

The most striking comment from a client was that "there has been absolutely no deterioration of service." Given the objective to design an intervention that would do no harm to a good group, this response was gratifying. Beyond this, the clients had little to say about changes since the retreat. The lack of any positive change reported two months after the retreat seems reasonable, however, given the company's already high performance. The clients did have some things to say about the interview process, which was designed using Appreciative Inquiry principles. They felt a "little surprised about the questions used." One client said, "I felt like this was a little bit of a game but played it as a willing player. I have learned not to be surprised, but rather to expect the unexpected from you. I figured there was a rationale." They felt that it was appropriate to have an "information broker."

The staff most enjoyed and valued their interviews of one another.

I also interviewed some of the staff a few months after the retreat. I wanted to know what their perceptions of the process were after they had time for some thought and whether they saw any changes to the business as a result of the retreat (see appendix 8 for the interview protocol for the staff).

The staff's reactions to the process in the retreat were mixed, ranging from feeling fully engaged in the process to feeling removed from it. Those interviewed seemed to think that the feelings of removal had something to do with preparation for the retreat: they felt that they had had none. **Early communications about the retreat had led staff to think that they were going to a retreat similar to past retreats, where they had just sat around and talked about things.** When they arrived at this retreat and discovered that they had to do something very different, they felt unprepared. I had told them that no preparation was necessary but because they expected one type of activity and found another, the lack of need for preparation didn't really matter to them. For some, the retreat was the first facilitated working session they had participated in. All this led to a feeling of uncertainty and may have affected their receptiveness to Appreciative Inquiry.

Despite feeling unprepared and being expected to use a theory they had never heard of before, the staff all expressed a sense of joy about interviewing one another and discussing what they had heard in these interviews.

"I enjoyed the interviews best — getting to know those people better. I also liked the easy-going tone to a lot of it."
(Staff member about the experience)

Offsetting this joy is the staff's disappointment stemming from a perception that there has been no follow-up to the retreat. This perception has made them feel as if their work at the retreat does not matter. The irony is that some of the most important items of follow-up have been and continue to be acted on. But because the actions are not linked to the retreat, the staff doesn't perceive the commitment to the actions. As a result, some of the return on the investment in the process is lost.

The staff's sense that Appreciative Inquiry is not serious because it begins with the personal continues to be a barrier to their seeing the value of the approach. The staff's perception of Appreciative Inquiry may also relate to their statement about freedom. In their culture, privacy is part of the meaning of freedom, and the questions of the first Appreciative Inquiry instrument used may have felt too personal for this group. Interviewing staff beforehand would have identified this preference. I will not omit this step in the future.

Impact of the Work
on the Company

Some real actions have been taken by the company to achieve the possibilities defined at the retreat

After the retreat there was follow-up on several of the actions. The most important was giving staff the option — rarely used — to tell a client that they needed two days to review a product before delivering it. Quality standards were being upheld. **The company began posting congratulations and other good news from clients on the back of the office's front door so that anyone going out of the office can quickly see what clients are saying and why.** The sense of perspective was being reinforced. People planned a few activities for the staff that were not business-related. Solidarity was recognized as a need. "Yes," said one staff member, "we are moving in the right direction."

Some opportunities are being lost

At the time this chapter was written, a "welcome box" to help new staff get off to a good start had not been assembled. The notebook of the products of the retreats was not made generally available — or people didn't know that it was available. These failures have led to a feeling of disappointment. Although some actions are being taken, they are not referred to as coming from the retreat, so the connection and synergy is being lost. One staff member captured the staff's feelings well when she said, "I wish I had seen the notebook. The ideas are valuable but don't have meaning because they are not visible. The ideas

need to be used consciously." Another said, "If we could just get one thing worked out, it would give more of a feeling of accomplishment."

No company can stop conducting its business to focus entirely on internal matters and expect to survive. But even if only a few things on the action list can be done at a time, a reminder of what still remains to be done would signal that all the actions are important and will be attended to as soon as resources allow. "I wish we could continue the momentum to bring about improvements and make everybody more comfortable," remarked one staff member.

Lessons About the Process
and the Approach

Explanation of Appreciative Inquiry theory must begin from personal experience and conviction

The Appreciative Inquiry theory is only complex in the telling, and so telling about it should come from personal experience and conviction, to aid the process of learning. Academic references may be important to some groups, but not to all. A lesson for me from this project was that I needed to size up the group and explain only what needs to be explained and do so from myself first and then from others only when necessary. With Appreciative Inquiry, it is important to move confidently beyond the theory to its use — where learning is easier.

A group can define common ground quickly through Appreciative Inquiry

The group was made up of very bright people whose work focuses on the use of language. Once they had grasped what we were trying to do, they created real, quality products. They defined energizing factors that included some unexpected ones. Quality and challenge and impact were to be expected. But who would predict perspective, freedom, or even solidarity would all come from the same group? Yet once the words were in the open, the fit was comfortable, although this group had never before discussed what "made their company tick" or what it was about. As one member put it, "This was more difficult for this group. There is a lack of identity. We don't have an established image, so we were having difficulty seeing our identity and how we wanted to change it." The possibilities they defined for themselves were challenging but real and achievable. These possibilities described a dynamic, responsive group of people who can do nothing less than make clients love them.

People whose work centers on the use of language find the vocabulary of Appreciative Inquiry to be off-putting

This was a group of very young individuals who found the expression *life giving forces* to be simply too much. But then they found Appreciative Inquiry and Provocative Propositions difficult to use as well. The new names they have given to these concepts — energizing forces rather than life-giving forces, and possibility statements rather than provocative propositions — have been used in this chapter. They liked them better and felt they would tell their story more effectively.

The characteristics of the group directly contribute to the product

Three things helped the work of this group. First, the group had good working relationships among themselves, which came out clearly as they discussed points with quiet openness. One said, "It is nice to take time to focus on the individuals and experience of working together rather than just seeing yourself as a part of a patchwork." Second, the group members had a strong command of the English language and so were able to express complex ideas through simple statements that were easy to understand even for someone not part of the discussion that created them. This was a gift for a group asked to do something in far less time than it normally takes to do well. Third, the group has clients who value it just as it is and appreciate the good services it provides, while at the same time desiring more. Clients who want the company to succeed are the right kind of clients to have. The challenge for the group is to keep listening to the feedback that even happy clients give and to be willing to respond.

Closing

Watching the energy levels in the room during the process is a means to gauge the effect of the process

As the group members' comfort grew, so did their energy. When the negative information was finally shared with them, they sagged visibly. I gave them time to get out their thoughts and feelings, allowing this time to let them process what the information meant. Skillful facilitation is important here to catch the point when the energy has just bottomed out to quickly capitalize on the upward movement of energy. Managing this renewal of energy after negative information is shared is critical. Scheduling another exercise after this briefing gave them time and distance to recover their energy.

Negative comments are not needed but can serve a creative purpose if managed

Most remarkable was that the negative comments from the clients did not change the possibilities that the staff had defined before hearing the comments. Instead, the negative comments sharpened the actions that the group developed to help achieve the possibilities. Without the client feedback, my speculation is that they would have defined an action plan fully effective in meeting their client's demands. But the client feedback gave them confidence in their action plan, and prompted them to make some of the actions more specific. One participant felt that "most useful were the possibilities and developing solutions." Another said, "I did feel the possibilities would solve our problems."

Appreciative Inquiry increases the probability of creating a good working climate for the group, or, said in reverse, lowers the risk of creating a disruption in the work

The objective of not dampening the group's high level of enthusiasm appears to have been achieved. As one of their most conservative clients said in a post interview, "There was absolutely no degradation of service." And this is a real compliment in their arena of work and the company's client-base. While the staff were not always happy with the process until they understood it, they always felt that they were in control of the outcomes. And the positive feedback they received about themselves from one another and from their clients appeared to strengthen the solidarity they named as one of the factors that energizes them. A staff member remarked, "I liked the collaborative exercise best – just coming together as a group to do things, including the interviews". "The day to day actions haven't changed, yet there is an awareness that can be tapped for further work. The activity has now *primed* us for further organizational development activity," was the comment of another.

© M. BLAIR, 1998

ABOUT THE AUTHOR

MADELYN BLAIR Ph.D.has been the president of Pelerei since 1988. Pelerei, specializing in international organizations, is a management consulting firm recognized as a leader in complex analytical studies for management, organizational development, team building, managing knowledge, and training. She is dedicated to working with clients in a unique manner – one that encourages understanding of the potential at hand and opens the "black box" so that the client understands how the work is done. The customer base of Pelerei includes the World Bank, the International Monetary Fund, the Bank of Canada, and numerous other international public and private organizations.

Dr. Blair has extensive line management experience. Prior to her work with Pelerei, Dr. Blair was a division chief in the World Bank. Dr. Blair also spent five years as Director of Institutional Research at the Universities of Colorado and Maine. Her most recent work has been in applying appreciative inquiry to teamwork and in coaching instructors in distance learning design techniques.

Dr. Blair received her doctorate in organizational psychology from the University of Tilburg, The Netherlands. She has written extensively and is called upon frequently to speak. She is a wife and a mother and an enthusiastic gardener.

For more information, contact:
Madelyn Blair
e.mail: mblair@pelerei.com
or visit Pelerei's web site at www.pelerei.com

Interview questions for clients

Introductory Comments (in brief)
Thank you for agreeing to be interviewed. This is a project to help CDI plan for the future in order to assure that quality is maintained as they grow. Often quality is diminished as companies grow. Their concern has led to this review of CDI. Your comments will not be identified to you individually unless you wish them to be. Any questions before we begin?

Selection (why)
BACKGROUND

1. Just to give me some context. Describe briefly what — is all about and what it does? Describe the work you do here at — ?

2. How long have you used CDI services?

3. What is the typical project for which you call upon CDI to do something?

4. Describe the project from your perspective. What does it mean to you? Where does it begin for you? What are the major steps for you? What is the last thing you do that means that the job is completed to your satisfaction?

5. What major experiences influenced your decision to try the services of CDI?

PERFORMANCE

6. Have you had any problems with CDI's services? Have you let them know it? How did they respond? Was it sufficient to satisfy your needs? What could they have done to do so?

7. Describe a time when CDI performed in a way that made you feel totally satisfied. What made it so?

8. If I were to give you three wishes that we could make happen in the way CDI performed for you, what would those three wishes be?

9. If there was an opportunity for you to be present at CDI's planning session, what would you say to them?

10. What is your perception of CDI's long term planning comparative advantage? What would be your vision for them? What would you recommend they do to get there? Are there gaps they should fill? What is the one thing you would not recommend they change?

Feedback from clients

Clients were asked to describe a time when CDI performed in a way that made them feel totally satisfied. What made it so? Their answers were grouped into messages that were captured into the statements listed below in italics. Below each statement are listed actual quotations from the clients that relate to the statement.

- *When we were working like partners; the communication between us was a comfortable give and take.*

personal relationship
collaborative process
commitment to listening
client could shape the product without having to save it
effective client relationships
partnership
personal relationship
being on the same intellectual wavelength
personal, professional assistance
flexibility

- *When the work looked good and read well.*

good work
reads well
looks good
quality high
excellence
good job
layout professional
reasonably high professional product (reliable)
quality

- *When the deadline was met regardless of the amount of lead time given.*

speed

responsive

good on deadlines

early warning of problems

deadlines

responding to their needs

delivers

competent judgment

- *When you showed real leadership and we were able to do more than we could do ourselves alone.*

leader to the client

do something the client cannot do for himself or herself

giving solutions which up the ante

setting standards

setting expectations

growing together with the client

- *When you do things which are ahead of the crowd and are willing to take that risk.*

balance point between creative chaos and organizational rigidity

intellectual leadership

investing in new ways of doing things

vision (especially of information management)

understanding the utility of information

sense of being a learning organization (experimentation, non-rigid about the budget and deliverables)

making transformation from print to on-line

Energizing Forces Defined in Retreat

The staff preferred to call their life-giving forces "energizing forces". They developed their energizing forces by first interviewing each other and then discussing what they learned from the interviews in a plenary session. When their comments were captured on newsprint, they began to look for trends and categorized their comments — discovering their energizing forces together.

QUALITY

- on-time
- you can go to the next step and trust it was done right
- consistency of right choices
- common understanding on both sides
- care
- you know your role and are responsible for your part
- realistic deadlines
- enemies of quality — late changes; budget constraints; uneducated clients; lack of control
- balance
- realism of deadlines
- going beyond the expectations
- amazing people — dedicated
- small projects, easygoing clients, well-defined,
- small team — these facilitate producing quality results

FREEDOM

- free to make decisions, take charge
- need to know where you stand (clear understanding of all important factors)
- allowed to make mistakes
- absence of control and punishment
- clear goals
- flexibility
- freedom from nonsense
- some need more guidance
- "billable hour"
- more likely to ask for help when we need it
- free to say or do or try flexibility to work "at home" so can balance other responsibilities
- feeling trusted — gives confidence

IMPACT

- even one more person
- eliminating bullshit
- indirect by helping our clients
- introducing technology
- hard to gauge because we don't know what happens to our products
- we don't get much feedback from clients (tends to be only to one person if given)
- we create really serious products (of substance)
- "built the Taj Mahal"
- enables the client to see more clearly
- our role is to extend the client's impact
- partnering
- help the client see more and wider

PERSPECTIVE

- graciously appreciate feedback from authors who don't understand
- never hear a raised voice
- clients enjoy working with us
- sense of disengagement
- deadlines are more flexible than they appear
- almost always feels a sense of perspective
- important to have other interests
- sense of security
- bonding with co-workers
- keep a sense of humor

CHALLENGE

- helping clients say what they want to achieve
- any deadline
- freedom to improvise — especially when you don't know what to do
- makes you think to produce something extraordinary
- good challenge — well-defined problem
- bad challenge — poorly defined problem and is not satisfying
- "see what you come up with" — dare to challenge yourself
- "reading Bruce's mind"
- learning the changing environment
- always jumping out of the box
- healthy when you have a sense of security to take a risk

SOLIDARITY

- having well-defined team
- clearly defined project
- clear idea of process and good sharing of information
- comes out of creative chaos — always flexibility and fluidity
- working with someone gives you a place to bounce ideas
- small team under high stress creates solidarity
- have to trust in the capabilities of team members
- physical separation works against solidarity
- caring that what you do reflects on the company
- takes time for new people to learn

Questions for improving quality as we grow

Developed in Day 1 of retreat

QUALITY (includes control)
- Think of the projects that you have worked on.
- Which product (publication) best exemplifies quality? Describe.
- What does "quality" mean to you?
- Describe a particular project (process) that, for you, worked well in producing a quality product.
- What things are needed to meet your expectations for a fine product?

FREEDOM
- How does freedom affect your performance? Your work environment? Your relationships with clients?
- Describe a situation where freedom played an integral role? Facilitated your work?
- Describe a situation when you were in control.

IMPACT (making a difference, effort)
- Describe something you've done that's made an impact.
- How do you feel you have made an impact – on yourself? Your coworkers? The company? Your clients? The world?
- What kind of impact could (or should) we have on the 5 categories above?
- Describe any feedback you've gotten on an impact you've made. How did you go about getting that feedback?

PERSPECTIVE (wit, humor, connection to the world and clients)
- Why do you think perspective is important?
- Give an example of a time when perspective was important (when executing a task or working with a client).
- How have you sharpened or strengthened your perspective?

CHALLENGE
- Describe a challenge that you found satisfying.
- How do you define a good challenge?
- What elements make for an environment in which you feel you can rise to challenges and take risks?
- How can we keep our jobs challenging?
- What are the sources for challenges in your job (yourself, clients, company, world, peers)?

SOLIDARITY
- When do you feel most like part of a team? What was happening that made this happen?
- How does it enhance the way we work?
- Describe an instance where solidarity helped when responding to client needs or when it contributed to the quality of your work?
- How do you get solidarity?

APPENDIX 5

Possibilty statements [1]

What CDI Might Look Like

- We and our clients have an explicit understanding of what quality means and we are vanquishing the many enemies of quality.
- We insist on a 2-day window for quality assurance.
- We communicate in writing the tradeoffs between meeting deadlines and quality.
- We train all rookie editors and desktoppers in our style.
- We have a list of enemies of quality.
- Our commitment to freedom is enhanced by a comprehensive tracking site. This backbone tracks the details of each project – its team members, scope, budget, client contacts – so that everyone involved has efficient access to a project's status.
- This tracking frees CDI employees to focus on substantive work and skills-building.
- CDI's strong reputation allows it to set limits at the start of projects with regard to timetables, design, and scope. We understand the time it takes to produce a quality project. We decline or reshape those that do not allow us the time or freedom to produce to our standards.
- We contract out more mundane tasks, allowing employees to develop their own skills.
- We follow up with the client and ask them how the product was used, whether it was effective, and if they would have done anything differently. We put this on the tracking system.
- Whenever we get feedback from a client, we send e-mail to everyone.

- Cool heads prevail – clients come running
- Our work reflects our awareness of clients' perspectives and the feedback we solicit helps us refine our work
- Sabbaticals and employees' pursuit of outside interests enrich our lives and work environment
- CDI has established a reputation for quality. We continue to expand our range of projects (i.e., taking on projects outside of our traditional fields).

This allows employees to:
- learn new subjects and fields
- work with new clients (and old ones in new ways)
- expand imaginatively
- build new skills
- spend more time working directly with clients
- Within our traditional fields of expertise, we find new ways to expand our clients' reach, exploring new platforms of communication. We bring them into new technologies while expanding our own knowledge base.
- Project leaders organize teams with well-defined tasks and goals.
- Cooperation, collaboration, and communication come out of creative chaos. Mentors give feedback and guidance to fellow employees. Trust grows from this experience.
- Frequent social functions – like parties-increase collaboration and bring together our widely dispersed employees. Despite recent growth, CDI keeps the closely-knit, small-company feel.

---

[1] Staff preferred to refer to the provocative propositions as possibilities.

Actions for improving quality as we grow

1. Have a party

2. Appoint a project leader for each project

3. Begin to introduce clarity to bills – attach notes

4. Create a proof-reading checklist

5. Create a DTP checklist

6. Create a list of "what's expected"

7. Amy calls clients at end of each project to ask questions (few) on satisfaction and use

8. Disseminate feedback from clients

9. Solve Benton web site problem

10. Start web site meetings and announce – Debbie schedules

11. Check the web site for possibilities of tracking -- everybody

12. Feed data and information for web site tracking

13. Identify whether Anna can be proofreader for Bank

14. Identify whether Meg can be proofreader for HQ

15. Prepare welcome "boxes" for new people

16. Type results of this retreat and have each person augment it for medium and long-term actions

17. Let clients know about recent products

18. Schedule changes are communicated to clients in writing and cite implications and options

19. Write list of enemies of quality

20. Assign names and dates to each item above

21. Prepare notebook on products of this retreat

Interview for clients after the retreat

INTRODUCTORY COMMENTS

Thank you for being willing to be interviewed again. This time your feedback is for a paper which I am writing about the process I used with Bruce's group. It was successful according to Bruce. I would like to see if it was also effective for you.

QUESTIONS

1. Thinking about the original interview, how did you find it from your perspective?

• What was it about that interview that you found useful, enjoyable, of high quality?

2. Did you receive any feedback from Bruce on what happened with your feedback?

• Did he share with you any of the other feedback he received?

3. Is there any way you wish we had done the exercise differently?

• How could we have made the exercise more useful to you?

4. I realize that it has been a very short period of time since our exercise, but have you seen any change in the way your work is being handled?

• Describe it to me. What works better? Has anything suffered?

5. From your perspective, do you think that the exercise was successful?

Interview for staff after the retreat

Thank you for being willing to be interviewed. The purpose of your feedback to me is for a paper which I am writing about the process we used. It was successful according to Bruce. I would like to see if it was also effective for you.

1. What did you like best about the planning process we used?

2. When you were the most comfortable about the process, what portion was it of the process, what were you doing, what was happening around you?

3. If you were given three wishes about the exercise, what would they be?

4. Since the exercise, do you see any changes in your work? In the way you work? In the work environment? In your colleagues?

5. The purpose of the exercise was to give you a chance to develop a plan for change that would help CDI to keep quality while growing and to learn some new skills. From your perspective, do you think that the exercise was successful? How?

*The group hug has been fine. I enjoyed it
and think it did a lot for the team.
Now I want to know if we really mean it?
Because if we do not, I have better ways
to spend my time.*

— BRIAN

APPLICATION OF THEORY

DO WE REALLY MEAN IT?

BY JACK BRITTAIN

Background

Telesystems is an international leader in the development and manufacture of telecommunications hardware components. Telesystems has a long history with teaming and a deep cultural respect for participation.

The wni (wireless network interface) Design Team was working on a new generation interface destined to provide the connection between current long distance transmission systems and emerging PCS wireless technologies The wni Design Team consisted of 16 engineers. All the members had experience working on teams and worked well together in the beginning, but approximately 9 months into the 20-month project schedule, problems started appearing in the design coordination process and deadlines started slipping. Because the wni design was highly visible, management reacted to the first sign of problems. A series of management interviews with team members followed, and the result was a belief that the team had "people problems." Based on this assessment, the manager of the interface-engineering group brought in a human resources generalist to work with the wni Design Team.

Problem Solving [1]

The approach used with the wni Team was standard practice: get the team with the "problem" together, share management's concerns with the team, and ask the team to come up with a solution.

This approach is based on sound organizational behavior principles. It does not emphasize blame, it gives the team an opportunity to understand the problem and the management issues involved, and it allows the team to come up with its own solution, greatly increasing the probability that the solution will actually be implemented. The company had great success with this approach, and used it frequently to solve a wide range of problems, although the problems involved tended to be technical. A human resources generalist facilitated the solution generation process in this case because the team had "people problems."

The wni Design Team met with the interface group engineering manager and the human resources representative on a Friday afternoon for a problem solving session. The manager, Fred Williams, presented information on the number of change orders generated by the team and the schedule slippage to date, along with his assessment of what this meant for meeting the team's delivery deadline. Because the team was among the first to use a new approach to design qualification that integrated testing with the design process in an attempt to shorten the overall product delivery schedule, much of the initial discussion focused on the coordination processes involved, especially for software. The team generally was very favorable toward the new integrated process and did not have any specific recommendations for improving or changing it.

---

1 The events in this section are reconstructed based on interviews with the interface-engineering manager, the human resources representative, members of the team, and the project leads. I have made every effort to be unbiased in my assessments. And there is really no reason to be judgmental; no one failed here, the problem-solving approach just could not work. Everyone involved acted professionally, responsibly, and worked very hard to solve the problems as he or she perceived them.

After spending two hours reviewing processes, the team was no closer to solving its problem than when it began. Fred reiterated the major symptom: the team was behind schedule. The team then began brainstorming to develop solutions that would get the team back on schedule. After brainstorming a list of options, the team began discussing each and trying to evaluate whether it would help them accelerate the development process. There was a high level of participation in the discussion, but the outcome was inconclusive. The team seemed to actually be doing most of the things that were suggested, and those they were not doing did not offer much hope for schedule acceleration.

At 5:00, everyone was tired, including Fred. It had been a long week. Most of the team members had worked at least 60 hours that week, and they just wanted to go home. There was a lot of activity at 5:00, including individuals packing briefcases, putting on coats, and looking at watches. **Basically, the team did everything but bolt for the door.** This made Fred mad, and he chewed everyone out and expressed his disappointment in the team's "unwillingness to do anything about the scheduling problem." The wni Team members shared furtive glances with one another as Fred continued lecturing them, but no one responded. In exasperation, Fred sent them home and told them to come back Monday morning with solutions.

Jerry and the Software Qualification Process

Jerry Rogers was responsible for software testing. He was a key team member because his tests provided feedback on the interface's performance in conjunction with a wide variety of equipment supplied by other manufacturers. In addition, as part of the qualification subteam, the testing he did was required for the design to be released to manufacturing.

In the past, the testing and qualification process had come after an initial design was completed. But because testing invariably identified problems, designs would have to go back to a design team that had subsequently been assigned to other projects, plus problems were often identified in the software that required hardware solutions, creating further problems in getting the design finalized. It was not unusual for the redesign process that came after testing to take as long as the original design process and then the design would still have to clear testing and qualification before it was released to manufacturing.

Based on successes at other companies, Telesystems had adopted a new approach to testing and qualification that placed testing engineers on the design team. The test engineers began test development in conjunction with the specification of design objectives, which allowed them to better understand the design and communicate qualification problems at the very beginning of the design process. In addition, the test engineers could begin subcomponent testing and preliminary testing as various parts of the design emerged, thereby providing early feedback if they identified any problems. This early feedback was very valuable to the design team in making hardware versus software tradeoffs in the design. This approach had been shown to reduce the time for design to manufacturing by 50%, which is why Telesystems was so enthusiastic about it.

It was not unusual for testers to work all night and have results back to the design team the next morning, and because they worked odd hours and were called on to perform heroic acts, the testers were given a lot of latitude in their work hours. They also generally worked unsupervised and were accountable only to their team. Again, this was a practice that had worked well for the company and was understood by the design teams.

The wni Team's Tester, Jerry, had been with the company for three years. Jerry's disposition was somewhat aloof, and he did not socialize with the other members of the team, most of whom were about 10 years younger. But Jerry was well liked, in part because he brought fresh-baked muffins to work for the team every Monday morning without fail. It was Jerry's way of showing he cared while not over committing himself on a personal level.

About 6 months into the project, Jerry's mother moved into his home. She was dying of cancer, had no health insurance, and at 60 was not eligible for Medicare. Much of the burden of caring for her fell on Jerry's wife, but Jerry also felt an obligation to spend time with his mother and help his wife. The team knew about his situation and was very sympathetic.

As his mother's health worsened, Jerry became more and more distracted and the testing process became more sporadic. It was not that Jerry wasn't doing his job, but tests that had been done in two days were now taking two weeks, in part because Jerry was not working nights anymore. And because the design process kept moving, feedback that took two weeks often identified problems that required design changes that might not otherwise have been required and caused work to be redone that might otherwise have not been done in the first place. In addition, Jerry was not as aware of the design activities, and so sometimes problems identified by the tests were not design flaws, they were test flaws.

The team did not doubt that it was missing schedule milestones, but who was to blame? Everyone was doing their jobs to the best of their ability, everyone was working long hours, and the design work was actually generating some exciting results. There was a lot of communication about Jerry's personal situation, and members of the team helped him as they could, but ultimately the delays and confusion around testing were having an impact on the schedule. The team did not blame Jerry, however. Instead, they tended to blame management for trying to stick to a schedule that was overly ambitious and did not allow for slippage due to the personal difficulties of key team members.

When the schedule problem got management's attention, the members of the team were reluctant to talk about Jerry's problem, plus there was a sense the schedule was unrealistic. So during the interviews, they tended to talk about unresolved "people problems," although even the members of the team were not sure what this meant. Nor could anyone on the team very clearly articulate how Jerry's personal problems were impacting the schedule. As far as the team was concerned, everyone was doing his or her job and the team was falling behind schedule. It was no one's fault.

Monday Morning

Fred rounded up everyone at 9:00 to resume the problem-solving session. The human resources representative, Debbie, was not around and Fred did not want to wait for her. Everyone crowded into the conference room, Jerry's muffins in hand, and Fred launched into another lecture. **Fred had taken everyone's desire to go home on Friday as a personal affront, and he had been stewing about it all weekend.** He had decided to let them know that he thought they were not committed to the project. Rough them up a little and get them motivated to prove him wrong, he thought. So he waded in and let them know in no uncertain terms that he thought they were overly complacent, unmotivated, and did not care about their work. Furthermore, he pointed out that they obviously did not realize that their jobs could be on the line if the wni design did not meet its delivery deadline. His parting words were "Now get back to work and I want to see some solutions."

Many team members were angry, and the rest of the morning was spent talking about what Fred had said. Most of the team had been putting in very long hours, and they had been working even

harder since it became apparent that the schedule slippage was giving management major heartburn. Based on what had just happened, they perceived that Fred clearly had not appreciated their contributions, and most of the team agreed that they would be going home at 5:00 every day from now on.

The problem-solving approach had clearly not worked as planned. A team with some relatively minor schedule slippage – they were about 3 weeks behind schedule – was now angry at their manager, plotting revolt, and no closer to dealing with their team issues than before. What had been a minor problem had become a major problem, and the process had created problems that had not existed before. And the conflict with management would have an effect on the team over the next two months as team members began to blame one another as work hours were reduced and Fred reacted with anger as more milestones were missed.

Appreciative Inquiry

By the eleventh month of the project, the schedule had gone from 3 weeks to 6 weeks behind. It was at this point that Fred decided he had lost control of the project and needed the help of an outside consultant. Debbie had been attending local Organization Development Network meetings and had participated in an appreciative inquiry exercise. She thought the appreciative inquiry philosophy looked interesting and suggested to Fred that a fresh approach might get the wni Team back on track. Fred was desperate and agreed to meet with a consultant to talk about the situation. After meeting with the consultant, Fred decided to go forward, not because he was convinced it would work, but more because he realized the team was disintegrating and needed some kind of intervention to bring it back together. At this point, Fred still thought he needed to eventually get the team back together for another problem-solving session.

The appreciative inquiry was scheduled for Thursday and Friday of the following week. The session began with an individual appreciation exercise in which the participants taped a 5x8 card on their backs and everyone anonymously wrote one thing they appreciated about the individual on every card. Fred participated with the team at the consultant's urging, and based on the consultant's coaching, he made sure he wrote something on every card. Only about a third of the team wrote something on Fred's card, but he was also coached not to take this personally. Individuals were asked to share items on their cards during the debrief and comment on their own positive experiences with the team. The debrief set a very positive tone. The individual members of the team clearly had a great appreciation for the efforts of others, and a lot of information was surfaced about heroic acts and hard work. Fred used his opportunity to speak to acknowledge the team's hard work and to comment that, based on the exercise, he had a new appreciation for the dedication that had been exhibited by the team. This was not something Fred had been coached to do. **The structure of the exercise exposed him to information that he had no other way of knowing, and it changed his perception of the team.**

After the opening exercise, the participants were broken into pairs and began the appreciative interview. As is typical with this part of the process, things began somewhat quietly. But as the morning progressed, the volume of the conversations increased, laughter could be heard with some regularity, and the energy and engagement noticeably increased.

The group reassembled after lunch to share interview information and to begin to organize a description of the team at its best. One of the events that surfaced during this discussion was something that had happened in the previous month. Jerry's wife was having trouble getting his mother in and out of the house, so he was planning to build a ramp on the front of his house so his wife could use a wheel chair. He mentioned this to one of the members of the team, and the team then surprised him by organizing to help him with the job that Saturday morning. With lots of help and too many engineers, the job was done quickly. Jerry's wife picked up barbecue and beer for lunch, and they sat around in Jerry's backyard all afternoon sipping beers and talking. They talked a lot about work, the team, the project, life, their hopes, and even a little football. It had meant a lot to the entire team, and they had experienced it as a kind of best that they had never had in the workplace. **The team spent most of the afternoon debriefing that Saturday at Jerry's house, what it meant, and identifying parallel times when they were both effective and satisfied with results at work.**

In addition to the teamwork description that surfaced and appreciation for task ownership, this discussion was pivotal because it was the first knowledge anyone outside the team had of Jerry's personal problems. Debbie immediately got to work on finding some help for Jerry, and by the next week had identified some non-profit agencies that could help Jerry fund home nursing assistance and would help him with some of the medical access issues he faced. Fred was also able to approve an equipment purchase to set up an office in Jerry's home so he could telecommute in the evening and at times when he was needed at home, providing him with greater flexibility in working with the team. This also contributed to mending Fred's relationship with the team.

While the appreciative inquiry process brought some relief for Jerry, problem-solving Jerry's personal issues was not going to get the team to peak performance. Instead, the issue was how the team was dealing with the performance challenges of Jerry's personal problems. The team had experience meeting challenges, dealing with schedule delays and process issue, and coming up with creative technical solutions to seemingly impossible situations. But they had not applied what they knew how to do to their team because they were focused on problems that they did not know how to deal with instead of challenges they were well equipped to meet. **The appreciative inquiry process was significant because it got the team focused on what they knew.**

On Friday morning, the team began working on its provocative propositions, taking the descriptive material from the day before and turning it into statements that captured what the team was when performing at its best. The team devoted a great deal of time to this task, continuing the discussion through lunch with sub-teams trying to find exactly the right wording for each proposition.

The working propositions were posted on flip chart sheets after lunch and the team began discussing the final wording. This is when Brian issued his challenge. "The group hug has been fine. I enjoyed it and think it did a lot for the team. Now I want to know if we really mean it? Because if we do not, I have better ways to spend my time."

Commitment to Living the Propositions

It is not unusual for discussions of appreciative inquiry to stop at the provocative propositions. And with good reason. There is a sense of accomplishment in defining the team at its best, in the realization that, though the propositions may be challenging, they describe a level of performance that has been achieved and can be replicated again. And people who have participated in the appreciative inquiry often would also like to stop at this point as well. To paraphrase Brian, they enjoy the group hug, so it seems like a good place to stop.

But the real challenge of appreciative inquiry is to make the group's propositions a reality. And this is very hard work that requires an individual and group commitment to trying to work at peak levels all the time. Furthermore, it may require a commitment on the part of individuals and groups to make changes in the status quo. Achieving at a group's peak level of performance often requires a continuous learning process and engagement with change that is simply more work than sticking with the way things have always been done. So how do you make the group's propositions a reality?

Wni Design Team

Brian had asked the question that needed to be asked, even if he had not waited until the propositions were edited. The team sat silently and the facilitator did not intervene.

The silence was maintained for a good four minutes as everyone thought about what Brian had asked. Then Ted asked, "What do you mean?"

Brian responded that he thought everyone meant well and had shown enthusiasm for the process of creating the propositions, but he seriously doubted that anything would be different on Monday. In fact, he added, he did not think anything would be different that afternoon when they went back to their offices to try to clear things up before going home for the weekend.

Various team members now stepped forward to challenge Brian, arguing they thought the process had been good and that they realized some things about working as a team that they had not realized before. But Brian was not backing down.

"Yeah, you know some things you did not know yesterday. But what are you going to do? What is going to change and how are you going to make it change?"

Some members of the team were becoming upset with Brian, who had a reputation on the team for disagreeing and "causing trouble." A couple of participants tried to humor him into going along by joking that "Brian can find the dark lining inside every silver cloud." Then Henry appealed to the facilitator to "get the group back on track," but the facilitator declined to intervene.

This is when Brian again stumped the team. Pointing at the posted flip chart sheets, he said, "Look at what we have up there. Item number 9. We challenge the process. But when I challenge the process, the first thing you do is try to shut me down. That is what I mean. We do not intend to live these propositions. We are assuming that writing these propositions will change who we are, but I do not think we are going to do any of this."

That the team was already violating its own values probably had the greatest impact on everyone present. Again, there was a long period of silence. There were no glances from person to person. Instead, everyone was concentrating and trying to come to terms with the challenge before them.

Robert, normally quiet and reserved, was the first to speak. "You know, it makes me sad to think that we may not be able to live up to what we would like to be. But I think Brian's questions are fair. Do we want to live our values? I want to. And I would like to know how we can do this as a team."

Henry, who had tried to get the facilitator to quiet Brian, was next to speak. "Brian is right. We were not living our values. But I would like us to respond by acknowledging Brian is right to challenge the process and by accepting his challenge. We need to live our values starting right now."

The discussion that followed went on for two hours. Every member of the team spoke, they listened to one another, and they discussed in great detail what it would mean to live the values reflected in the propositions. This discussion was not facilitated. Once Henry had accepted Brian's challenge, the whole group took ownership for everything that happened next. Members of the team asked about boundaries of obligation, they shared expectations and negotiated roles, and they talked about the next Monday as if it were the most important day of the rest of their work career.

After two hours, the team quickly completed the initial word-smithing of the propositions and gave them to Brian, Henry, and Robert to do the final edit. Then they went around the table and had every person make an individual commitment to the team to try to live the propositions. The facilitator had not played any role in the entire afternoon session and the team left that afternoon with complete ownership of the propositions, including all the capture and distribution.

Socially Constructing Reality and Individual Commitment

One of the things we know about group processes is that if there is a dispersion of perceived volition, the result can be weak individual commitment to action. There are also some widely used solutions. The one most frequently used is the action item commitment. In some environments this becomes a formal document that must be filed in triplicate. The purpose of the action item is to have each individual define a next step in order to get implementation started. It also takes advantage of the public forum of the decision group to increase accountability and volition, two variables that are shown to greatly increase the level of commitment on the part of individuals.

While holding individuals accountable to a group may work fine for well defined individual deliverables like a project plan or meeting a deadline, it is less clear that it is sufficient in a situation where a commitment to shared values is expected. This describes the kind of situations where appreciative inquiry is frequently used. The problem with using the commitment lever alone is that the participants may not have a shared interpretation of what commitments are being made. **It is one thing to agree with one's own interpretation of the provocative propositions that come out of an appreciative inquiry; it is quite another thing to commit to a shared understanding of what the provocative propositions mean in practice.**

The process that Brian drove for the wni Design Team was a social construction process. The team not only agreed on the provocative propositions, they agreed on what they would mean for actual day-to-day behavior on the job. This is no small thing, and the commitments that occurred as a result of this social construction were not taken lightly. Indeed, much of what happened in the final commitment process had strong similarity with the role agreement process (rap), which emphasizes shared, negotiated understandings of role expectations. But the social construction that occurred within the wni Team went far beyond work roles, including how people were treated as individuals and the team's concept of success and failure.

While some social construction occurs in the process of writing the propositions, it is probably not enough. There are two reasons for this. First, the process of proposition writing tends to summarize related and similar, but not identical, statements. While the facilitator can make every effort to retain meaning, invariably different participants are going to see different slants on the propositions based on which of the draft propositions they personally wrote or most closely identify with. So from a straight perception standpoint, there is an important social construction process that needs to take place around the final propositions. And the second reason for the social construction process is that it adds meaning to the propositions and turns them into defined behaviors that all participants understand. A group's propositions may not have a great deal of meaning to those outside the process, and this is because the meaning is created through the process of constructing the statements. In other words, there is no meaning in the propositions per se. Rather the meaning is in the shared understanding that the group develops through the social construction process (also known as the co-construction of reality). Because this social construction creates the reality of living the words, it is important that appreciative inquiry not stop with the word-smithing.

FACILITATING SOCIAL CONSTRUCTION

WHAT BRIAN DID FOR THE WNI TEAM IS SOMETHING EVERY FACILITATOR NEEDS TO ENSURE HAPPENS FOR EVERY TEAM OR GROUP THAT PARTICIPATES IN AN APPRECIATIVE INQUIRY. THE FACILITATION GOALS ARE:

1. Team must have time allocated for the social construction process, and this time must be significant. How much time is needed depends on the size of the group involved in the appreciative inquiry, but the units are hours, not minutes.

2. The team or group must grapple with the "Do you mean it?" question. The appreciative inquiry process, because it is positive, makes it easy for participants to go along. The problem is they can enjoy the process without committing to the results.

3. The group must live their values throughout the social construction process. And if they are not living their values during the social construction process, they must be challenged to do so. It is in the struggle to immediately put their provocative propositions into effect that groups construct the behavioral meanings that become work behavior.

4. The social construction process is difficult, and teams may want to avoid it. The process of constructing the propositions tends to be affirming and generates a lot of enthusiasm. Dealing with meaning and accepting the challenge of living the propositions is serious and at times emotional. Difficult issues need to be resolved, understandings articulated, and personal commitments made. The tone of this process tends to be serious. It is still affirming, but making a face-to-face personal commitment to the team is a sobering experience.

5. The propositions must leave the room with the group. If they are to become a day-to-day reality, the group needs to take control of them and all that happens with them. If the facilitator is doing the final processing, then the propositions are the facilitator's, not the groups.

Again, note that the closing process is not just about commitment, it is about social construction and commitment. Commitment has a role, but the commitment that should come out of an appreciative inquiry is a commitment to the shared meaning of the propositions, not the idiosyncratic meanings of the individual participants.

Wni Team Practice

One of the profound things about the wni Team's appreciative inquiry was that most things did not change. Jerry still brings fresh muffins to the wni Team on Monday mornings, team members still work longer hours than is probably healthy, and Brian is still challenging the process. But important things did change, and they have made a difference in how effective the team is. Now the team listens to Brian, Jerry asks for help when he needs it, and Fred gives constructive suggestions instead of criticizing. In addition, team members know a lot more about each other and they have an occasional barbecue on a Saturday afternoon to let off steam and talk about work issues. Instead of seeing the project as a collection of individual deadlines, the team accepts responsibility for team deadlines, which was Fred's initial objective when he launched his problem-solving process. But Fred's problem-solving approach created problems because that was its focus, whereas appreciative inquiry challenged the team to be at its best because that was its focus.

The social construction process did not stop with the development of the provocative propositions (see Appendix A). The wni Team had cards made up, and they continue to review these cards at team meetings. After several months, the values are well understood and committed to memory, but the team seems to enjoy reviewing what they have achieved. Because the provocative propositions are the Team's, they take pride in living up to their own expectations.

The wni Design Team

At the time of the appreciative inquiry, the team was 11 months into a 20-month project and six weeks behind schedule.

THE WNI DESIGN TEAM:
- Completed its work in a total of 19 months
- Delivered a product that performed significantly above specifications for less than the expected cost.
- Developed improvements to the concurrent design and testing process that are expected to produce reductions of time to delivery of about 10% on all future design projects.

Telesystems is now using appreciative inquiry as its primary team development tool for all product design teams, Fred still has an occasional problem solving session, and Jerry and his wife are adjusting to life following the death of his mother. All the members of the wni Team attended the funeral.

© J. BRITTAIN, 1998

Wni Design Team's Provocative Propositions

SUPPORTIVE ENVIRONMENT

- We achieve together.
- We ask for help and give help when asked.
- We give credit to others in a timely manner.

OPEN COMMUNICATION

- We listen first.
- We give constructive feedback.
- We value each other's opinions, even when we agree to disagree.

CHALLENGE

- We accept challenges as a team, not as individuals.
- We own the process, and we challenge the process.
- We challenge each other to learn and tackle new tasks.

TEAMWORK

- We meet our commitments to the team.
- We take the time to know each other.
- We have fun and look for the humor in every situation.

ABOUT THE AUTHOR

JACK BRITTAIN is Dean of the David Eccles School of Business at the University of Utah. Prior to this position, Jack was an Associate Professor of Organizational Behavior, School of Management, University of Texas at Dallas. He joined the UTD faculty in 1989 after receiving his Ph.D. from the University of California, Berkeley. In 1993, Jack earned the University of Texas Chanellor's Council Outstanding Teacher Award and the School of Management's Outstanding Teaching Award in 1992. His expertise is in the fields of change management and business education. He founded the Appreciative Inquiry Listserv, which serves hundreds of participants worldwide. Visit: http://lists.business.utah.edu/mailman/listinfo/ailist

For more information, contact:
Jack Brittain
e.mail: Brittain@Business.Utah.edu

𝓕ind the good and praise it!

— PHOEBE BEASLEY

APPLICATION OF THEORY

EXIT
INTERVIEWS
WITH AN "APPRECIATIVE EYE"

BY LIA BOSCH

Introduction

Exit interviews are a long-standing "institution" in some organizations; unfortunately, they end up being like one of those family stories that has been passed down from generation to generation — told so many times that the original facts get distorted. The practice of conducting exit interviews may have started in your organization with good intentions of gathering meaningful information to help improve the way the organization does things. However, often the natural course of events in an organization looks like this: the human resources professional follows the policy of diligently gathering feedback from the departing employee, who is actually quite reluctant to give honest feedback for fear of "burning bridges." The feedback gathered gets summarized and filed away. If you work in a progressive organization, perhaps the feedback gets forwarded to senior executives who may read the information, but discount it because they question the openness of the departing employee.

Can we trust the information obtained from exit interviews? Is there any value in the data collected? Why do we conduct these interviews anyway? These are age-old questions that human resources professionals have asked themselves. Improvements in interviewing techniques and refinements in the exit interview process continue to be made in an effort to increase the value and the outcomes from exit interviews. Now, there is another approach that takes a unique perspective to exit interviews that shifts our traditional paradigm. Using appreciative inquiry premises and techniques, the exit interview can take on an "appreciative eye" rather than a "problem-solving eye." The appreciative perspective turns the interview with a departing employee into an opportunity to discover the organization's core life giving factors, and how to build upon those, rather than a routine discussion to identify the organization's problems, and ways to fix these problems.

Traditional Exit Interviews

Generally, exit interviews are conducted to find out why employees are leaving. Among organizations and professionals, there are mixed practices and mixed feelings about the value of exit interviews. Two separate studies conducted attest to these mixed reactions. For example, according to Brotherton (1996), a survey conducted by Robert Half International Inc. in 1994 indicated that of 150 executives, 93 percent thought that exit interviews provided useful information. Specifically, respondents thought that the data would serve the following purposes:

PURPOSE	
42%	Learn ways to improve specific department
34%	Find ways to improve overall company policies
17%	Suggest how specific supervisors can improve skills
7%	No valuable information

Yet, another study of 18 major organizations conducted in 1980 by Pamela Garretson and Kenneth Teel found that only a little over half the companies (58 percent) actually made use of the data collected in exit interviews. These researchers concluded that the other group of companies (42 percent) merely conducted exit interviews as a symbolic gesture. For those companies that made use of the information, typical outcomes from the interviews included: making changes to working conditions such as pay and redesign of work areas, dismissal of ineffective supervisors, early identification of problems, or confirmation of the existence of problems (Garretson & Teel, 1982).

Two of the most serious concerns about exit interviews are convincing employees to open up in exit interviews, and that data collected in such interviews are of a one-sided nature. The skepticism about the value of exit interview information is mainly related to the concern about employees being open in interviews. As stated by Phaedra Brotherton (1996) in her article, Exit Interviews Can Provide a Reality Check, "employees who are leaving may be concerned about getting a good reference and not burning bridges." In addition, she emphasizes that, "employees really may have nothing to gain from an exit interview. In fact, they may be more concerned about using the interview as an opportunity to meet their own political goals." Another author adds a psychological element to the concern about employees being open and truthful in exit interviews. Charles McConnell (1992) highlights that departing employees "having acted upon the decision to resign, simply do not care to expend the time or energy necessary to participate fully in an exit interview." Emotionally, these employees may already have "severed contact and they no longer especially care a great deal."

Traditional exit interviews ask questions of a one-sided nature, generally concerned with why the employee is leaving and what improvements the organization should make. According to Garretson and Teel, the most common topics covered in exit interviews include:

- Reason for leaving
- New job and salary
- Things liked best about the job
- Things liked least about the job
- Rating of current job, supervision, pay, advancement opportunities
- Suggestions

It is interesting to note from the above list that only one topic specifically asks for the positives of the current employment situation, i.e. what things were liked best about the job. Most of the questions asked in exit interviews focus on collecting constructive criticism. For example, employees are asked their opinions on specifics such as the job, supervisor, pay, working conditions, as well as their suggestions for improvement, or ways the company could have prevented the resignation (Garretson and Teel, 1982).

The problem-solving paradigm is well entrenched in the traditional exit interview process. The tone of traditional exit interviews is generally negative.

Interviewers "dig for dirt" about the company, supervision, and the job. With this frame of mind, questions by interviewers lead employees to highlight the negatives or focus on constructive criticism. As a result, exit interviews tend to be energy draining on both the interviewer and the employee. As we have learned, although the problem-solving model can provide useful information on issues, consequences, and possible solutions, few organizations use this information. More organizations need to conduct exit interviews with a purpose in mind. This purpose provides a framework for the questions to be asked. After all, the information we get is based on the questions we ask.

Appreciative Approach to Exit Interviews

Appreciative Inquiry presents an opportunity to change the traditional approach to exit interviews — a more purposeful approach to gathering important data. It can improve the quality of the data gathered and the chances of the data leading to improvements within the organization. The underlying premise of appreciative inquiry is that learning from the things we do well can be just as, if not more, useful than learning from the things we do not do well. I recently experimented with developing a new exit interview approach using some appreciative concepts and methods. Ideally, by turning the experience into a positive one for both the exiting employee and the company, the goal of the new approach was to improve the quality of data gathered, and encourage senior management to act upon it. Specifically, I wanted the employee to leave the organization with a good feeling about the company, and perhaps wondering if he or she had made the right choice in leaving. In turn, the departing employee is reminded of the positives, which would serve to enhance the company's reputation as a good employer in the industry, and in the overall community. For the company, I hoped that the experience would highlight what is truly unique about our management practices that lead to our success, and what we should continue to build upon in the future.

Using a core model of an appreciative interview questionnaire, from David Cooperrider's work, I developed a specific questionnaire to be used in an exit interview process. The topic areas selected for the interview were defined based on:

A. My personal experiences from previous interviews

B. My understanding of work motivation and related theories

C. My knowledge of the company's culture and espoused values.

This approach is different from what is recommended by David Cooperrider, in that it only reflects my opinion of what the topic areas should be, and does not incorporate the experiences of a

group of people in developing topic areas. I chose this approach because I wanted to experiment a little with appreciative inquiry before presenting the merits of this approach to senior management. I expected the group to be resistant to taking a number of individuals away from their busy schedules to generate topic areas, without some reassurance that the experiment would produce valuable results.

The four topic areas I chose were:
- **FACTORS MAKING THE COMPANY**
- **ATTRACTIVE/UNIQUE**
- **BEING "THE BEST"**
- **SHARED COMMITMENT**
- **PEOPLE AND TEAMWORK**

For each of these topics, I developed a set of questions to collect data that would get at the core of each topic. The questions for each topic area are listed on the following pages.

INTERVIEW QUESTIONS IN TOPIC AREAS

Factors behind what makes the company attractive and/or unique

A. Starting back at the time you joined the company...
- What attracted you to the organization?
- What were your initial impressions when you joined?
- How have your impressions changed since then?

B. Looking at your entire experience with the company, tell me about a time when you felt most excited, most involved, most engaged in this company...
- What made it an exciting experience?
- Who were the significant people involved? Why were they significant in the event?
- What were the most important factors in the company that helped to make it a peak experience? (e.g. leadership qualities, structure, rewards, systems, skills, strategy, and relationships)

C. What do you value most about the organization? Why?

D. What is the single most important thing the company has contributed to your life?

The company prides itself in "being the best"

A. In your opinion, what do you think makes us unique or stand out above others in the industry?

B. What is the most important achievement of this company that you can recall that illustrates the spirit of "being the best"?

C. What is the most outstanding or successful achievement or piece of work you have been involved in that you are particularly proud of?
- What made it outstanding?
- What unique skills/qualities did you apply in achieving this result?
- What organizational factors helped to create this achievement?
(e.g. leadership, teamwork, culture)

SHARED COMMITMENT

Organizations work best
when people at all levels
share a basic
common vision...

A. In your mind, what is the common mission or purpose that unites people at this company? How is this communicated and nurtured?

B. Describe a time you felt most committed to the company and its purpose.
- Why did you feel such commitment?
- Give one example of how the organization has shown its commitment to you.

PEOPLE AND TEAMWORK

Our company's strength
rests with its people.
We believe that we have
among the best people in the
industry working with us.
How these people work
together is also considered
to provide us with an
advantage over others...

A. Can you think of a time when there was an extraordinary display of teamwork between individuals or diverse groups in the company?
- What made such teamwork possible? (e.g. planning, communication, leadership, incentives, skills, team development techniques, other).

B. Can you give me an example of the most effective team or committee you have been part of? What are the factors/skills that made it effective?

C. What individual qualities are most valued in this company? What qualities are necessary for people to excel?

D. People in this company tell me that they want the chance to "make a difference"...
- What is the best example of when the company provided you with the chance to "make a difference"? How did that feel?

As is customary in the appreciative approach, I concluded the interviews with two questions: one focused on having the individual identify the one core factor that gives life to the organization, and the other asking the individual to outline three wishes or suggestions for heightening the organization's effectiveness. The interview plan and questionnaire also included brief notes to explain the appreciative inquiry approach, and to introduce each topic area. The purpose of the general introduction to the appreciative interview process was to explain and reassure people that the feedback we were seeking was of value to the company, but that it was being collected from a perspective different from what they may have expected. The message was that the organization was seeking information that would help us focus on reinforcing practices, skills, and values that would keep the company functioning at its best. Our interest was to learn from their personal experiences with the organization, and their impressions of what distinctive values, management practices, and skills make the company unique.

Appreciative theory presents an alternative approach to gathering information of a sensitive nature in what is often an emotional time for a departing employee. This approach can overcome the two greatest obstacles faced in collecting important information in exit interviews; that is, convincing employees to open up in interviews, and getting information about why people stay with the organization, not just why people leave.

In appreciative exit interviews, employees are asked to talk about the organization when it is at its best. As a result, there is less of a chance to create anxiety in employees who may be concerned about burning bridges. In addition, for the person who is trying to sever emotional ties with the company, an appreciative approach to the interview may ease the transition. Recalling his or her experiences with the company at its best will produce a positive end to the relationship. As well, in the appreciative process, probing for specific examples will encourage people to more actively engage in the interview.

Traditional exit interviews focus on asking employees why they are leaving the organization and what their opinions are on specific organizational issues, such as supervision, morale and promotional opportunities. Answers to these questions may not lead to answers about why employees remain in the organization. This one-sided view of organizational issues could result in an organization missing part of the equation of what makes the company attractive to those who stay (Hughes and Flowers, 1987). The appreciative perspective ensures that the strengths of the organization are highlighted, with a large majority of the questions focused on building upon the positives and understanding why employees first joined the organization

Results of Appreciative Approach

My efforts in applying appreciative practices to exit interviews started in the spring of 1995, and continue to be work-in-progress today. So far, I have selectively tried the appreciative exit interview in about half a dozen cases. The one key learning for me has been that old habits are hard to break. It is difficult to get employees who are leaving the organization to stop talking about their suggestions for improvement. These individuals often use the "sandwich" approach to feedback; that is, a negative comment is sandwiched between two positive ones. As an interviewer, it is also difficult to keep focused on the appreciative agenda if your training has ingrained your thinking with the problem-solving model. I found myself wanting to ask about the suggestions brought forward, and having to think about rephrasing my questions to be more appreciative.

Although my experience so far is based on a few interviews — certainly not statistically significant — I have noticed some difference between the two interview approaches. Specifically, the appreciative interviews have resulted in a larger number of positive comments being made by the employee, and the information gathered in these interviews has been more specific. Most notable was that suggestions for improvement in appreciative interviews were limited to three or four, whereas in the traditional interviews, the suggestions provided far outnumbered the factors valued about the company. I believe this is a direct outcome of the questions asked. In fact, an underlying premise of appreciative inquiry is that people create their worlds, and that the questions we ask lead to

what we find, and subsequently to what we imagine. The general nature and the problem-solving tone of the questions asked in traditional interviews lead to general answers, and encourage people to focus on issues that are foremost in their minds; that is, the "cons" they identified in making their decision to leave. In appreciative interviews, the questions are more specific, and employees are asked to identify three suggestions or wishes for enhancing the effectiveness of the organization. The limit of three results in the individual identifying the three most important wishes or suggestions. In reviewing the feedback from the interviews I was also curious about whether suggestions were positively worded. Only one employee stated two of his three suggestions positively. For example, his suggestions were to "increase openness around compensation issues" and "continue to bring the goal of a flat management structure into reality."

When asked about what was valued most about the company, employees in appreciative interviews tended to provide the same answers as employees in traditional interviews. For example, employees mentioned that they valued the people who work in the organization, the company picnics and other events, the additional benefits provided for fitness and recreation, the flex days and extra holidays, and so on. The majority of the comments reflect the extrinsic elements of employment arrangements. With the purposeful nature of appreciative questions, I expected the appreciative interviews to surface more intrinsic responses such as comments about valuing opportunities provided for professional growth, the chance provided to make a difference, being made to feel like part of the team, and others. A human resources trained individual naturally looks for the intrinsic; however, it may be unrealistic to expect individuals to describe what they value about a company from an intrinsic perspective, unless they are purposely seeking to satisfy those needs by moving to another organization. As a result, further probing of the employee's answer is needed to understand the underlying intrinsic factors. As with traditional interviews, the practice of in-depth probing is important with appreciative interviews in order to capture the real essence of the organization.

The question that seemed easiest for employees to answer was the first one asked, that is, what had attracted them to the company. The answers were remarkably consistent regardless of when they had joined the company. The common factor, however, was that they all had resigned shortly following a significant downsizing, and were perhaps disillusioned with the company. These employees talked about how the company had a good reputation in the industry, and how it had been a vibrant, aggressive, and enthusiastic company at the time they joined. All of them also proceeded to talk about how the environment had changed over the years, and that the company needed to recapture the spirit it had shown when they first joined. In traditional interviews, employees rarely talk about why they joined the company, and spend most of their time talking about why they are leaving. In the appreciative interviews, hearing about what attracted employees to the company provided me with a better sense of what these employees valued,

and what had made the company an employer of choice at the time.

A noticeable difference between the two types of interviews was the level of detail provided by appreciative interviews. The questions in the appreciative approach are more purposeful, and result in specific examples. In particular, the question asking the individual to provide an example of when he or she felt most excited, most engaged, most involved in the company led to answers specific to the individual's job and circumstances. A senior manager recounted his experience in managing a project to build a gas plant that achieved success by meeting the high technical standards set at tight cost targets. On the other hand, a more junior employee talked about her experience working on a team in which she was considered a full member of the team, and expected to provide advice to more senior personnel on land administration matters. Both these individuals vividly remembered how they felt at the time.

At this point, although it is inconclusive whether there are substantial benefits from using appreciative practices in exit interviews, I am encouraged enough to continue experimenting further. Reflecting upon my experience so far, I can see some specific areas in the process that can be improved upon. My learnings and ideas for improving the process are listed on the following pages.

LEARNINGS AND IMPROVEMENTS

LEARNINGS	IDEAS AND ACTIONS FOR IMPROVEMENTS
1. I lack experience in using an appreciative approach, and, as a result, lack confidence to rigorously follow through with the approach in an interview where the individual proves unwilling to remain in an appreciative perspective. As a result, I have found myself switching back and forth between the problem solving and appreciative approaches within interviews.	• Continue to practice appreciative interviewing, and commit to follow the interview protocol developed. • Provide an advance copy of the exit interview questions and an explanation of the appreciative approach to allow for adequate preparation by individuals. This also commits me to follow the questions developed. • Make notes on the interview plan or question- naire to ensure focus on appreciative questions and answers.
2. The individual may have a psychological need to distance himself or herself from the organization to ease the transition. As a result, the individual is unwilling and uncommitted to dig deep to talk about what is valued about the organization. Individuals leaving an organization may be afraid to re-live the peak experiences they have had with the organization because of a concern about hav- ing made the wrong decision, or simply do not care any longer about the organization.	• Help individuals with the transition by identify- ing the exit interview as a process for "closing the current chapter", and by sharing in their excite- ment about their new endeavor. • Continue to probe for specifics when superficial answers are provided. • Increase confidence of employees to talk about issues by getting them to talk more about their own accomplishments within the company before moving into organizational issues. • Encourage employees to share experiences by emphasizing the importance of contributions.
3. Appreciative interviews take time. I have found that the one hour allotted for the interviews has not been enough to get to the real core, especially in four topic areas. I originally set the one hour for traditional interviews because it seemed to allow employees to adequately cover the important issues, without making the interview repetitive or allowing for too much "complaint" time.	• Test shortened version of questionnaire which focuses on two topic areas rather than four. • An alternative may be to modify the question- naire to include all four topic areas but limiting the questions within each topic to a maximum of two. • Expand the time allotted for interviews from one hour to one and a half to cover the four topic areas.

LEARNINGS AND IMPROVEMENTS

LEARNINGS	IDEAS AND ACTIONS FOR IMPROVEMENTS
4. The individual lacks experience with an appreciative approach. When people are invited to exit interviews, they expect to be asked problem-solving type questions. The appreciative interview questions take people by surprise, and perhaps make them skeptical in an exit interview situation. Most employees come prepared for the interview with their "suggestions for improvement" sprinkled with a few positives. When using the appreciative questions, I often wonder if employees think the company is skirting the issues or rejecting any "constructive" criticism.	• Provide an advance copy of the interview questions. • Increase the communication about appreciative practices with both exiting employees and senior management. • These practices should decrease anxiety about the interview and make employees more comfortable with the appreciative approach. • Use appreciative approaches in other areas of organizational work, such as team building, so that appreciative methods become a natural part of organizational life.
5. Exit interview feedback, whether collected appreciatively or traditionally, has had little impact on the company. From the appreciative approach, the real value of the data collected from the interview lies in the sharing of the data and the experiences with as many people as possible. At this point, senior managers are the only ones who have access to the information collected. However, management has not noticed a difference in feedback received and has not asked questions about the data. As well, the information is presented to them in written format, which is not as powerful as hearing individuals talk about peak experiences and what is valued about the organization.	• Spread responsibility for exit interviews throughout the company, after providing interviewers with appropriate training in appreciative methods. • Create a new format for exit interview summaries that reflect the appreciative focus instead of highlighting reasons for leaving and suggestions for improvement. • Collect "quotable" quotes from interviews to place on large and visible bulletin boards. The quotes would reflect the spirit of the company, and are symbols of the "gifts" provided to the company from departing employees. • Act upon suggestions by employees. Show the importance to all of the feedback provided. • Engage senior management in the process of developing topic areas so as to create ownership of information collected during exit interviews, and increase the likelihood of changes being implemented.

As I continue my experiments with appreciative exit interviews, new learning will surely develop to help build upon the small successes achieved so far. In turn, recognition of this success will lead to more experimentation and acceptance by others in the organization. **I believe that appreciative inquiry can provide a refreshing alternative in the practice of organizational change.** The exit interview experiment is just a small example of such case. **As people recognize its value, appreciative inquiry is bound to spread like wild fire!**

© L.BOSCH, 1998

References:

Brotherton, P., "Exit Interview Can Provide a Reality Check." *HR Magazine* 41, no. 8 (August 1996) pp. 45-50.

Garretson, P., and Teel, K.S. "The Exit Interview: Effective Tool or Meaningless Gesture?" *Personnel Journal* 59, no. 4 (July/August 1982) pp. 70-77.

Hughes, C.L., PhD, and Flowers, V.S., PhD, "Why Employees Stay is More Critical Than Why They Leave." *Personnel Journal* 66, no. 10 (October 1987) pp. 19-28.

McConnell, Charles R., "The Exit Interview: Locking the Barn Door." *Health Care Supervisor* 11, no. 2 (December 1992) pp. 1-10.

ABOUT THE AUTHOR

LIA BOSCH, is an organization development professional with over 18 years of human resources management and executive experience in private industry. She is an advocate of A.I. philosophy and brings a practical perspective to the application of A.I. in an organizational nad personal context. Taking a strategic and innovative view of organizations, Lia helps her clients identify ways to optimaze both business and human potential.

For more information, contact:
Lia Bosch
Creative Edge Consulting & Books
16 Country Lane Court
Calgary, AB T3Z 1H7
phone and fax: 403.286.2050
e.mail: creative.edge@cadvision.com

I have seen many people die
because life was not worth living. From this I
conclude that the question of life's meaning is
the most urgent question of all.

— CAMUS

CREATING OPPORTUNITIES FOR LEARNING AI

BY MARY CURRAN
AND GAIL WORK

Introduction

One need not be a philosopher to know that Camus was on to something. Had he been an organizational consultant, he may well have been drawn to Appreciative Inquiry as a means of ferreting out life's personal and professional possibilities. Camus' provocative quote and the powerful potential of Appreciative Inquiry (AI) intrigued a group of students at the California Institute of Integral Studies in San Francisco and motivated us to launch an inquiry into this most urgent question of all. Since our class was designed as an introduction to Appreciative Inquiry, our selected topic and the approach used in AI seemed like a great match.

AI is a powerful tool for collaborative exploration. Based on the writings of Suresh Srivastva and David Cooperrider (Srivastva, S., Cooperrider, D., 1992), it was developed out of frustration with the traditional approach to organizational consulting. The traditional approach begins with an awareness of problems and remains in problem-solving mode, seeming to view life as a series of problems to be addressed. Appreciative Inquiry, on the other hand, first looks at an organization when it is functioning at its best rather than focusing immediately on what is considered problematic. This establishes a context of success, positive energy, hopefulness, and a sense of a collectively desired future — a context within which to examine present reality and shared images of the future.

By asking employees to remember a time when they felt the most positive about being involved with the organization, the interviewer facilitates a relationship among the interviewee, the interviewer, and the inquiry process itself. Whereas in a problem-solving model, data proceeds from fearful and discouraging memories, in Appreciative Inquiry, data consists of vital memories of successful, empowering, and energizing experiences. **The Appreciative approach generates energy and excitement as an inquiry progresses: Both interviewer and interviewee alike become more interested and committed along the way.**

Knowing this potential and curious about how best to apply it, students in a seminar on Appreciative Inquiry created a team-based field experience for the participants using Appreciative Inquiry. Our purpose was to document and analyze our findings in order to further refine a curriculum design, a training framework, and a consulting approach. The application was collaboratively designed, and participants considered multiple possible approaches at each stage of the study. For our purpose, the actual content of the study was far less important than the practice field being created to learn more about AI. The practice field was temporary and the stakes were not high; the topic was chosen out of the interest and curiosity of the interviewers.

AI Design

To prepare ourselves for a collaborative type of inquiry, we began the study with an introduction to AI and to a collaborative inquiry process as described by Peter Reason in *Human Inquiry*. In this sourcebook of new paradigm research, Peter Reason and John Rowan state: "We have to learn to think dialectically, to view reality as a process, always emerging through a self-contradictory development, always becoming; knowing this reality is neither subjective nor objective, it is both wholly independent of me and wholly dependent on me. This means that any notion of valid knowledge must concern itself with both the knower and what is known, and be a matter of relationship."

Knowing that our collaborative inquiry essentially would be relationship building, we wanted to choose a topic that would have interest for all of us. We brainstormed themes from the many topics that we considered: *Creating one's life* and the *Integration of self into life and work* were the most intriguing. We combined the two as an inquiry into the freedom/creativity people claim in creating the life they want. Generally speaking, in our exploration of personal-development topics, we are continually encouraged to envision the life we want, as a first step toward recovery, happiness, success, or salvation. Yet within our group, there was a widely held perception that most people struggle just to get by, with little chance to actually live the life they choose. This discussion made our inquiry topic even more inviting.

Realizing that in qualitative research, the researcher is an integral part of the process, we started by brainstorming our initial assumptions about what we would find, developed possible questions, and held a short training for the interviewing process.

The assumptions were not meant to be a part of the interview; rather, they were put aside and referred to after the interview data had been collected. The training format was as follows: As we were all familiar with traditional interviewing methods, we knew that for this nontraditional process, it would be essential to free interviewees from a state of mind of "answering" our questions; instead, we would encourage them to tell their own stories.

We began by asking them to remember a time when ..., rather than have them answer a question. Then we listened and only asked directive questions as needed.

We each then agreed to interview six people who appeared to have led interesting and intentional lives. There were six interviewers, which gave us a total sample of 36 interviews. Since this inquiry was done primarily for the purpose of learning, the criteria we used in selecting interviewees as a life history or lifestyle that indicated directions taken outside of the average, or traditional, choices.

The interview structure was meant to serve as a doorway into the person's meaningful recollections, not just to provide a means of gathering focused data.

Questions reached for the essence of how interviewees made life's choices. At times, this included probing questions meant to lead the story line into an expression of values, and to discover how a person's essential values impact their most important life decisions.

Another key aspect of the project's design was that the team itself generated the interview questions. The rich discussion that crafted the wording, the intention, and the goal of each question enhanced the team's commitment. Crafting the questions together allowed the group to highlight and clarify the focus, scope, and purpose of our inquiry. Some of our best thinking happened during this meeting, a result of the high degree of interest participants had in the content and meaning of the questions, as well as positive anticipation of the AI interviews.

Each interviewer carried this focused intention and enthusiasm into the interview. If the interview questions had been prescribed in advance, the team would have not experienced the excitement and understanding that came out of careful consideration in structuring the interview.

Because this was a practice field created for our own learning, it was not necessary to focus on a client's agenda. For client-centered AI interventions, however, client-generated questions are an essential step in tailoring this process to the client's needs.

After two months, each of us had completed the six interviews and we met again to pool our interview material. **Each of us reported experiencing a deep connection with the interviewees, and a profound experience for both parties, as the interviewer followed the journey of the explorer into the possibilities and limitations of the interview.**

The engaging topic — why a person made his/her most essential choices in life — logically accounted for part of the connection between interviewer and interviewee. And the focus — the most alive times in a person's life — accounted for the depth of the interviews. During this meeting, we recounted our interview experiences, re-evaluated our original assumptions, and looked for themes that had emerged from our interviews.

This was such a powerful research approach for us that we felt the design, process, and results were worth sharing. This project revealed promising results from design nuances that are readily accessible for AI applications. For this reason, we wanted to offer in more detail our methodology, process, findings, and the remaining questions we discovered, in the hopes that therein you will find new possibilities for further research.

Appreciative-Inquiry
Question Construction

In constructing our questions, we were very aware of taking the locus of control away from the inquirer as quickly as possible in order to give free rein to the interviewee. To achieve a fluid nature, our bias was to invite the interviewee into the storytelling mode, without intrusion by the interviewer.

The inquiry was contextualized with this question: "To what extent do you feel you are able to create the life you want?" The interviewee was then asked to remember a time when s/he felt the most able or had the most freedom to create the life s/he wanted. Subsequent leading questions probed further into the experience the interviewee was relating. A natural rhythm developed with the AI interviews, similar in some distinct ways to other forms of interviewing. **Listening for the underlying message, interviewers would pace themselves, being careful not to jump to the next question, but rather, lingering with a thought and leaving time for silence and reflection.**

Awareness of our initial assumptions allowed interviewers to remain vigilant for their own biases. Listening on multiple levels for the essence of the message required watching for body language, listening for change in tone of voice, and moving the inquiry in the direction of the interviewee's own excitement, as they shared the meaning of their life choices.

There were ten interview questions; however, few interviews went beyond two or three because the interviewers were facilitating storytelling, leading and listening rather than directing. In some cases, the full ten questions were addressed, but these interviews tended to be less rich than the ones that focused on the initial few questions. Why was this? Because of the weight of the topic — creation of a meaningful life — a simple answer would not do justice to the question. We sought breadth by soliciting the sequence of life choices, as well as depth by further probing into one or two of those choices.

We asked two types of questions: first, *foundation questions* that made up the inquiry format, and second, *probing questions* that further explored the content and experience of the foundation questions. Some interviewees took longer than others to involve themselves in storytelling, as they preferred a more standard format of questioning. We found it important to be prepared for both types — those who could more easily engage in storytelling and those who considered interviews to be a task to be completed. It was also important to be prepared for some interviews to last well over the initial time estimate. Some interviews went as long as two to three hours, while ordinarily they would last one to one and a half hours. We found that the richest material often came well into the interview, when the interviewee was comfortable with the pacing and the reward of sharing meaningful discourse. Because the sample of interviewees was likely to want to speak to the meaning of life, we rarely had the challenge of the interviewees' going off on tangents. These were people who had already thought about the larger questions of creating a life, so they were generally eager to talk about those choices. The interviews were consistent in remaining focused: When people were asked to speak about their most significant life choices, they tended not to trivialize or sidetrack the story. These were not conversations; they were interviews, with the spotlight on the interviewee's experience, not on answering the questions.

This project was designed to offer participants learning experiences at both the individual and group levels. Adult learning theory clearly shows that learning from doing and learning within groups are highly effective modalities. "Learning, change, and personal growth, according to Lewin's Experiential Learning Model, are facilitated best by a process that begins with an experience followed by the collection of observations about that experience. This information is then analyzed and the resulting conclusion used by the learners to modify their behavior and select new experiences."[1] Meetings provided the group with a learning opportunity, and the inquiry process gave each participant experience in reflecting on what and how they learned.

---

[1] Renner, P., 1994. Originally published in *Experiential Learning: Experience as the Source of Learning and Development* by David A. Kolb. Englewood Cliffs, NJ: Prentice-Hall, 1984, p. 21.)

Storytelling

Storytelling is a powerful tool in the interview process. Normally in a question-and-answer formatted interview, specific information is sought, which keeps the interviewee in the framework of answering the interviewer's questions. Evoking a story from the interviewee's experience, however, turns control over to the storyteller and encourages a deeply personal journey.

Anthropologists generally view storytelling in indigenous cultures as the major means of passing on meaning and tradition. Storytellers were often the tribes' healers, who shared the stories of past lessons to carry forward wisdom through folklore. There are many instances in our own culture in which telling stories — such as after a disaster or a funeral — provides healing and a sense of social connection. Often the most memorable family gatherings include storytelling by the elders, to acknowledge the history and recognize the significant meaning held in shared experiences.

In storytelling, the speaker is less likely to be concerned with whether or not s/he is giving the "right" or "wrong" answer. This contrasts with a prescriptive question, which requires the respondent to structure the answer to conform to the limits of the question. For example, consider the difference between A) "Tell me about a time ..." and B) "What are the top three successes for you ..." The context of storytelling is robust, which is not the case with prescriptive interviews. A prescriptive approach asks for specific extraction of information, while a storytelling approach asks for flow, meaning, and description of both essential and outlying factors that influenced a situation. Through the rich content of the stories, we were able to recognize themes as well as feel the social bonds of relationship being created.

Assumptions

Knowing, from Peter Reason, that reality is neither subjective nor objective, but both wholly independent of us and wholly dependent on us, we began the study by identifying our initial assumptions, and stayed cognizant of these biases during the interviews. Filtering our experiences through the assumptions launched us on three parallel learning tracks: first, the content of the data itself; second, the experience as interviewer; and third, the meta-learning from self-reflection. Later, we revisited our original list of assumptions to compare our expectations with what the data revealed.

• We defined "assumptions" as our biased expectations of what we would hear from the interviews. These assumptions were understood to mean a filter through which we were likely to hear the stories of our interviewees.

• We chose to focus on assumptions as an important interpretive concept because they form the foundation of beliefs, values, and actions. Critical

building blocks of perception, these filters were closely examined to determine the effect they might have on our work.

• Although assumptions are generally unspoken, we made ours conscious by verbalizing them. The resulting environment invited self-reflection and learning through shared disclosure of bias, blind spots, and projections.

• We revisited the initial assumptions when we convened to share our data. The comparison of our first assumptions and the actual data made us realize how much assumptions can change, once they are tested. The gap caused us to look more closely at where the assumptions may have originated.

• Using the assumptions to articulate the attachment the interviewers had to their perspective allowed us to look at how much interviewers might be protective of their assumptions. The degree to which the interviewer was challenged by disconfirming data offered an opportunity to ask why this perspective was important to hold on to.

• After the interaction between interviewer and interviewee, we discussed how our assumptions and beliefs had been affected; this process reinforced the learning stance of the project.

The following list represents our first set of assumptions. The discussion from revisiting the data is in italics.

1. There was a general initial belief that one has to "give up to get" — give up a piece of one's self in order to succeed. One has to risk giving something up in order to succeed. Our population did not generally support or deny this. *A larger sample would show more results, either way, of what we discovered.*

2. Most people feel played upon by life rather than composers of it. *Our research didn't tell us about this, although our sample of interviews was done with people who have a predilection for being self-starters.*

3. People will have a major difficulty connecting reflectively to their lives. *This was not the case in the sample we used; however, this population was selected for a likely ability to be reflective.*

4. People don't see life as an ongoing process but rather as a fragmentation of self-identity, a series of separate chapters. *We found some of this. People tend to compartmentalize their lives; however, this may generalize to a larger population sample.*

Revisiting our assumptions validated for us Peter Reason's exhortation to "think dialectically, to view reality as a process, always emerging through a self-contradictory development, always becoming … ." We found a significant difference between our original assumptions, the findings, and the assumptions generated after the interviews. A return to the list of first assumptions suggested taking a further look at the impact of the process on the researchers as well as the participants. The shift between the initial and the later assumptions was wide enough to indicate that we were as influenced by our assumptions as by what we were hearing. Reading through each original assumption generated rich topical discussion. While we did not discuss in detail the later assumptions, we noted the gap between the two sets of assumptions.

A Few Conclusions

The interview data about creation of a life created an awareness of paradox/duality and an opening to see and learn about "both/and" rather than "either/or." This aspect of the learning came out of discussing the gap between original and the changed assumptions. This ambiguity was helpful in increasing participants' ability to accept and learn from the contradictory data while distilling the themes. Given the need for many organizational members to increase their ability to live with ambiguity and uncertainty in these changing times, the value of this insight became clear.

Themes emerged from the interviews that seemed common to everyone attempting to create a life that is satisfying, creative, and worthwhile. Each of the interviewers looked for repeated themes in the data culled from the six interviews, highlighting words, phrases, or ideas that were repeated within their collection of stories. Before our data-comparison meeting, each of us reviewed the assumptions we had collected before the interviews, to look for confirming or disconfirming evidence of the initial assumptions. A few of the themes follow, others are in Appendix A.

• Initiation into a "life-creating" consciousness requires an entry point or awakening; then there can be interplay between the initiation and further opportunity for the development of this awakening awareness.

• This is an essential process, evoked from the core of being a person, which is experienced as both learned and given. It contains a mysterious, elusive quality and is often both a revelatory process and a spiritual identification.

• It is necessarily a collaborative and social process, requiring that one be able to experience life as relationship.

• An element of service was mentioned frequently, sometimes expressed as the desire to make a contribution that would last over time.

• An ability to live outside the norm seemed to be required — an ability to be authentic to oneself when social acceptance was in question, a capacity to respond rather than react to life. It was noted that people in a minority or less-advantaged group usually have to create their own paths — one not set in advance — because they are born outside of the norm.

• People with a high need for external structure and approval have less sense of being able to create a life. High internal structure may allow for more creativity in composing one's life.

Key learnings

One of the key learnings from this project was that combining the AI research process with documentation of before-and-after assumptions provided a critical step for self-examination. At each stage of the inquiry, interviewers were asked to recall their original assumptions and make note of both confirming and disconfirming data from the interviews. By articulating both the individual and group assumptions at the onset and conclusion of the study, interviewers were invited into a reflective mode, from which to glimpse of their own perspective. This illumination of perception filters led to a further key learning: This AI research approach is different from traditional qualitative research in some distinct ways.

First, assumptions create a *filter* for each participant, allowing them to see movement of their assumptions during the course of the project, and to discuss implications of these changes with other participants. Second, by using a qualitative approach to research, researchers become aware of the biases and perspective s/he brings to the process so that s/he can be an active participant rather than an "objective" observer. If the researcher remains unaware of the assumptions s/he carries, this may distort what is being said. Since AI attempts to build rapport rather than to collect information, interviewers attend as much to the quality of understanding as to the actual data. Third, AI is more than an inquiry — it is also a visioning process. The hope and vision of the interviewee captured in the data collection serve as a foundation for the possibility statements that further refine the group vision.

Finally, by collecting data through the crafting of positively focused questions, interviews highlight the "best and most hopeful" vs. a problem-solving focus. The positive feelings and inspiration that the interviewees are left with have an energy: Herein lies the generative capacity of AI, and the foundation for building a future of possibilities.

Future Applications

The two applications of AI referred to here involved a practice field for our own learning purposes, and work with a not-for-profit community organization. We also see many possibilities for applying AI in the business sector. In a business environment, a work team or department could use Appreciative Inquiry as an introduction tool, to examine and make note of assumptions and later reexamine them. AI could be particularly effective when cross-functional teams are getting started on a new project or just getting to know each other. In the case of mergers or acquisitions, AI could facilitate cultural alignment by forming positive norms at the beginning of work and relationships. As a tool for understanding the whole person, AI goes beyond the social, business, and formal relationships and can quickly create the context for meaningful conversation.

The question of using indigenous vs. imported questions for the inquiry became an intriguing subject for our group. Our topic's relevance to communication and learning and the wording of the questions arose as a possible future research. One of our greatest learnings from this inquiry was that the questions have a power of their own above and beyond the answers. This realization came from the precision with which we crafted the questions, and the conversations that took place as we worked toward these agreements.

Within an organization, the inquiry process could be used to build the AI capacity, to build trust, to collect information, to create readiness for change, to raise cultural awareness, and to enhance the web of relationships. The creation of possibility statements as a form of visioning could be useful in finding and building shared meaning among members. By highlighting what is most energizing and alive in the organization, the AI process takes the spotlight off of a problem-solving mentality. This emphasis on hope, curiosity, and wonder is the foundation of the visioning process.

© M. CURRAN AND G. WORK, 1998

Data Analysis:

The group also identified themes from the interviews in both content and process contexts. Examples of these follow:

CONTENT — A theme originating from the topic of inquiry.
A. To conceptualize the creation of one's life requires resources, intelligence, and self-esteem.

B. This approach allows people to discover connecting points in their life histories, and the opportunity to "tell their story" leads to unleashing this discovery.

C. People of color and those who grew up outside of the norm tended out of necessity to create their lives, as the norm was so often others' construction of reality rather than their own. The norm is defined here as the mainstream lifestyle of the dominant culture. Making choices outside of the norm required external presentation of conformity while developing a separate internal reality.

PROCESS — A theme originating from the use of AI.
A. AI can be used as a continuous, iterative process of checking assumptions against others' perceptions, thus creating an opening to find a new way of seeing. The AI process can create fundamental change. An AI interview can be an empowering experience for the interviewee as well as the interviewer. Having people remember stories provides a sharp contrasting experience to the habit of perceiving in negative and powerless thought patterns.

B. When asked to remember a time when s/he felt free, powerful, competent, or had other positive remembrance, the interviewee stands in a place of strength, which can then be used as a resource. "Learned helplessness," as described by Martin Seligman in *Learned Optimism* (Seligman, M. 1990), is a habit of perceiving in negative and powerless ways. An AI interview offers instead the possibility of learned empowerment and can reinforce self-affirming memories for the interviewee.

References

Crabtree, B. & Miller, W. (1992) *Doing Qualitative Research*, vol. 3, Newbury Park: Sage Publications.

Marshall, C. & Rossman, G. (1995) *Designing Qualitative Research*, Second
Edition, Thousand Oaks: Sage Publications.

May, T. (1993) *Social Research: Issues, Methods & Process*. Buckingham: Open University Press.

Reason, P., (1981) *Human Inquiry*, Wiley, Chichester, England.

Renner, P., (1994) *The Art of Teaching Adults*, Vancouver: Training Associates.

Seligman, M., (1990) *Learned Optimism*, New York: Pocket Books.

Srivastva, S., Cooperrider, D., (1992) *Appreciative Management and Leadership*, San Francisco: Jossey-Bass.

ABOUT THE AUTHORS

MARY CURRAN, PH. D. has worked with appreciative inquiry for the past 10 years in her Organization Development consulting practice of 25 years. She has taught organization development courses at the California Institute of Integral Studies, Pepperdine and JFK University. She is now living in Redwood Valley, Ca. between a Buddhist and a Byzantine monastery as a stained glass artist, a therapist and an organizational consultant and trainer. She considers herself partially retired.

For more information, contact:
Mary Curran
phone: 707.485.5249
fax: 707.485.9390
e.mail: maryc123@sonic.net.

GAIL WORK is a consultant to organizations pursuing strategic change, organizational learning, or team effectiveness. Her work integrates strategic planning with the human impact of change. She offers a participatory approach to groups seeking high-performance change, and customized consulting in work-flow analysis and redesign, team learning, culture change, best practices, and group facilitation.

For more information, contact:
Gail Work
22400 Skyline Blvd. Box 18
Lattonda, CA 94020
phone: 650.948.1707
fax: 650.559.0460
e.mail: g_work@earthlink.net.

THEORY

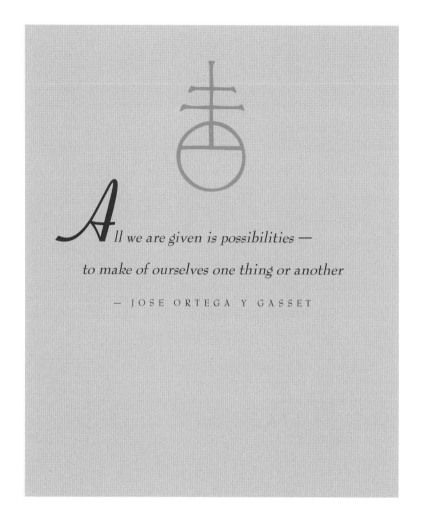

All we are given is possibilities —

to make of ourselves one thing or another

— JOSE ORTEGA Y GASSET

A SPIRITUAL PATH

TO ORGANIZATIONAL RENEWAL

BY GREGORIO BANAGA JR.

While Appreciative Inquiry is considered by many as a methodological process for organizational analysis and development, I believe it is also a "spiritual path", a way to spiritually renew an organization. It embodies a set of attitudes that can shed light on, shape, and give meaning to, every phase of the methodological journey, thus transforming it into a lived Christian spiritual experience. In 1996 I facilitated a strategic planning process for a Catholic religious organization with a team of eight professionals, all members of the same organization. From the beginning, I wanted to use a process that was aligned to the faith-based objectives of the organization, respectful of its traditions and spiritually regenerating for the facilitating team. I chose Appreciative Inquiry. How does one make sense of the inquiry and planning process in the light of Christian faith and spirituality? How can we as a team consider the work we were doing as an expression of our faith and an opportunity to encounter God who inspired the founding of this organization and continues to sustain it even today? How can our intervention into this organization connect us to the wellspring of faith-based values as well as the other life-giving elements that are already present within the organization? These and similar questions guided our process and gave rise to this essay. I offer it as an initial attempt to look at Appreciative Inquiry from a Christian and spiritual perspective.

Appreciative Inquiry: A New Way of Seeing

Appreciative Inquiry is a new way of seeing. Since "beauty is in the eye of the beholder", one has to develop a new eye or rather retrain one's eye to see differently. Jesus alludes to the importance of the eye and its power when he said: *The lamp of the body is your eye. When your eye is sound, then your whole body is filled with light, but when it is bad, then your body is in darkness.* (Luke 11:34; Matthew 6:22)[1] And the English poet William Blake: *"As a man is, so he sees. As the eye is formed, such are its powers."*[2]

The fox in The Little Prince expressed it in another way: *"It is only with the heart that one can see rightly; what is essential is invisible to the eye"* (Saint-Exupery 1971, p. 87). The essence of an organization and the life-giving elements that sustain it often escape the physical, rational, scientific and analytical eye of an observer or consultant. One has to go beneath the surface and with the "eye of the heart", search for the mystery of life.

With an eye made quiet
  by the power
Of harmony,
  and the deep power of joy,
We see into the life of things.[3]

St. Paul refers to a similar appreciative approach in his letters to the Philippians and to the Ephesians: *Finally, brothers, whatever is true, whatever is honorable, whatever is just, whatever is pure, whatever is lovely, whatever is gracious, if there is any excellence and if there is anything worthy of praise, think about these things. Keep on doing what you have learned and received and heard and seen in me. Then the God of peace will be with you.* (Philippians 4:8-9)

May the eyes of (your) hearts be enlightened, that you may know what is the hope that belongs to his call, what are the riches of glory in his inheritance among the holy ones, and what is the surpassing greatness of his power for us who believe... (Ephesians 1: 18-19)

Appreciative Inquiry does not turn a blind eye on "negative" situations or "deficit-oriented" realities in organizations; it does not substitute a "rosy" and "romantic" picture for an "objective" and "realistic" one.
It accepts these realities for what they are — areas in need of conversion and transformation; they are part of "creation (that) is groaning in labor pains," awaiting redemption and liberation from slavery to corruption (Romans 8: 21-23). But AI intentionally shifts the focus of the inquiry and intervention to those realities that are sources of vitality and that manifest the marvels of God within an organization. This approach is based on the convictions that "organizations are the products of the affirmative mind" and that "when beset with repetitive difficulties or problems, (they) need less fixing, less problem-solving, and more reaffirmation – or more precisely, more appreciation" (Srivastva, Cooperrider, 1990).

To contemplate with love is another way of describing an appreciative eye.
To contemplate is to look at attentively and thoughtfully; to consider carefully and at length, to meditate on.[4] Appreciative Inquiry is an act of contemplating an individual or an organization with love, focusing on "what is best" and on "what it can become". The late psychiatrist Victor Frankl (1963) describes how a loving look can impact an individual:
Love is the only way to grasp another human being in the innermost core of his personality. No one can become fully aware of the very essence of another human being unless he loves him. By the spiritual act of love he is enabled to see the essential traits and features of the beloved person; and even more, he sees that which is potential in them; which is not yet actualized but yet ought to be actualized. Furthermore, by his love, the loving person enables the beloved person to actualize these potentialities. By making him aware of what he can be and of what he should become, he makes these potentialities come true (p. 113-4).
St. Mark also narrates how on at least one occasion, Jesus cast a loving glance on a rich man whom he perceived had potential for greatness (Mark 10:21). Indeed, appreciative contemplation builds up individuals and groups.

---

[1] All Scriptural quotations are from *The New American Bible* except where indicated differently.
[2] W. Blake, letter of 23 August 1799. Published in the *Letters of William Blake*.2
[3] W. Wordsworth, Lines Written A Few Miles above the Tintern Abbey, 1798. Published in *Lyrical Ballads*, 1789.
[4] *The American Heritage Dictionary of the English Language*, 3rd Ed.

The art of appreciation does not come easily for those raised in a Western Christian spiritual tradition. For many centuries Christianity has emphasized the deficit/negative side of spirituality that revolved around the doctrines of the fall of Adam and Eve, sin, death, judgment and redemption by Christ. St. Augustine (354-430 AD) started this spirituality of human deficit and debility by his doctrine of "original sin".[5] The classical theological explanation of original sin teaches that every human being is by nature prone to sin and weakness and, consequently in need of redemption. The flip side of this doctrine — that every human person is graced and created in the image and likeness of God (Genesis.1: 26) — was forgotten or at most, received little attention. "What has been most lacking in society and religion in the West for the past six centuries," Matthew Fox (1983) laments, "has been a Via Positiva, a way or path of affirmation, thanksgiving and ecstasy" (p. 33). He suggests the development of "creation spirituality" to straighten this imbalance. "Creation spirituality" affirms that no person enters the world a sinner or an enemy of God. From the first moment of conception, a human being becomes a creature of God, surrounded by unconditional love. Every human being comes into the world as an "original blessing" rather than as an "original sin". We have to recover the concept of "original blessing" which Fox claims "is far more ancient and more biblical a doctrine than original sin and must be the starting point for spirituality" (p. 47-49).

1. Discovery

Appreciative inquiry starts with discovery. This initial phase involves a diligent search for "what is best" in an organization. There may be different ways of doing this. Usually the search includes asking people about what they appreciate most in themselves, when they felt most alive, most committed and most excited about their organization and, their hopes and dreams for their organization. **Interviews and story telling are preferred methods for gathering data because these methods make people get in touch with the human spirit and make them share from the heart.** People love to share because sharing affirms them as human beings. Some start bashful about themselves but once rapport is established, time flies. Often interviews last longer than planned. The collective wisdom and strengths of an organization gradually emerge from these narratives. The inquirer's task is to pull these stories together and highlight the best and the most inspiring ones.

The spirit behind the initial step of discovery is similar to the biblical practice of "interpreting the signs of the times". In Matthew 16: 1-4, Jesus makes this observation:

The Pharisees and Sadducees came, and to test Jesus they asked him to show them a sign from heaven. He answered them, "When it is evening, you say, 'It will be fair weather, for the sky is red.' And in the morning, 'It will be stormy today, for the sky is red and threatening.' You know how to interpret the appearance of the sky, but you can-

not interpret the signs of the times (New Revised Standard Version). In the Old Testament (e.g., the Book of Exodus) "signs" often refers to the "saving deeds" of Yahweh (God). In the New Testament it connotes a demonstrative wonder and is associated with "portents and wonders" (McKenzie 1965). The expression "interpreting the signs of the times" refers to the act of shifting through external appearances and events in order to discover the unseen presence of the Spirit of God. In biblical times both prophets and people used this mode of discernment. The discovery phase is an invitation to "interpret the signs of the times" within a particular context. It is pinpointing and emphasizing the marvels of God's presence and action within an organization.

This preliminary phase often evokes a sense of awe, wonder and reverence at what the Spirit is doing within an organization. One can then consider it as a sort of sacred ground that should be tread with reverence because within its boundaries are signs of God's work among human beings: generosity, industriousness, goodwill, commitment, creativity, synergy, bonding, integrity, leadership, etc. Organizations are the handiwork of God who inspires the human imagination to create them. *"You have made all your works in wisdom"* (Psalm104: 24). A perceptive inquirer will always find signs of life and hope even in organizations that struggle with difficulties or problems.

"Give thanks to the Lord for he is good, for his kindness lasts forever" (Psalm 106:1).
A feeling of gratitude accompanies appreciation. One who brings to light the "best of what is" in an organization cannot but see how blessed an organization is. The recollection of the past and present often reveals other covert "blessings" in the form of unrecognized talents and untapped potentials. **Inquiry affirms the good that is present and unleashes potentials, thus giving people reasons to be grateful.**
"Everything God created is good; nothing is to be rejected when it is received with thanksgiving..." (1 Timothy 4:4).

Appreciation leads to faith, hope and love. Acknowledging the "best" in people reinforces belief in one's abilities and faith in others, which are foundations of esprit de corps, partnership and teamwork. Affirmation likewise sparks hope in the future of the organization and begets loyalty and commitment.

---

5 Jewish and Christian scholars affirm the absence of the concept of original sin in the Old Testament. M. Fox (1983), *Original Blessing: A Primer in Creation Spirituality.* Santa Fe: Bear & Co. See also R. McBrien (1980), *Catholicism*, NM: Winston Press, pp. 162-167.

2. Dreaming

It will come to pass in the last days, God says, 'that I will pour out a portion of my spirit upon all flesh. Your sons and your daughters shall prophesy, your young men shall see visions; your old men shall dream dreams' (Acts 2:17).

Dreaming about the future of the organization is the next step in the process. After inquiring into the "best of what is" one sets sights on "what could be" or possibilities. The heart of the appreciative process is the construction of a desired and compelling image of the future. Every organization contains within itself latent possibilities that are like seeds waiting to burst to life. *"Without vision, people perish"* (Proverbs 29:18). *A positive image of a future state (a "dream") can ignite the imagination of people, arouse action and call forth commitment* (Srivastva, Cooperrider 1990).

The imagination, more than direct appeal to minds and wills, becomes most important at this stage. Wilder (1976) asserts that *"human nature and human societies are more deeply motivated by images and fabulations than by ideas. This is where power lies and the future is shaped."*

Jesus knew the power of imagery and employed it often in his preaching. At the inception of his public ministry he declared his mission in graphic and dynamic images: *The Spirit of the Lord is upon me, because he has anointed me to bring glad tidings to the poor. He has sent me to proclaim liberty to captives and recovery of sight to the blind, to let the oppressed go free, and to proclaim a year acceptable to the Lord* (Luke 4: 18-19).

The evangelist Luke later commented how *"all eyes in the synagogue looked intently at him"* and how *"all spoke highly of him and were amazed at the gracious words that came from his mouth"* (Luke 4: 21-22). Vast throngs of people were so captivated by the vision of life that he preached about that they followed him (Luke 6:17; 11:29; 23:27; Matthew 4:25).

He saw greatness in every person and showed his would-be followers a vision that was inspiring and empowering. *"Follow me and I will make you fishers of men,"* He told a group of fishermen as He walked along the Sea of Galilee. They immediately dropped their nets and followed him (Matthew 4:18-22). In describing the future — the Kingdom of God — he employed familiar yet attractive metaphors and images. He likened it to a buried treasure and a pearl (Matthew 13:44-46), to a mustard seed (Mark 4:30-32), and to a wedding feast (Matthew 22:1-14). The disciple John writing for a different audience uses another type of imagery to describe what awaits us in the future:

Then I saw a new heaven and a new earth. The former heaven and the former earth had passed away, and the sea was no more. I also saw the holy city, a new Jerusalem, coming down out of heaven from God, prepared as a bride adorned for her husband. I heard a loud voice from the throne saying, "Behold, God's dwelling is with the human race. He will dwell with them and they will be his people and God himself will always be with them (as their God). He will wipe every tear from their eyes, and there shall be no more death or mourning, wailing or pain, (for) the old order has passed away" (Revelation 21:1-4). Christians believe this vision of the future is already here but will be fully realized in the next life.

The visioning phase is a participation in the task of creating the earthly city of God. Through the creative use of our imagination we become partners and fellow workers with God in giving birth to organizations that reflect the values of the Kingdom such as truth, life, justice, love and peace (1 Corinthians 3: 9).

Crafting an organization's future requires the freedom of the imagination.[6] **The imagination cannot soar if the memory of the past or the limited horizon of present possibilities or fear of an uncertain future weighs it down.** Painful memories of failed plans; chaotic structures and persistent problems can restrict the visioning process. **Skeptical and cynical remarks like, "it cannot be done" or "it is not worth trying again" or "what is this, another fad?" can dampen bold dreams and high hopes.** One must be on guard against critical and depreciating talk within the organization. We have to liberate the memory that ties us to the past and begin living out of our imagination in order to see possibilities.

Success can also thwart visioning. The success of present plans and satisfaction with structures and processes can often lull us to complacency. There is a need to let go of "success" and to challenge the organization to take risks, to shift gears, and to leave the comfort zone. Success stories are leverages for growth, not deadweights.

Fear and self-doubt can also clip the wings of possibilities. It is not easy to leave well-known routes for unexplored paths. The possibility of failure scares people to be less daring and imaginative with the future. Self-doubt dampens boldness and makes people "realistic" and "reasonable". St. Paul reminds Christians not to "fall back into fear" because they are led by the mighty power of the "Spirit of God" (Romans 8: 14-15).

The articulation of a vision is creativity in action. It is not to be identified with daydreaming or the idle use of the imagination. Nor is it an exercise in futility similar to "building castles in the air." It is an act that is firmly rooted in the reality of an organization, in the "best of what is". Dreaming is the first act of giving birth to a new organizational reality. While dreaming may connote the creation of something external to a person or a group, it can be a deeply transforming process. One becomes what she or he creates. A sense of excitement and anticipation characterizes this

---

[6] I am indebted to the Movement for a Better World for some of the ideas in this section and in other parts of this essay.

phase of the process. God through human effort and cooperation is giving birth to something new. *Lo, I am about to create new heavens and a new earth. The things of the past shall not be remembered or come to mind. Instead, there shall always be rejoicing and happiness in what I create* (Isaiah 65:17-18).

3. Design/Dialogue

At this stage of the process the vision — usually conceived by a small group or a committee within an organization — is brought back to the entire organization. The purpose is to give the members an opportunity to look at it in order to see whether it truly represents their aspirations for the organization. This process involves dialogue at different levels of the organization until a shared vision develops.

Dialogue thrives on diversity. It is premised on the belief that each of us is different and that it is our uniqueness that fuels and enriches dialogue. Covey (1996) writes: *"If two people have the same opinion, one is unnecessary. I don't want to communicate with someone who agrees with me. I want to communicate with you because you see it differently. I value the difference."* (Monthly Compass, 1996) Genuine dialogue builds organizations. It satisfies the human hunger to be understood, to be affirmed, to be valued, and to be appreciated. (Covey 1989, p. 241). St. Paul encouraged dialogue to build the Church, the community of Christ gathered in faith, hope and love.

But speaking the truth in love, we must grow up in every way into him who is the head, into Christ, from whom the whole body, joined and knit together by every ligament with which it is equipped, as each part is working properly, promotes the body's growth in building itself up in love...Let no evil talk come out of your mouths, but only what is useful for building up, as there is need, so that your words may give grace to those who hear. (Ephesians 4:15-16 New Revised Standard Version) Moreover Jesus pledged to be present among those who engage in dialogue in his name: *"Where two or three are gathered in my name there I am in their midst"* (Matthew 18:20).

Using dialogue to create a shared vision empowers people to achieve their goals. Members of an organization who come together to interact and to design a shared future, unleash synergy. Synergy means that the power of the whole is greater than the sum of the individual parts. Its force lies in valuing differences, in respecting them, and in building on them.

The search for a shared vision connects people; it binds them to a common cause and a journey, giving them the strength and determination to carry on in the midst of difficulties. There is power when everyone shares in a common vision.

4. Delivery

The final step in the process is delivery or action planning. It involves deliberating, deciding and planning the most appropriate steps to take in order to move the organization from its present situation to its desired ideal. This is a step where one has to address the *means* needed to *deliver* the goal. *Means* refers to processes to achieve objectives; it answers questions related to *how to.*

The transition from "where we are" to "where we want to be" is very critical. One has to search for innovative ways or strategies to move the organization closer to the ideal. The issue of speed and quality of changes must also be addressed. **Moving too fast may create unhealthy tension and instability within the organization; moving too slowly may cause frustration and apathy.** One has to hold these extremes in creative tension and take many other things into consideration in making decisions. For this, some kind of "organizational wisdom" or prudence is needed. In advising his disciples on prudence Jesus tells them to be *"shrewd as serpents and simple as doves"* (Matthew 10:16).

There are often several routes to reach a particular objective or goal. Some are better than others are. One has to discern the most appropriate path to take. From a faith perspective, discernment is the art of looking at a particular situation in order to discover the Will of God in the practical choices that have to be made. Authentic discernment in St. Paul's mind presupposes transformation of the mind:

Do not conform yourselves to this age but be transformed by the renewal of your mind, that you may discern what is the will of God, what is good and pleasing and perfect (Romans 12:2).

Planning can start once goals are determined. Planning is a series of choices that are logically sequenced and aimed at reaching a goal. **There should be nothing haphazard in it because the future of an organization is at stake.** It requires anticipation and discipline. Jesus counsels planning before initiating any endeavor. *Which of you wishing to construct a tower does not first sit down and calculate the cost to see if there is enough for its completion? Otherwise, after laying the foundation and finding himself unable to finish the work the onlookers should laugh at him and say, 'This one began to build but did not have the resources to finish.' Or what king marching into battle would not first sit down and decide whether with ten thousand troops he can successfully oppose another king advancing upon him with twenty thousand troops? But if not, while he is still far away, he will send a delegation to ask for peace terms* (Luke14: 28-32).

Planning is grounded in hope – hope in the strengths of an organization: the achievements of the past, the successes of the present and the possibilities of the future. It is based on a firm belief that God who sustained the organization in the past will always be present among his people. *"I am with you always until the end of time" (Matthew 28:20).*

Some attitudes such as courage and commitment should accompany visioning and planning. **Courage makes one ingenious and determined to overcome obstacles in the pursuit a goal.** *"Whatever you can do, or dream you can, begin it. Boldness has genius, power and magic in it"* (Goethe). A Christian can rely on an additional source of courage: God's power already at work in the world. *Now to him who is able to accomplish far more than all we ask or imagine, by the power at work within us, to him be glory in the church and in Christ Jesus to all generations, forever and ever...* (Ephesians 3: 20-21).

Finally, there is need for commitment. It is the driving force behind implementation. Without it the most ambitious plans remain in paper. Commitment means doing whatever it takes to cause something to happen. It implies discipline and sacrifice. In Christian spirituality, this is where carrying the cross and losing one's life comes into play. (Mt. 10:38) Sometimes it may even entail unexpected sacrifice. (John 21: 15-19) Commitment means to keep one's focus on the goal and not to turn back. *"No one who sets a hand to the plow and looks to what was left behind is fit for the kingdom of God."* (Luke 9:62)

Conclusion

Appreciative Inquiry is much more than a technical and methodological tool for organizational analysis and effectiveness. Undertaken in a spirit of faith and informed by Christian Scriptures, it can become a powerful means for corporate spiritual renewal.

© G. BANAGA JR., 1998

ABOUT THE AUTHOR

GREGG BANAGA, JR. is a Filipino Roman Catholic priest and a doctoral candidate in Organizational Behavior at Case Western Reserve University, Cleveland, Ohio. He was the East Asia Coordinator of the Movement for a Better World (an NGO affiliated with the United Nations) for many years and did consulting work for parishes, dioceses and religious organizations in some Asian countries. Presently he works for the Philippine American Ministry in the Diocese of Cleveland.

For more information, contact:
Gregg Banaga Jr.
959 San Marcelimo St
Box 2013, Ermita, Manila, Philippines 1000
phone: 63.522.0016 and 63.524.2011
fax: 63.400.0923
e.mail: glbanaga@hotmail.com

References

Blake, W. *Letters of William Blake* (23 August 1799). Microsoft CDROM Bookshelf '95. Also in Columbia Dictionary of Quotations. NY: Columbia University Press, 1993.

Covey, S. (1989). *The seven habits of highly effective people.* NY: Simon and Schuster. (1996). Weekly compass.

Fox, M. (1983). *Original blessing: A primer in creation spirituality.* Santa Fe: Bear & Co.

Frankl, Victor. (1963). *Man's search for meaning From death camp to existentialism.* Boston: Beacon Press.

McKenzie, J. (1965). *Dictionary of the Bible.* Milwaukee: Bruce Publishing Co.

Saint-Exupery, A. (1971). *The little prince.* NY: Harcourt Brace Jovanovich, Inc.

Senge, P. (1990). *The fifth discipline: The art and practice of the learning organization.* NY: Doubleday Currency.

Srivastva, S. & Cooperrider, D. (1990). *Appreciative management and leadership: The power of positive thought and action in organizations.* San Francisco: Jossey-Bass.

The American Heritage Dictionary of the English Language. 3rd Ed.

The New American Bible, St. Joseph Edition, 1970.

Wilder, A. (1976). *Theopoetic: Theology and the religious imagination.* Philadelphia: Fortress Press.

Wordsworth, W. Lyrical Ballads, 1789. *Columbia Dictionary of Quotations.* NY: Columbia University Press, 1993.

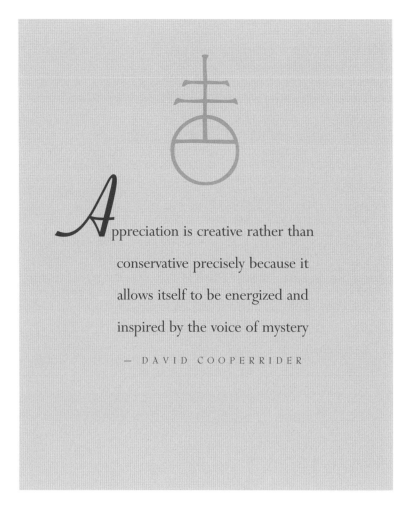

Appreciation is creative rather than conservative precisely because it allows itself to be energized and inspired by the voice of mystery

— DAVID COOPERRIDER

CROSS CULTURAL
EXILE INTO AI

BY KEN MURRELL

Introduction

This chapter will focus on the background of the concept known in the U.S. as "appreciative inquiry". Special attention is given to the historical roots I experienced in both the intellectual contributions of Sir Geoffrey Vickers and in the application of a process parallel to AI practiced by development professionals in the Middle East and Africa 20 years ago. The applied approach, developed by the Coverdale group of the UK (Taylor, 1979) was based on finding and documenting successful practices and interventions used to assist rural development projects, particularly small village development. I also include a set of core assumptions that I believe are implicit in the emerging theory of AI and a sampling of cases where I tested and developed my assumptions.

International and Intellectual Roots of AI

Intellectual roots of AI for me go back to the work of Sir Geoffrey Vickers, who could be compared to the current English writer Charles Handy. His published work became available in the late 50's and early 60's. As a new OD professional in the early 70's I was particularly taken by two of Vickers more influential, though not widely known books. Reading his *Art of Judgement* and *Freedom in a Rocking Boat: Changing Values in an Unstable World* helped me and many others at that time to form a new understanding of the concept of *appreciation*. Vickers notion of appreciation was:

"The appreciated world is selected by our interests; for only some interest would lead us to notice any of its constituents" (Vickers, 1965)

What I understood from his work was that there is only the appreciated world because that is what we choose to see. If a better world is desired, then we should start to pay special attention to the elements of our world, which are already better. Let us pay attention, i.e., *appreciate*, that of the world we can value along with that which we feel must change. This positive expectation was a core dimension of Vickers work as well as a clear description of how what we appreciate becomes what we can see more clearly, through a deeper level of understanding and acceptance.

I was highly influenced by Vickers and at the same time; I read an emerging literature best represented by the very popular work, *The Social Construction of Reality* by Berger and Luckman.

This new way of seeing science was also well articulated by Thomas Kuhn's notion of scientific paradigms as developed in *The Structure of Scientific Revolutions*. He shows how one could have considerable influence over the nature of reality one was experiencing if the worldview they live within led one into believing and thus seeing a certain set of assumptions about what is accepted as normal. **If that were possible why not go about choosing to see as well as trying to create more humane and satisfying worlds for ourselves?**

Fortunately for me a few years later in 1977, I was living in Cairo, Egypt and given a chance to use these theories. **Anthropologists claim that leaving one's home culture is often what it takes to better understand the culture you were raised in.** This experience and the "new" theory led me to dramatically restructure how I thought about the whole field of OD. I, like so many others I know, ended up learning far more about my professional role and myself by being very far from home.

The Assumptions of the Expert

Leaving the country was an easy decision. Giving up my assumptions about the importance of being the OD expert was not as easy. Living and working outside my home culture, it became abundantly clear that there were many different ways of seeing and making sense of the world. In Egypt where civilization dates back several thousand years before Europe, it was imperative for

me to see and appreciate what this historical record meant to the assumptions I brought to my role as a change agent and professor.

I was a product of work and educational bias reflected in the common western management fixation with problem solving. I believed in process consulting ala Schein (1969) and others but I had never truly appreciated how deep the problem solving emphasis negatively affected relationships even when finessed with process. Within this world-view, it is very easy to be seduced into thinking you are the expert bringing the gift of OD to the world, particularly when the audience also expects that of you. **As an outsider I had to learn quickly to suspend judgement and observe, as any good process consultant should do.** I also had to learn to ask to be educated. In learning to seek out that, which should be appreciated, I became educated, and my relationships were built on mutual respect. Such are the learnings from being far from home and open enough to try humility when arrogance is too often expected

I also found that trying to practice an honorable and ethical form of OD without knowing the local situation simply demands taking on the responsibility to learn long before I began to make recommendations and in many cases before I attempted to offer feedback. And in cultures where time is valued enough to allow this to occur, the relationships formed and work done is of a significant qualitative difference. Time in these parts of the world is far more valuable than money.

ASSUMPTIONS

• OD is first and last a human relationship based activity. If in starting to form that relationship I begin with a critique I may never be able to see and appreciate the local situation for what it is and can be.

• People can be very gracious to an outsider, and even one who is bent on discovering all their problems, but very little will be accomplished once that rather obnoxious outsider gets on his or her jet to return home.

• Problem oriented consulting done outside one's home culture is much like the impact the carpetbaggers from the north had on the south following the civil war. Of course they had authority but they lacked any real influence because of their aggressive style and arrogance and it took generations to have their agenda given the least bit of respect.

• In many non-industrialized countries the role of work in how they live their lives is less important than spiritual and family roles. This differs greatly from my observations of the addictive behavior of work in the western world-view.

• Long term sustainable development is not built from short-term problem fixing and we are very limited in our work if we cannot commit to staying longer than a quick visit. I have seldom seen any OD consultant accomplish anything if the person is not able to invest him or herself in the situation for a significant period of time.

• People tend to trust and respect visiting consultants who don't have all the answers but show genuine interest and empathy for their situation. Appreciative eyes and ears go much further than quick wit and brilliant diagnoses. Paying attention to what has worked is often the most powerful intervention in that it helps raise local respect and build a strong foundation for the future.

• Finally, great harm can be done by anyone who is so presumptuous to assume they will have any real impact on human systems that have taken generations to form. This is particularly true in the way of local politics and in appreciating how one's visit might simply be used as a power play that the outsider has no way to decipher.

A Sampling of AI Oriented Cases

My experience with an appreciative frame in both Egypt and Sudan in the seventies, centered on mobilizing local groups and villages to document and then share the successful practices each location had developed over the years. In some cases these were managerial and technical improvements, for example in irrigation or harvesting methods. I was able to learn how important this was for forming relationships and contacts that respected and appreciated the local situation. From this my OD work evolved in many different forms.

A few years later (1983-92) I found myself working for the UN Development Program (UNDP) on missions to Gambia, Kenya, Somalia, and Ethiopia. **In each case I took what I considered a combination of process consulting based models and a highly appreciative stance to conduct a series of interventions focused on helping to develop the capacity of local Management Development Institutes.** A local partnership team was developed whose purpose was to evaluate and recommend what the UNDP and the host country could do to strengthen the capacity and sustainability of their development activities. In these cases the focus of attention was placed on the unique strengths and successes already experienced in order to build an even stronger future state. Many times this caught several stakeholders off guard because the traditional approach had been aimed at finding problems and evaluating individuals.

Both aims of the UN evaluative work, to assist and to audit, were accomplished but the evaluative steps were redefined as preliminary findings where the local staff was given a chance to immediately design improved measures to respond to their unmet challenges (Murrell, 1993). Giving the local leadership an early chance to address the issues and start forming solutions from what they knew they could do well put a double emphasis on finding what had worked as well as building commitments in discovering more successful practices.

Working collaboratively to both collect and to examine the records and the history of events was a method I often used. First, I built a team of local researchers to be a part of the evaluation process instead of conducting the evaluation as an inquisition. In this way the critical elements of the report were formed as catalysts for change proposals on how to design better future states. **Considerable attention was given to the successful practices, and given the nearly impossible conditions many of these projects were formed under, these successes were quite significant.** We encouraged the public display and open discussion of the lessons learned and in a few cases helped to write up these lessons for publication. In all countries the local staff was treated with respect, and attention focused on all their good work wherever it could be found. Having lived in these environments myself, as had the other team members, it was easier to recognize the hurdles placed on these projects and very important to offer encouragement and affirmation.

Over the years of doing management development and administrative work in the places I frequently traveled, the toughest cases were in Ethiopia, Somalia and Yugoslavia. **Those cases were several levels more difficult than anything I had ever experienced in the West because management decisions at times were a life and death issue, not just a career issue. To be a good manager anywhere in the world is asking a lot, to do so in non-industrialized and less than affluent setting is asking for a heroic capacity.** I learned to appreciate them and the role of spiritual and family support necessary to be a good manager.

In Ethiopia I was asked to evaluate the management development programs of an Institute that was formed under one government, lived through and even continued working throughout a very difficult period under another regime, and then was in the midst of the formation of a completely new government as the evaluation project was taking place (Murrell, 1992). Through all of this; programs were offered, managers assisted and a respectable management development institute was developed that worked with professionals from around the world. If you can appreciate the amount of change that has occurred in this country from the Haile Selasie period through the communist regime of Mengistu and into a new coalition government and the creation of two countries where there once was one, you can begin to understand the special qualities of many managers from worlds where chaos is more than an interesting new theory.

In my role as a program and project evaluation consultant for the UN and the U.S. Agency for International Development I learned to look for the critical strengths of a system. I did this through in-depth interviews, often over coffee or in some more relaxed setting. I also used young well-educated professionals who as graduate students were willing to work with me to learn as I paid them a reasonable salary in their local economic terms. At some point problem issues were normally raised but the difference in response was quite amazing. When the right appreciative tone was set and mutual respect built in, the energy to correct deficiencies and improve methods came. **Using a team based appreciative stance in contrast to an outside evaluator role, the chance to really learn what had occurred and what potential existed was increased.** In every case it was important to work with as many local managers and government officials as possible. I often insisted that the meetings and discussions be conducted in the local language. A local team member would brief the team members without the language skills, on what we needed to understand. When we did this in Somalia it was literally the first time the local language had been used and the group did an excellent job of keeping us informed. More importantly, the work created in this form became something they owned and not just a glossy copy of one more outsider's report.

I also conducted team-building exercises
where my trust for the team and the team
leadership was again demonstrated by
insisting the work be done in their language.
I facilitated and helped the team leader but the
team owned the process (Murrell and Valsan,
1985). All involved had experienced outside evaluation tensions before and had witnessed how
often this produced nothing more than denial or
defensiveness. In each of the cases using an
appreciative stance, it was apparent that after the
evaluation, the local group still had the desire as
well as the capacity to improve and commit to the
projects they had created.

Another group of development experts using a
similar practice of sharing successes was the
Institute of Cultural Affairs, which is the subject of
an AI case just published in *the OD Practitioner*
by Tojo Thatchenkery. Back in the 70's the ICA
had projects in nearly every time zone around the
world and though their formal process was not
then defined as an appreciative model it contained some early features. **I was particularly
impressed with its work with song and celebration. As Ron Lippitt often said, the cele-
bratory event is a basic ritual not practiced
nearly enough.** Today the Global Excellence in
Management program funded by our US Agency
for International Development and led by David
Cooperrider, Jane Watkins and others is doing
some amazing work by gathering together people
who have learned to accomplish everyday miracles in very difficult situations.

Closer to Home

Over the last three years I've worked with several
different hospitals and health care systems that are
experiencing nearly as much stress and turmoil as my
African managers had to deal with. In each case the
approach I used was to design an intervention using
an appreciative stance. In the most dramatic case, I
was asked to serve as the sole external consultant to
a 500-bed hospital facing serious competition in
what was labeled then, at the height of the re-engineering frenzy, a re-engineering project. Quickly the
executive level sponsor group agreed to put the
emphasis not on downsizing but on restructuring the
whole hospital operating process. We set out to do
this with 100% staff involvement. Three large teams
of managers were assigned to carefully review each
operation of the hospital from patient input; treatment
and output oriented functions rather than from the
traditional flow of separate activities designed around
particular specialties. **Over the next four months
everything possible was done to help the teams
carefully consider all the strengths and capabilities currently existing and to then design a new
future state of operating at a much improved
level.** The appreciative side of this activity was built
on a commitment to the people in the organization
and an agreement by senior management to provide
all the help and assistance needed by the design
teams to do their work.

All through this process the issue of what was working well was blended with bench marking other system's examples of successful practices. This was not
conducted as a problem to be fixed but as a way to
reinvent health care delivery in a rapidly changing
environment. The dedication and skill of the 40-60

managers devoted to the design effort was greatly appreciated by the hospital community. The impact of the redesign was minimal on staffing levels as compared to many so-called re-engineering projects driven by outside consultants. One of the most useful elements of the whole process was in confirming to the managerial staff that they could indeed determine more of their own fate rather than have a group of external consultants determine it for them.

Lessons Learned

To learn some of life's more valuable lessons often takes a rather long journey. Being an exile to a distant and strange land paid off well for me. The route to learning more about AI is not necessarily in the physical journey but in the journey to redirect one's perspective from a dominant problem solving focus towards a philosophy of collective empowerment where the visions we dream for a better organization can be achieved by working together. Finding the soul and spirit within systems is critical for renewing the motivation to help an organization develop further and that all starts with a full and deep appreciation of what already is. To reach for the stars and to create the futures we aspire to starts with us seeing and appreciating how much distance we have traveled and in setting our shared goals to go even further. As each new successful case is described we increase our options for how to use AI in our lives and in our work with organizations around the world.

Within this book, I am confident we are building the knowledge base for even more exploration. I personally am very excited about this journey and to discover how many others are engaged in traveling some of these same roads. **Appreciative Inquiry is also an inquiry on itself.** It is this reflective and in particular self-reflective form that is so important. As we begin a new century it is comforting to know we always have at our fingertips the lessons from the past thousands of years to learn from. One of the most important things I believe is for us to learn to value what we have achieved and to deeply appreciate how far we have come. With that energy I feel like staying in this OD profession well into the future and find that even our concern for whether our computers can manage a date change pales in comparison to what we can accomplish given the record of accomplishments our human species has so far achieved.

ABOUT THE AUTHOR

KEN MURRELL is Professor of Management at the University of West Florida in Pensacola. He is also president of Empowerment Leadership Systems, a consulting firm working with a large variety of organizations. His most recent interest is in combining the values of community and spirit in organizations. Ken has traveled and worked in more than 50 countries and has consulted with the United Nations Development Programs for more than ten years. He is co-author with Judith F. Vogt of *Empowerment in Organizations: How to Spark Exceptional Performance* (Pfeiffer & Co, San Diego, 1990), and author of over 80 articles, reviews and technical reports. Ken is a part of the Taos Institute and co-authored *Empowering Employees* (McGraw Hill, 2000).

For more information, contact:
Ken Murrell
3149 Deep Water Circle,
Milton FL 32583
phone and fax: 850.474.2308
e.mail: Kmurrell@earthlink.net

References

Bellman, Geoffrey (1990). *The Consultant's Calling.* San Francisco: Jossey Bass.

Berger, Peter & Luckman, Thomas (1966). *The Social Construction of Reality.* Garden City, N.Y. Doubleday.

Kuhn, Thomas S. (1970) *The Nature of Scientific Revolutions.* 2nd Edition, University of Chicago Press, Chicago, IL.

Murrell, Kenneth L. (1993) "Action Research and Evaluation in The Gambia, West Africa," *International Journal of Public Administration,* Vol. 16, No. 3, pp. 341-356.

Murrell, Kenneth L. (1997) "Emergent Theories of Leadership for the Next Century: Towards Relational Concepts." *Organization Development Journal,* Vol. 15, no. 3.

Murrell, Kenneth L. (1992) *"Evaluation Mission Report on United Nations Development Program for Strengthening of the Ethiopian Management Institute",* ETH 016/019.

Murrell, Kenneth L. (1993) "Process Consulting Guidelines for Development Assistance, with Case Study (Somalia)." Chapter in Handbook of *Organizational Consultation* edited by Robert R. Golembiewski, published by Marcel Dekker, Inc., New York.

Murrell, Kenneth L. (1985) "A Team Building Workshop As An Organization Development Intervention in Egypt," co-authored with Dr. A. H. Valsan, American University in Cairo. *Leadership and Organization Development Journal,* Vol. 6, No. 2.

Schein, Edgar. (1969). *Process Consultation: Its Role in Organization Development,* Addison Wesley, Reading, Mass.

Taylor, Max. (1979). *Coverdale on Management,* Heinemann, London.

Thatchenkery, Tojo J. (1996) Affirmation as Facilitation: A Postmodernist Paradigm in Change Management. *OD Practitioner.* Vol. 28 no. 1.

Vickers, Sir Geoffrey. (1965). *The Art of Judgement.* New York, Basic Books.

Vickers, Sir Geoffrey. (1970). *Freedom in a Rocking Boat.* Middlesex, England, Penguin Press.

Vogt, Judy and Murrell, Kenneth L. (1990) *Empowerment In Organizations: How to Spark Exceptional Performance,* Pfeiffer, San Diego.

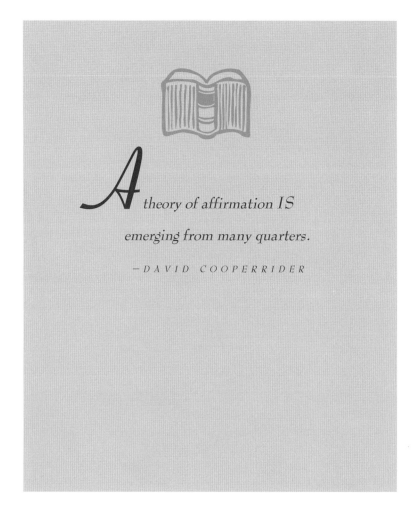

A theory of affirmation IS

emerging from many quarters.

—DAVID COOPERRIDER

RESOURCES

BY DAWN DOLE

Resources

Barrett, F. J. (1995). Creating Appreciative Learning Cultures. *Organizational Dynamics,* 24(1), 36-49.

Barrett, F. J. (1998). Creativity and Improvisation in Jazz and Organizations: Implications for Organizational Learning. *Organization Science,* 9(5). 605-622

Barrett, F. J., & Cooperrider, D. L. (1990). Generative Metaphor Intervention: A New Approach to Intergroup Conflict. *Journal of Applied Behavioral Science,* 26(2), 223-244.

Bowling, C., Ludema, J., & Wyss, E. (1997). *Vision Twin Cities Appreciative Inquiry Report. Cleveland,* Ohio: Case Western Reserve University, Department of Organizational Behavior.

Bunker, B. B. (1990). Appreciating Diversity and Modifying Organizational Cultures: Men and Women at Work. In S. Srivastva, D. L. Cooperrider, & Associates (Eds.), *Appreciative Management and Leadership: The Power of Positive Thought and Action in Organizations* (1st ed., pp. 126-149). San Francisco, CA: Jossey-Bass Inc.

Bushe, G. R. (1995). Advances in Appreciative Inquiry as an Organization Development Intervention. *Organization Development Journal,* 13(3), 14-22.

Bushe, G. R., & Coetzer, G. (1995). Appreciative Inquiry as a Team Development Intervention: A Controlled Experiment. *Journal of Applied Behavioral Science,* 31(1), 13-30.

Bushe, G. R., & Pitman, T. (1991). Appreciative Process: A Method for Transformational Change. *Organization Development Practitioner,* 23(3), 1-4.

Chaffee, P. (1997 Fall). Ring of Breath Around the World: A Report of the United Religions Initiative Global Conference. *United Religions, A Journal of the United Religions Initiative* (4).

Chaffee, P. (1997). *Unafraid of the Light: Appreciative Inquiry and Faith Communities* (Unpublished Manuscript). Interfaith Center at the Presido: San Francisco, CA.

Chin, A. (1998). Future Visions. *Journal of Organization and Change Management,* (Spring).

Collins, James., & Porras, Jerry (1994). *Built to Last.* New York: Harper Business

Cooperrider, D. L. (1986). *Appreciative Inquiry: Toward a Methodology for Understanding and Enhancing Organizational Innovation.* Unpublished Doctoral Dissertation, Case Western Reserve University, Cleveland, Ohio.

Cooperrider, D. L. (1990). Positive Image, Positive Action: The Affirmative Basis of Organizing. In S. Srivastva & D. L. Cooperrider (Eds.), *Appreciative Management and Leadership: The Power of Positive Thought and Action in Organizations.* San Francisco, CA: Jossey-Bass.

Cooperrider, D. L. (1995). Introduction to Appreciative Inquiry. In W. French & C. Bell (Eds.), *Organization Developement* (5th ed.,): Prentice Hall.

Cooperrider, D. L. (1996). The "Child" As Agent of Inquiry. *Organization Development Practitioner,* 28 (1 & 2), 5-11.

Cooperrider, D. L. (1996). Resources for Getting Appreciative Inquiry Started: An Example OD Proposal. *Organization Development Practitioner,* 28(1 & 2), 23-33.

Cooperrider, D. L., Barrett, F., & Srivastva, S. (1995). Social Construction and Appreciative Inquiry: A Journey in Organizational Theory. In D. Hosking, P. Dachler, & K. Gergen (Eds.), *Management and Organization: Relational Alternatives to Individualism* (pp. 157-200). Aldershot, UK: Avebury Press.

Cooperrider, D. L., & Bilimoria, D. (1993). The Challenge of Global Change for Strategic Management: Opportunities for Chartering a New Course. *Advances in Strategic Management,* 9, 99-141.

Cooperrider, D. L., & Dutton, J. (Eds.). (1998). *No Limits to Cooperation: The Organization Dimensions of Global Change.* Newbury Park, CA: Sage Publications.

Cooperrider, D. L., & Khalsa, G. (1997). The Organization Dimensions of Global Environmental Change. *Journal of Organization and Environment,* 10(4), 331-341.

Cooperrider, D. L., & Pasmore, W. A. (1991). The Organization Dimension of Global Change. *Human Relations,* 44 (8), 763-787.

Cooperrider, D. L., & Srivastva, S. (1987). Appreciative Inquiry In Organizational Life. In W. Pasmore & R. Woodman (Eds.), *Research In Organization Change and Development* (Vol. 1, pp. 129-169). Greenwich, CT: JAI Press.

Cooperrider, D. L., & Srivastva, S. (1998). An Invitation to Organizational Wisdom and Executive Courage. In S. Srivastva & D. L. Cooperrider (Eds.), *Organizational Wisdom and Executive Courage* (1st ed., pp. 1-22). San Francisco, CA: The New Lexington Press.

Cooperrider, D. L., & Thachenkery, T. (1995). Building The Global Civic Culture: Making Our Lives Count. In P. Sorenson, T. Head, N. Mathys, J. Preston, & D. Cooperrider (Eds.), *Global and International Organization Development* (pp. 282-306). Champaign, IL: Stipes Publishing L.L.C.

Cooperrider, D. L., & Whitney, D. (1998). When Stories Have Wings: How "Relational Responsibility" Opens New Options for Action. In S. McNamee & K. Gergen (Eds.), *Relational Responsibility*. Thousand Oaks, CA: Sage Publications.

Cummings, T. G. (1990). The Role of Executive Appreciation in Creating Transorganizational Alliances. In S. Srivastva, D. L. Cooperrider, & Associates (Eds.), *Appreciative Management and Leadership: The Power of Positive Thought and Action in Organizations* (1st ed., pp. 205-227). San Francisco, CA: Jossey-Bass Inc.

Curran, M. (1991). Appreciative Inquiry: A Third Wave Approach to OD. *Vision/Action*, December, 12-14.

Frost, P. J., & Egri, C. P. (1990). Appreciating Executive Action. In S. Srivastva, D. L. Cooperrider, & Associates (Eds.), *Appreciative Management and Leadership: The Power of Positive Thought and Action in Organizations* (1st ed., pp. 289-322). San Francisco, CA: Jossey-Bass Inc.

George, Evan., Iveson, Chris., Ratner, Harvey. (1990). *Problem to Solution: Brief Therapy with Individuals and Families*. BT Press. London. Available in the US through The Thin Book Publishing Co, Plano, TX.

Gergen, K. J. (1990). Affect and Organization in Postmodern Society. In S. Srivastva, D. L. Cooperrider, & Associates (Eds.), *Appreciative Management and Leadership: The Power of Positive Thought and Action in Organizations* (1st ed.,). San Francisco, CA: Jossey-Bass Inc.

Gibbs, C., & Ackerly, S. (June 1997). *United Religions Initiative Global Summit Summary Report*. Paper presented at the United Religions Initiative Global Summit Summary Report, San Francisco, CA.

GTE. (1997). GTE Asks Employees To Start a Grassroots Movement To Make GTE Unbeatable in the Marketplace. *GTE Together*, Published by GTE Corporation, Dallas, TX, 15-19.

Hammond, S. (1996). *The Thin Book of Appreciative Inquiry*. Plano, TX: Thin Book Publishing.

Harman, W. W. (1990). Shifting Context for Executive Behavior: Signs of Change and Revaluation. In S. Srivastva, D. L. Cooperrider, & Associates (Eds.), *Appreciative Management and Leadership: The Power of Positive Thought and Action in Organizations* (1st ed., pp. 37-54). San Francisco, CA: Jossey-Bass Inc.

Hopper, V. (1991). *An Appreciative Study of Highest Human Values in a Major Health Care Organization*. Unpublished Doctoral Dissertation, Case Western Reserve University, Cleveland, Ohio.

Hubbard, B. M. (1998). *Conscious Evolution: Awakening the Power of Our Social Potential*. Novato, CA: New World Library (See chp. 11 on AI).

Johnson, P. (1992). *Organizing For Global Social Change*. Unpublished Doctoral Dissertation, Case Western Reserve University, Cleveland, Ohio.

Johnson, P. C., & Cooperrider, D. L. (1991). Finding A Path With Heart: Global Social Change Organizations and Their Challenge for the Field of Organization Development. In R. Woodman & W. Pasmore (Eds.), *Research in Organizational Change and Development* (Vol. 5, pp. 223-284). Greenwich, CT: JAI Press.

Johnson, S., & Ludema, J. (Eds.). (1997). *Partnering To Build And Measure Organizational Capacity: Lessons From NGOs Around The World*. Grand Rapids, MI: Christian Reformed World Relief Committee.

Johnson, S. P. (1998). *Straight to the Heart: Cleveland Leaders Shaping the Next Millenium*. Unpublished Doctoral Dissertation, Case Western Reserve University, Cleveland, Ohio.

Kaczmarski, K., & Cooperrider, D. L. (1997). Constructionist Leadership in the Global Relational Age. *Journal of Organization and Environment*, 10(3), 234-258.

Kaczmarski, K., & Cooperrider, D. L. (1998). The Birth of a Worldwide Alliance: The Story of the Mountain Forum. In D. L. Cooperrider & J. Dutton (Eds.), *No Limits to Cooperation: The Organization Dimensions of Global Change*. Thousand Oaks, CA: Sage Publications.

Khalsa, G. S., & Kaczmarski, K. M. (1997 Summer). Chartering and Appreciative Future Search. *Global Social Innovations, Journal of the GEM Initiative, Case Western Reserve University*, 1(2), 45-52.

Khalsa, G. S., & Kaczmarski, K. M. (June 1996). *The United Religions Initiative Summit Conference Summary*. Paper presented at The United Religions Initiative Summit Conference Summary, San Francisco, CA.

Liebler, C. J. (1997 Summer). Getting Comfortable With Appreciative Inquiry: Questions and Answers. *Global Social Innovations, Journal of the GEM Initiative, Case Western Reserve University*, 1(2), 30-40.

Lord, J. G. (1995). *The Philanthropic Quest: A Generative Approach for Professionals Engaged in the Development Process*. Cleveland, Ohio: Philanthropic Quest International.

Lord, J. G. (1998). *The Practice of the Quest: Evolving a New Paradigm for Philanthropy and Social Innovation - A Casebook for Advancement Professionals Grounded in the Quest*. Cleveland, Ohio: Philanthropic Quest International.

Ludema, J. (1993). *Vision Chicago: A Framework For Appreciative Evaluation*. Cleveland, Ohio: Case Western Reserve University, Department of Organizational Behavior.

Ludema, J. (1994). *Vision Cities As Partnerships That Build Community: An Appreciative Inquiry Into Vision Chicago*. Cleveland, Ohio: Case Western Reserve University, Department Of Organizational Behavior.

Ludema, J. (1996). *Narrative Inquiry*. Unpublished Doctoral Dissertation, Case Western Reserve University., Cleveland, Ohio.

Ludema, J., Wilmot, T., & Srivastva, S. (1997). Organizational Hope: Reaffirming the Constructive Task of Social and Organizational Inquiry. *Human Relations*, 50 (8), 1015-1052.

Mann, A. J. (1997 Summer). An Appreciative Inquiry Model for Building Partnerships. *Global Social Innovations, Journal of the GEM Initiative, Case Western Reserve University*, 1 (2), 41-44.

Miller, Marlane. (1997). *BrainStyles: Change Your Life Without Changing Who You Are.* Simon & Schuster. New York.

Pages, M. (1990). The Illusion and Disillusion of Appreciative Managment. In S. Srivastva, D. L. Cooperrider, & Associates (Eds.), *Appreciative Management and Leadership: The Power of Positive Thought and Action in Organizations* (1st ed., pp. 353-380). San Francisco, CA: Jossey-Bass Inc.

Rainey, M. A. (1996). An Appreciative Inquiry Into the Factors of Culture Continuity During Leadership Transition. *Organization Development Practitioner,* 28(1&2), 34-41.

Robinson-Easley, C. A. (1998). *The Role of Appreciative Inquiry In The Fight To Save Our Youth.* Unpublished Doctoral Dissertation, Benedictine University, Naperville, IL.

Royal, Cathy, L. (1997). *The Fractal Initiative: Appreciative Inquiry and Rethinking Social Identities.* Dissertation: The Fielding Institute. Santa Barbara, CA.

Royal, Cathy, L. (1994). *The NTL Diversity Study, The Use of Appreciative Inquiry to discover Best Experiences around Diversity in a Professional OD organization.* NTL Institute for Applied Behavioral Science. Alexandria, VA.

Royal, Cathy, L. (1996). *What is Appreciative Inquiry?* Occasional Paper for the MacArthur Foundation.

Royal, Cathy, L. (1996). *Appreciative Inquiry, Community Development and Sustainability.* Occasional paper for the MacArthur Foundation.

Sena, S. O., & Booy, D. (1997 Summer). Appreciative Inquiry Approach to Community Development: The World Vision Tanzania Experience. *Global Social Innovations, Journal of the GEM Initiative, Case Western Reserve University,* 1(2), 7-12.
Senge, Peter. (1990). *The Fifth Discipline.* Doubleday.

Senge, Peter., Ross, Richard., Smith, Bryan., Roberts, Charlotte., Kleiner, Art. (1994). *The Fifth Discipline Fieldbook.*   Doubleday.

Srivastva, S., & Barrett, F. J. (1990). Appreciative Organizing: Implications for Executive Functioning. In S. Srivastva, D. L. Cooperrider, & Associates (Eds.), *Appreciative Management and Leadership : The Power of Positive Thought and Action in Organizations* (1st ed., pp. 381-400). San Francisco, CA: Jossey-Bass Inc.

Srivastva, S., & Cooperrider, D. L. (Eds.). (1998). *Organizational Wisdom and Executive Courage* (1st ed.). San Francisco, CA: The New Lexington Press.

Srivastva, S., Cooperrider, D. L., & Associates (Eds.). (1990). *Appreciative Management and Leadership: The Power of Positive Thought and Action in Organizations* (1st ed.). San Francisco, CA: Jossey-Bass Inc. Now available through Williams CUstom Publishing, Cleveland, OH.

Srivastva, S., & Fry, Ronald (Eds.). (1992) Executive and Organizational Continuity. San Francisco, CA: Jossey-Bass Inc.

Stavros, J. M. (1998). *Capacity Building: An Appreciative Approach, A Relational Process of Building Your Organization's Future.* Unpublished Doctoral Dissertation, Case Western Reserve University, Cleveland, Ohio.

Thachenkery, T. J. (1996). Affirmation as Facilitation: A Postmodernist Paradigm in Change Management. *Organization Development Practitioner*, 28(1), 12-22.

Watkins, J. M., & Cooperrider, D. L. (1996). Organizational Inquiry Model For Global Social Change Organizations. *Organization Development Journal*, 14(4), 97-112.

Weisbord, Marvin. (1992). *Discovering Common Ground.* Berrett-Koehler Publishers. San Francisco, CA.

White, T. W. (1996). Working In Interesting Times. *Vital Speeches Of The Day*, LXII(15), 472-474.

Whitney, D. (1998). Appreciative Inquiry: An Innovative Process for Organization Change. *Employment Relations Today.* Spring, 11-21.

Whitney, D. (1998 Summer). An Appreciative Inquiry Approach to Organization Change. *Career Development International, UK, Special Edition.*

White, David (1994). *The Heart Aroused.* Doubleday

Williams, R. F. (1996). Survey Guided Appreciative Inquiry: A Case Study. *Organization Development Practitioner,* 28(1&2), 43-51.

Wilmot, T., & Ludema, J. (1995). Odyssey Into Organizational Hope. In D. Marcic (Ed.), *Organizational Behavior Experiences and Cases* (3rd ed.,). New York: West Publishing Company.

Wilmot, T. B. (1996 Summer). Inquiry & Innovation in the Private Voluntary Sector. Global Social *Innovations, Journal of the GEM Initiative, Case Western Reserve University,* 1(1), 5-12.

Wishart, C. G. (1998). Toward a Language of Human Abundance: *The Holistic Human Logic of Sustainable Development.* Unpublished Doctoral Dissertation, Case Western Reserve University, Cleveland, Ohio.

ABOUT THE AUTHOR

DAWN DOLE has worked in various organizations including non-profit, health care, corporate, and educational institutions. She has held positions as manager/director, teacher, and consultant/trainer. Dawn holds a master's of Organization Development and Analysis degree from Case Western Reserve University, a master's of Education degree from John Carroll University and a bachelor's of Recreation Administration and Outdoor Education degree from George Williams College.

Currently Dawn works with organizations designing and conducting experiential teambuilding programs. She is also the chief administrative officer for the Taos Institute.

For more information, contact:
Dawn Dole
63 Maple Hill Dr.
Chagrin Falls, OH 44022
phone: 440.338.3543
e.mail: coopdole@modex.com

For Taos Institute questions call toll-free at 888-999-TAOS or visit www.taos institute.org

ABOUT THE DESIGNERS

ALISANN MARSHALL (ART DIRECTOR) stays busy with her young family and points her design skills towards the setting of her faith. She is currently involved in a host of creative venues at Lovers Lane United Methodist Church in Dallas. Prior to becoming a parent, Alisann designed books and magazines for Meredith Corp (*Better Homes and Gardens*), Horchow Corp, and created the first in-house art department for American Airlines (*American Way Magazine*). During her days at American Airlines, Alisann and her team recevied over 40 awards for art. She has been featured in national and international design publications and has served as guest speaker and judge of design and photography competitions. She has a Bachelor of Fine Arts from Colorado State University. Family life, church and community service bring fullness to her life.

For more information, contact:
Alisann Marshall
5623 Caladium
Dallas, TX, 75230
phone: 214.750.4824
e.mail: alisannm@aol.com

KYLE DREIER (COVER ILLUSTRATOR) started his career at age five with abstract drawings on the family furniture. These initial forms of expression were not well received, but after years of discipline he has found a more receptive audience, and a different medium. Kyle's work is produced digitally, yet somehow he still manages to come home with paint on his elbows. Kyle was a graphic designer for a number of years before deciding to pursue illustration as a career. Kyle is based in Franklin, Tennessee and does work for clients from NY to LA and places in between. You can see more of his work at www.dreier.com.

For more information, contact:
Kyle Dreier
1.800.546.4714
e.mail: Kyle@dreier.com
www.dreier.com